Rush
and Philosophy

Popular Culture and Philosophy®
Series Editor: George A. Reisch

VOLUME 1
Seinfeld and Philosophy: A Book about Everything and Nothing (2000)

VOLUME 2
The Simpsons and Philosophy: The D'oh! of Homer (2001)

VOLUME 3
The Matrix and Philosophy: Welcome to the Desert of the Real (2002)

VOLUME 4
Buffy the Vampire Slayer and Philosophy: Fear and Trembling in Sunnydale (2003)

VOLUME 5
The Lord of the Rings and Philosophy: One Book to Rule Them All (2003)

VOLUME 9
Harry Potter and Philosophy: If Aristotle Ran Hogwarts (2004)

VOLUME 12
Star Wars and Philosophy: More Powerful than You Can Possibly Imagine (2005)

VOLUME 13
Superheroes and Philosophy: Truth, Justice, and the Socratic Way (2005)

VOLUME 17
Bob Dylan and Philosophy: It's Alright Ma (I'm Only Thinking) (2006)

VOLUME 18
Harley-Davidson and Philosophy: Full-Throttle Aristotle (2006)

VOLUME 19
Monty Python and Philosophy: Nudge Nudge, Think Think! (2006)

VOLUME 23
James Bond and Philosophy: Questions Are Forever (2006)

VOLUME 24
Bullshit and Philosophy: Guaranteed to Get Perfect Results Every Time (2006)

VOLUME 25
The Beatles and Philosophy: Nothing You Can Think that Can't Be Thunk (2006)

VOLUME 26
South Park and Philosophy: Bigger, Longer, and More Penetrating (2007) Edited by Richard Hanley

VOLUME 28
The Grateful Dead and Philosophy: Getting High Minded about Love and Haight (2007) Edited by Steven Gimbel

VOLUME 29
Quentin Tarantino and Philosophy: How to Philosophize with a Pair of Pliers and a Blowtorch (2007) Edited by Richard Greene and K. Silem Mohammad

VOLUME 30
Pink Floyd and Philosophy: Careful with that Axiom, Eugene! (2007) Edited by George A. Reisch

VOLUME 31
Johnny Cash and Philosophy: The Burning Ring of Truth (2008) Edited by John Huss and David Werther

VOLUME 32
Bruce Springsteen and Philosophy: Darkness on the Edge of Truth (2008) Edited by Randall E. Auxier and Doug Anderson

VOLUME 33
Battlestar Galactica and Philosophy: Mission Accomplished or Mission Frakked Up? (2008) Edited by Josef Steiff and Tristan D. Tamplin

VOLUME 34
iPod and Philosophy: iCon of an ePoch (2008) Edited by D.E. Wittkower

VOLUME 35
Star Trek and Philosophy: The Wrath of Kant (2008) Edited by Jason T. Eberl and Kevin S. Decker

VOLUME 36
The Legend of Zelda and Philosophy: I Link Therefore I Am (2008) Edited by Luke Cuddy

VOLUME 37
The Wizard of Oz and Philosophy: Wicked Wisdom of the West (2008) Edited by Randall E. Auxier and Phillip S. Seng

VOLUME 38
Radiohead and Philosophy: Fitter Happier More Deductive (2009) Edited by Brandon W. Forbes and George A. Reisch

VOLUME 39
Jimmy Buffett and Philosophy: The Porpoise Driven Life (2009) Edited by Erin McKenna and Scott L. Pratt

VOLUME 40
Transformers and Philosophy (2009) Edited by John Shook and Liz Stillwaggon Swan

VOLUME 41
Stephen Colbert and Philosophy: I Am Philosophy (And So Can You!) (2009) Edited by Aaron Allen Schiller

VOLUME 42
Supervillains and Philosophy: Sometimes, Evil Is Its Own Reward (2009) Edited by Ben Dyer

VOLUME 43
The Golden Compass and Philosophy: God Bites the Dust (2009) Edited by Richard Greene and Rachel Robison

VOLUME 44
Led Zeppelin and Philosophy: All Will Be Revealed (2009) Edited by Scott Calef

VOLUME 45
World of Warcraft and Philosophy: Wrath of the Philosopher King (2009) Edited by Luke Cuddy and John Nordlinger

Volume 46
Mr. Monk and Philosophy: The Curious Case of the Defective Detective (2010) Edited by D.E. Wittkower

Volume 47
Anime and Philosophy: Wide Eyed Wonder (2010) Edited by Josef Steiff and Tristan D. Tamplin

VOLUME 48
The Red Sox and Philosophy: Green Monster Meditations (2010) Edited by Michael Macomber

VOLUME 49
Zombies, Vampires, and Philosophy: New Life for the Undead (2010) Edited by Richard Greene and K. Silem Mohammad

VOLUME 50
Facebook and Philosophy: What's on Your Mind? (2010) Edited by D.E. Wittkower

VOLUME 51
Soccer and Philosophy: Beautiful Thoughts on the Beautiful Game (2010) Edited by Ted Richards

VOLUME 52
Manga and Philosophy: Fullmetal Metaphysician (2010) Edited by Josef Steiff and Adam Barkman

VOLUME 53
Martial Arts and Philosophy: Beating and Nothingness (2010) Edited by Graham Priest and Damon Young

VOLUME 54
The Onion and Philosophy: Fake News Story True, Alleges Indignant Area Professor (2010) Edited by Sharon M. Kaye

VOLUME 55
Doctor Who and Philosophy: Bigger on the Inside (2010) Edited by Courtland Lewis and Paula Smithka

VOLUME 56
Dune and Philosophy: Weirding Way of the Mentat (2011) Edited by Jeffery Nicholas

VOLUME 57
Rush and Philosophy: Heart and Mind United (2011) Edited by Jim Berti and Durrell Bowman

IN PREPARATION:

Dexter and Philosophy: Mind over Spatter (2011) Edited by Richard Greene, George A. Reisch, and Rachel Robison

Halo and Philosophy (2011) Edited by Luke Cuddy

Sherlock Holmes and Philosophy (2011) Edited by Josef Steiff

Philip K. Dick and Philosophy (2011) Edited by D.E. Wittkower

Spongebob Squarepants and Philosophy (2011) Edited by Joseph Foy

Inception and Philosophy (2011) Edited by Thorsten Botz-Bornstein

Breaking Bad and Philosophy (2012) Edited by David R. Koepsell

Curb Your Enthusiasm and Philosophy (2012) Edited by Mark Ralkowski

The Rolling Stones and Philosophy (2012) Edited by Luke Dick and George A. Reisch

For full details of all Popular Culture and Philosophy® books, visit www.opencourtbooks.com.

Popular Culture and Philosophy®

Rush
and Philosophy

Heart and Mind United

Edited by
JIM BERTI
and
DURRELL BOWMAN

OPEN COURT
Chicago and La Salle, Illinois

Volume 57 in the series, Popular Culture and Philosophy®,
edited by George A. Reisch

**To order books from Open Court, call toll-free 1-800-815-2280, or visit our
website at www.opencourtbooks.com.**

Open Court Publishing Company is a division of Carus Publishing Company.

Library of Congress Cataloging-in-Publication Data

Rush and philosophy / edited by Jim Berti and Durrell Bowman..
     p. cm.—(Popular culture and philosophy ; v. 57)
   Includes bibliographical references and index.
   ISBN 978-0-8126-9716-2 (trade paper : alk. paper)
    1. Rush (Musical group)—Criticism and interpretation. 2. Rock music—History
and criticism. 3. Rock music—Social aspects. I. Berti, Jim, 1977- II. Bowman, Durrell.
   ML421.R87R87 2011
   782.42166092'2—dc22

                                    2011005652

Contents

Listen to My Music, and Hear What It Can Do   vii

PART I
To the Margin of Error   1

1. Yesterday's Tom Sawyers
   RANDALL E. AUXIER   3

2. Barenaked Death Metal Trip-Hopping on Industrial Strings
   DURRELL BOWMAN   27

3. The Groove of Rush's Complex Rhythms
   JOHN J. SHEINBAUM   45

4. Nailed It!
   JOHN T. REULAND   59

5. Can't Hear the Forest for the Cave?
   ANDREW COLE   75

PART II
The Ebb and Flow of Tidal Fortune   87

6. Rush's Revolutionary Psychology
   MITCH EARLEYWINE   89

7. Rush's Metaphysical Revenge
   GEORGE A. REISCH   101

8. Ghost Riding the Razor's Edge
   JIM BERTI   111

9. Honey on the Rim of the Larger Bowl
   MELISSA L. BECK   121

10. How We Value a Gift Beyond Price
    KAYLA KREUGER   129

11. Free Wills and Sweet Miracles
   NEIL A. FLOREK   139

PART III
I Want to Look Around Me Now 157

12. A Heart and Mind United
   LIZ STILLWAGGON SWAN 159

13. More Than They Bargained For
   DURRELL BOWMAN 169

14. Contre Nous
   NICOLE BIAMONTE 189

15. The Inner and Outer Worlds of Minds and Selves
   TODD SUOMELA 201

16. Cruising in Prime Time
   NICHOLAS P. GRECO 211

PART IV
The Blacksmith and the Artist 223

17. What Can This Strange Device Be?
   TIMOTHY SMOLKO 225

18. Enlightened Thoughts, Mystic Words
   CHRIS McDONALD 239

19. Rush's Libertarianism Never Fit the Plan
   STEVEN HORWITZ 255

20. Neil Peart versus Ayn Rand
   DEENA WEINSTEIN and MICHAEL A. WEINSTEIN 273

21. How Is Rush Canadian?
   DURRELL BOWMAN 287

Co-produced By 307
Index 313

Listen to My Music, and Hear What It Can Do

Rush has largely remained outside of the mainstream, but it has also maintained a very large cult following, perhaps of "Rush-ians." Rush usually preferred to keep a low profile, and the band often stayed away from the typical frenzy of popular stardom. However, for those people who have not always found lasting value in other forms of popular culture (not that there's anything wrong with them) and thus remained on the fringes of popularity or success, Rush has offered a veritable lifeline, helping many to feel that it is okay to be different from the majority.

Many people have characterized Rush as a "thinking man's band." Despite often updating specific aspects of its approach, the band maintained a remarkably consistent, "individualist" mission and purpose over several decades. The group has done this partly through its virtuosic and structurally complex music and partly by calling attention to social, political, cultural, technological, and scientific issues. In fact, Rush achieved its most lasting artistic successes when it addressed such themes not only in its lyrics, but also in its music. Through the blending of "thoughtful" lyrics and "progressive/hard" music, Rush's style triggers in its fans an unusual combination of air-drumming, air-guitar, singing along, and fist-pumping with a type of thoughtful reflection that does not often typify hard rock music.

Conversely, Rush's style often triggers in non-fans a highly-negative response, including dismissive words of dislike or even of passionate hatred. Rush may thus be for you a band you "love to love" or a band you "love to hate," but in either case (or neither) you should be able to learn something from this book about philosophy, ideas, history, culture, and music. This book was not written by Rush fans trying to make you like their favorite band. (Thousands of Rush fans already try to do that on the Internet.) Rather, it was written by an assortment of Rush fans who usually write or teach about other topics (mostly philosophy or musicology), but who have also found that there are quite useful threads for discussion within Rush's lyrics and music.

Rush began in Toronto, Ontario, in 1968, with fifteen-year-old high school students who performed songs by Cream, Jimi Hendrix, Elvis Presley, Buffalo Springfield, and others. By the time the trio began recording in 1973, its repertoire included original songs that stylistically combined aspects of Led Zeppelin's British "eclectic" hard rock with US "blues and boogie" hard rock, such as KISS and ZZ Top. When drummer-lyricist Neil Peart replaced original drummer John Rutsey in 1974, Rush also began to explore elements of the structural, metrical, and lyrical complexity of British progressive rock. In the following decades, Geddy Lee's virtuosic bass playing and countertenor singing style, Alex Lifeson's emotive electric guitar riffs and solos, and Neil Peart's elaborate drumming and lyrics endured as the central features of Rush's sound.

Given the band's lack of Top 40 success in the US (1982's "New World Man" reached #21), its strong album sales, and its interest in performing the music of those albums live, Rush has subtly and continuously served as the very definition of "album-oriented rock" (AOR). This context includes the band's album *Moving Pictures* (1981), which features such well-known "album rock" songs as "Tom Sawyer" and "Limelight." By 2010, fans in various countries—especially the US and Canada, but also the UK, Germany, Japan, Brazil, and elsewhere—had purchased forty-five million copies of Rush's thirty-three albums (including live albums and anthologies) and at least fifteen million of the band's concert tickets. Twenty-four of Rush's albums sold in the US at gold, platinum, or multi-platinum sales levels (a total of forty-three album certifications), ranging from a half-million copies to four million copies sold of each of those albums.

Rush resonates widely for musician-fans and others interested in structural complexity, individualism, and a much wider range of literary and stylistic influences than is usually acknowledged by rock critics and others. The group has explored such genres as heavy metal and hard rock, progressive and synth-rock, and post-progressive "power trio," along with various secondary influences. However, the band has also wandered among such lyrical interests as relationships, fantasy-adventure, classical mythology, European and world history, science-fiction, libertarianism, atheism, science, and technology.

This book is meant for those who love to think, question, and reflect—and for those who are comfortable in their own skin, even if they fall outside of the "mainstream." As you read, try to think of each chapter as part of an ongoing dialogue, perhaps akin to Rush's own approach. Don't hesitate to break down each chapter and to think about how an author's subject matter or interpretation may apply to you, individually. The book explores the meaning of selected musical and lyrical passages found in Rush's music, and its "philosophical" fields of inquiry unite it with its siblings in this series.

Even if you have strong, existing views about Rush, the book provides a multi-faceted platform in which you might reconsider certain subject areas or specific topics (a song or an album, for instance) or to increase your general appreciation of Rush's contributions to musical culture. *Rush and Philosophy* might even help you come to an acceptance that being different—like Rush—is not necessarily a bad thing.

PART I

To the Margin of Error

1
Yesterday's Tom Sawyers

RANDALL E. AUXIER

It was October of 1977, the *Farewell to Kings* Tour, and Rush was coming to Memphis. They went almost everywhere but Parsippany on that endless tour—I mean, they made it to Dothan, Alabama, and Upper Darby, Pennsylvania, where they split the bill with Tom Petty (now there's a case of musical cognitive dissonance). I hadn't really heard of Rush. Like an idiot, I was still listening to the *last* band my friend "Brice" got me into three years before, Led Zeppelin (and I'm still listening), and in the week of which I will speak, I also had out my old Lynyrd Skynyrd albums, mourning the sky plunge of Ronnie van Zandt and friends. ("Old" is a highly relative thing; my favorite Skynyrd albums were simply *ancient*, you know—I got them when I was fourteen, two years before.)

Rush's *2112* had caught the ears of all the teen-aficionados-of-what's-next, and I certainly wasn't one such. But way across town, some thirty miles from my digs in a humble part of town, my friend from elementary school, "Brice Kennedy," was experiencing a serious meltdown. Brice Kennedy is not his real name, which is being withheld because, well, he's still out there, and he's now a Republican. Back then he wasn't, although I now understand why he made me play all these board games built around financial transactions, like *Monopoly*, and *Masterpiece*, and *Stocks and Bonds*—he taught me what leverage was and then amortized my ass, but good. Anyway, he was the guy, and every school had one, who *really* knew music, sort of what Chuck Klosterman must've been like in high school. This attention to the details and fringes of music actually makes you geeky at that age (or, in Klosterman's

3

case, geeky, narcissistic, annoying and self-indulgent, even if your taste in music is unmatched).

The meltdown came to this: Brice had somehow scored second row, center section seats for the Rush concert, and his very strict (and sometimes arbitrary) parents had just denied him permission to go to said concert. They had their reasons, I'm sure. Those were the glorious days when the rule was: the lights go down then the people light up. Even Brice's parents had caught on to that little feature of the youth culture. And unlike parents today, they could truthfully report they never themselves inhaled.

It's embarrassing in any generation to still be asking your parents' *permission* to go somewhere at sixteen. I mean you're just getting to the point that they sort of couldn't stop you, except with the "I pay the bills argument," an idle threat which invites one's own flesh and blood to contemplate homelessness and is oh-so-easy to see through. But old habits die hard, and at sixteen you don't quite want to test those waters, at least if they've been fairly good to you. I wouldn't say Brice's parents had been exactly "good to him," yanking him as they did from the public school system when bussing started and sending him to a very expensive prep school *for boys*. I mean, *no girls*, and rich assholes establishing their pecking order with *no girls* to make them feel insecure about it, and did I mention *no girls*? Frankly, I'd rather go to military school to be made into a man, and I think no jury of sixteen-year-old boys would have convicted Brice of failing to honor his mother and father if he'd told them to piss off. But Brice wasn't quite to the point of openly defying the elders. Rather, unbeknownst to them, he had, of necessity, become Tom-Sawyer-devious.

Philosophical Moments

Among fans, the themes and lyrical motifs in Rush's important early songs, especially on *2112*, are widely recognized as being driven by philosophical concepts. Unhappily, the "philosophy" they are supposedly advancing is the ideological individualism and "objectivism" of the pseudo-philosopher Ayn Rand. Now, before you go either grinning in approval or snarling at me, I don't call Rand a pseudo-philosopher as an insult. Like absolutely everybody else in the world, Rand had some philosophical ideas, and, being an aspiring novelist, those ideas informed her narratives and characters in thematic ways. But even a Hardy Boys mystery has *that much* philosophy (and as I now consider it, I'm pretty sure the Hardy Boys probably grew up to be Republicans too). I doubt it initially dawned on Rand to try to *be* a philosopher—up until people began to respond favorably to the philosophical aspects of her writing.

It's sort of like what happens when several people tell you independently "I like that hat on you." You're likely not only to wear it more, but to start buying hats based on their proximity to the one people like. It's only human. But that doesn't make you so much as a hatter, let alone a maven of fashion. If you then present yourself as hatter or maven, and ignorant people *believe* you, don't be surprised when the hatters are pissed and the fashion mavens are laughing. (This, by the way is called an "argument from analogy," and one difference between a follower of Rand and a philosopher is that philosophers both know and admit that analogies settle nothing, *and* also *know* when they are relying on one. Rand's entire philosophy is built on questionable analogies, and her following consists of people who either don't know that or won't admit it.)

All people have philosophical moments, but most people don't *credit* their own philosophical thoughts. They forget them quickly and certainly don't *do* anything about them. What is there to *do* about having a philosophical thought? Well, plenty, but like anything else, you'll have to practice, and learn, and read, and work at it to do anything very good with such ideas. Now some people have lots of philosophical moments, but not all of them become philosophers. Rand had a handful of philosophical ideas that she visited over and over, none of them original (but that isn't important in philosophy), and she also learned in a superficial way to stitch them together into the rudimentary semblance of a "philosophy." In this respect, Rand was like Mark Twain, George Orwell, Emile Zola, and even Tolstoy and Dostoevsky (who were operating on a higher plane), in that she had a lot of such moments, credited them, and put them to work in a more or less co-ordinated way. She was by a long stretch, as a writer and thinker, the inferior of all of those mentioned above, but in terms of successfully combining philosophical ideas with fiction writing, she was better than the average bear.

No one likes Rand better than tweenage males who think themselves misunderstood geniuses. It's a shame that people have hung the Rand-albatross on Neil Peart, just because he read some Rand at an impressionable age. It's especially unfortunate since, unlike the hordes of other infantile, self-regarding tweenage males so affected, Neil actually *was* a misunderstood genius. The hordes don't usually have much to show for their supposed genius, except a few, like Alan Greenspan, who have more to apologize for than to prove their pretensions of genius. It is far better to have a modest self-estimation and exceed it than to have a grandiose one and make others pay for the deficit.

My point is that when you look at Neil's lyrics from that time period (part of the proof of his genius is that he rather quickly outgrew all of this), what are you looking at? How is it that the lyrics and the music from Rush's "literary era" combine to make something that has, well, philosophical *value*, even if it isn't quite "philosophy"? Rush's music is way, way better and more valuable as a cultural contribution than anything Rand ever managed, in my opinion. I do think that there's something in that literary era of Rush that opens minds and that elevates the fans to places, good and worthy places, they might not otherwise go.

Halloween Traditions, or, Are You Down with What You're Up For?

The concert was scheduled for an inconvenient Sunday night, October 30th, downtown at Dixon-Myers Hall, which was where the Memphis Symphony Orchestra performed at the time (hell, maybe they still do). This was a concert hall, not a coliseum or arena. It promised incredible sound and proximity. UFO and Max Webster both opened. That was going to make it a late night. I have no memory of Max Webster and only the vaguest memory of UFO, that the lead singer, in mascara and bright green pants, spit a lot as he vocalized and we were in the danger zone.

Maybe you've got a similar experience in your history, but Brice and I were finding less and less to talk about after he moved to the rich side of town. As usual, friendship had been built on dozens of common activities—sports, playing board games, collecting football cards, and especially music, as I struggled to keep up with his ever expanding taste for progressive rock. To this day my album collection (yes, I still have it—hope you kept yours too) bears Brice's stamp. I felt sort of like a musical contrail behind his Lear jet. But now I was more like Roger Waters, finding all the talk about cars and money and rich people stuff a little off-putting.

Yet, since he moved, Brice and I had sort of started spending Halloween together. Two years before Rush, he came to my house for a sleepover (and neighborhood marauding), one year before Rush, I went to his neighborhood for the same. I don't think we were actually planning to make it a tradition, and I had already become, I think, something of a wrong-side-of-the-tracks embarrassment for him in his new social circles, but then came those amazing tickets and his parents' unbearable denial of concert privileges.

Now yesterday's Tom Sawyer was a modern-day warrior, and his mind was *not* for rent. So it occurred to Brice that there might be a way, just maybe, to get to that concert after all. His folks would surely believe that he was at *my* house for the now annual Halloween exchange, and since Halloween was on an unworkable Monday, well, we'd just have to do our annual get-together on Sunday (concert day). It probably crossed Brice's mind to try the whole plan without calling me at all, since another friend, let's call him "Jim" (whose emerging worldly values were closer to Brice's), was already promised the second seat. But Brice believed in hedging his bets, and Jim would just have to understand.

So Brice called me with the offer of a seat in exchange for, well, a willingness to join a conspiracy (displacing Jim, who eventually ended up further back in the crowd, with a one-off ticket of some kind). Now I'm no one's Huckleberry friend, but I was up for this. Brice proposed to make a weekend of it: Friday, Saturday, *and* Sunday, and this was intended to throw his folks off the trail, I believe. And I was down with that. But there was a problem. *My* parents would be out of town Friday and Saturday, and while they would willingly leave *me* for a weekend, no way would they leave someone else's kid, for whom they'd be responsible, etc., and no way would Brice's folks let him come to my house with the folks out of town . . . blah, blah, blah.

But I'll bet you've already figured out what we told them. You've seen *Risky Business*. This would be like that, minus Rebecca De Mornay, plus Brice Kennedy, minus Chicago, plus Memphis, minus Bob Seger, plus Geddy Lee. It's funny how parents' perceptions run. My folks thought Brice was probably a good influence on me, and his folks suspected I was a bad influence on him, when the truth was exactly the opposite. Parents, if you are reading this, be chastened, be very chastened. You really *don't* know. Remember your own youth and tremble.

Lyrical Motifs

It has crossed your mind many times that song lyrics are not something you usually grasp the first time you hear them. There are exceptions to this, of course—especially funny songs and story songs, where the music is just there for effect and the whole point is the words. You can recognize such songs almost immediately and then you sort of quickly *decide* whether you want to follow along or just tune it out. That quick decision process is a relatively recent phenomenon in human history. Music is so ubiquitous in our culture (God, I love having an excuse to use words like "ubiquitous"—I once managed to get antidisestablishmentarianism into an article, and have now managed it again, except that the last time it was legit and here it's utterly gratuitous and annoying), where was I?

Oh yeah, the ubiquity of music in our culture makes it easy to forget that not very long ago, music was a pretty special thing, not heard everywhere and anytime, but rather planned for, hoped for, anticipated, relished. Real instruments were expensive and actual musicians relatively sparse. The presence of music a hundred years ago rendered people rapt or ecstatic, or both in turns. It still has that effect on traditional peoples whose ears aren't ruined by the noise of modernity. In the days of yore, you wouldn't have *decided* whether to follow a story song. Rather, your body would grow still, unbidden, and everything *but the ear*, and its peculiar power of focus, would simply fall into the background.

You know it's hard work to follow lyrics, and the music has to be arranged to create the right sonic space for lyrics to punch through to the surface in perfect clarity. One thing that has to be pulled way back, almost to silence, is the bass. The rumbling in those sonic ranges created by bass cancels all clarity, takes the fine point off of enunciation, and it doesn't take much bass to prevent people from understanding the words entirely. On the other hand, when the bass ranges are prominent, it has the effect of blending and melting all the other ranges together; bass can unify the music and weld the percussive to the melodic.

The bass in Rush's typical music is actually mixed loud, but along with the kick drum, it is equalized thin to minimize this "cancellation effect" on the clarity of vocals and other instruments, but still you aren't going to get all the words in a Rush song. In fact, even with special attention and cranking up the stereo at home, you'll never understand them all until you read them somewhere. Rather, what happens is that when the music pulls back for a dramatic moment, you'll pick up a few words, usually the repeated ones, and then the music will swell and take the rest away from you. Go ahead, sing with me: "The world is, the world is love and light hmmm, hmmm. . . . Today's Tom Sawyer he gets high on you, hmmm hmm, hmmm, he gets by on you." I know you're with me.

Resistance Is Futile

This thing I just described actually has a name. The philosopher Susanne Langer (1895–1985) calls it "the principle of assimilation." Her claim is that wherever two or more fundamental art forms are *mixed* (in this case music and poetry), one of them *must* assimilate the other to itself. For example, where painting or sculpture is used to decorate a building, they would be *assimilated* to the art of interior design, or, if the sculpture is outside, to architecture. Most painting and sculpture really is just decoration, after all. An extreme case of this tension between art forms and assimilation is Frank Lloyd Wright's Guggenheim Museum building in New York, which assimilates interior design to architecture, and then ingeniously assimilates even the greatest painting and sculpture into simple decoration for *his* architecture. This is what Wright intended. That pisses off the interior designers and painters and sculptors, of course, but to the architects it seems about right.

On the other hand, if you visit the Academia in Florence (where Michelangelo's *David* is on display), you will see an entire architectural edifice assimilated to the purpose of showcasing Michelangelo's sculptural works, especially his *David*, which was originally commissioned to stand outside at the entrance of a government building, assimilated to the art of architecture or urban design, but was later deemed by a later generation to be too good for that pedestrian function and made into its own *raison d'être*. Does this "assimilation principle" hold true in every case? That's a long argument we can have some other time, but there are certainly many examples of it. It is clear that differing art forms are constantly in tension when combined. Some art forms, like film, are ravenous in their appetite for assimilating other art forms to their own primary structures. Film gobbles up drama, acting, photography, painting, writing, music, interior design, urban design, architecture, and more, turning them all into filmatic effects.

In music where words are being employed, there is a tension between poetry and pure music. In the singer-songwriter genre, generally the music just supports the poetry. With the music of Rush the lyrics are assimilated to the music, most of the time. "The Trees" and "Closer to the Heart" are exceptions, and there are some others, but for the most part let's just say you are not being encouraged to sing along. Rather, Geddy's voice is being used as a somewhat shrill lead instrument and the lyrics simply cause the aesthetic qualities of his voice to vary in interesting and pleasing ways. It doesn't matter very much what he is singing about; the point is what it *feels* like and *sounds* like to hear him sing. You may know that Neil was writing the lyrics because neither Geddy nor Alex had any real interest in doing so. Whether they had any talent for it I don't know, but lyrical *talent* wasn't really needed, only lyrical *competence*. This band wasn't going to be about lyrics, it was about music. So Neil got the job by default.

Now Neil Peart is not exactly the possessor of a great literary pedigree, but one thing I have noticed about songwriters of all sorts: nearly all of them are avid readers. They love words. I was just reading the autobiography of Keith Richards, and one learns near the end that he owns a massive library and is addicted to (among so many other things) British and Roman history. *Keith Richards*. Next to him, Neil Peart looks like a Harvard professor. So Neil was always a reader, and he read this and that, and found that he liked mythology, ancient history, and, unfortunately, in callow youth, before he had time to read widely, also Ayn Rand. No one who reads widely, and who gets the benefit of that reading, is likely to hold her in very high esteem for very long. Emotionally damaged people and those who simply cannot grow up are the exceptions, but then, they don't get the full benefit of their reading, do they? And in this they follow their heroine.

By the time of *Moving Pictures*, three years and some months after my night out with Brice, Neil was writing lyrics about what he really knew: his own experience. He still wasn't much of a poet and it still didn't matter. As I write this, Rush is preparing for a 2011 tour in which they will be playing the *Moving Pictures* track list in order, for its thirtieth anniversary. It's their best album and they know it. No Ayn Rand on that masterwork. Neil's lyrics are so much less contrived and closer to the heart even beginning with *A Farewell to Kings*, so the flirtation with objectivist ideas was pretty brief.

But even on *Moving Pictures*, if you try it, I think you'll see that the lyrics can't withstand the test of being pulled from the music and examined as poetry. Some lyricists *do* pass that test—Robert Plant writes in the same vein as Neil, for example, but is a much better poet; and Roger Waters is a bit like Neil in his minimalist mood, but far better poetically. Still, even the best lyricists have a hard time being taken seriously as poets because they often try to *rhyme* things, which just isn't hip in poetry these days. And thinking of Plant and Waters as other progressive rock lyricists, it is interesting that in Zeppelin, the lyrics are almost always assimilated to the music, while with Pink Floyd, most often the lyrics dominate the music whenever they are present. There isn't a single formula here, but a dynamic tension between two art forms.

It's natural for these musicians to put in the audible foreground whatever is artistically best at any given moment. When you've written lyrics as good as "Stairway to Heaven" or "Comfortably Numb," you don't drown that out with bass. When everything in a piece is outstanding—music, lyrics, melody, groove, tonal textures of the voice and guitars—well, in that situation, something is going to have to be sacrificed to the whole. One of the most difficult moments in the production of a recording is the moment when a musician has hit a riff that is so amazing *on its own* but it distracts the ear from some other musical element that is more necessary to the whole. Such a riff has to be left out (or, as we sometimes can do these days, moved to another place in the recording). It is tragic, but it happens constantly in the art of recording. Live performance presents similar dilemmas, and the visual presentation just complicates matters more.

Returning to the issue of assimilation of lyrics to music, as Rush favors, it creates a lower standard of poetry needed, and that's just fine. To provide another analogy: if you're part of the crew building the Notre Dame Cathedral and your boss says "sculpt me a Madonna for the roof," you don't need or want a Michelangelo for that spot. It would be a waste to put in that kind of time and detail for something no one ever sees up close. You want something that *feels* right from a couple hundred feet below, and while you can't afford to hire a sculptor who sucks, you do want one who *understands* that this is about the building, not his statue, and who sculpts accordingly. Rush's music is a veritable Notre Dame of both living and processed sound, and it just isn't about the lyrics, at least not very much.

J-Wags, or, Are You Down with What You're Up For?

The plan for *Friday* night (Rush, T-minus forty-eight hours and counting) was in Brice's hands. We were staying at my house, of course, while *his* folks believed *my* folks were home and *my* folks believed I was at Brice's house (and my sister was also gone somewhere that weekend, I don't remember where, but her absence becomes relevant at T-minus twenty-four hours). Brice actually knew of a bar where they wouldn't ask for our ID's (drinking age was eighteen back then). This is one reason to keep old friends even when you have little left in common; you might discover new uses for each other. A bar? That was way beyond my ken. I didn't think of myself as an innocent (I was, sort of, but I didn't like to *think* about it), but I had never been in a *bar*, and I certainly hadn't heard of this place called "J-Wags Lounge" in mid-town.

Anyone who knows Memphis is now saying "oh my God." J-Wags, which is still operating, later became a famous bar—a famous *gay* bar, that is. And here we were sixteen, straight, and clueless. Now I want to be very clear that when it comes to gay bars, I am totally down with it, even if I'm not up for it. Still, the worry is irrelevant because in 1977 J-Wags was just a neighborhood bar, not yet having evolved into its future niche, and I now know how *very* ordinary it was.

I was instructed by Brice to wear a powder blue pinpoint Oxford shirt with a button-down collar and khaki pants, and docksiders. This was all very important, I was told, because if you aren't dressed right, they might ask for your ID and then everything is ruined, right? Well, I was down with doing as told to by those attempting to corrupt me, and I was pretty much up for some corruption. But I had none of these clothes, so Brice lent me a shirt and I made do with that and Converse All-stars and jeans. Thus shod and shirted, we set out.

Brice's very cool and discreet older brother (he played a blue Stratocaster and was the prime source of Brice's cutting edge intelligence on what would soon be hip rock music among our younger and more ignorant masses) took us to within a dozen blocks of J-Wags (we hadn't told him the destination, so he had deniability), and from there we hoofed it a pretty fair piece to J-Wags. Jim (of the displaced ticket) had a car and was supposed to meet us there. And so he did. The concept of a "designated driver" did not exist in 1977, but Jim was far more interested in getting stoned than getting drunk, and a stoned driver, aged sixteen, is probably safer on the roads than the average sober adult: our average speed home, probably thirty miles per hour.

The evening was passed, and you just *won't* believe this, drinking *actual* beer in an *actual* bar and playing pool with *actual* bar patrons. Doesn't take much to thrill you at that age, does it? But the anticipation of a whole weekend of such forbidden adventures, to be culminated in a Rush, well, it was quite enough. Did I get drunk? Well, I had, like, four draft beers in three hours, with no resistance to alcohol, at 5' 7" and 115 lbs. You do the math. Did Brice? I actually don't remember much. I woke up in my own bed (alone). Jim must have somehow made it back to the rich side of town because he wasn't at my house Saturday morning, and somehow we *were*, and Jim was still alive Sunday night when Rush came to town. He must have puttered back to the rich side. (I never saw Jim again after that Sunday night, so I hope he turned out better than it looked like he would. But I'll bet if he's alive, he's a goddamn Republican.)

The Virtues of Virtual

Langer says that every basic art form accomplishes its "work" by taking some aspect of our actual experience and making a *semblance* of that experience in a *virtual space* and/or *time*. Now, I'm going to be honest with you, this is one honking big philosophical idea. It isn't quite as honking big as the idea of God, or freedom, or eternal life. (I'm not saying whether those ideas have any concrete reality corresponding to them, only that at the very least they *are* ideas, and you *can* think about them.) Those big boys would sort of be the Beethoven symphonies of philosophical ideas. This idea of Langer's is sort of more like a bitching Rush album of an idea. And hearing an idea like this just once is akin to trying to take in *2112* and "get it" the first time through. It isn't going to happen. But I've spent about twenty years thinking on this idea of Langer's, turning it over, trying to decide whether I agree with it, so maybe I can save you some trouble. You decide. I still haven't made up my mind, but I think it's a serious thought, sort of a way of cashing in on the claim that art imitates life, but richer. So I'm going with it.

What does that idea *mean*? Basically she's saying that the *reason* we recognize something *as art* when we encounter it is that it reminds us of something in life that it recreates in a virtual way, as an illusion. For example, painting, as an art form, makes a semblance in two dimensions of *what it is like* to actually *see* things in three-dimensional space. Its "primary illusion," then, is to reduce that experience of seeing to two dimensions and to use pigments and geometrical tricks of the eye to create the illusion. The "virtual space" is the space *inside* the painting. It sort of invites you to step out of your actual space and into the virtual space of the painting, at least if it's a good painting. This is true even with abstract paintings: they exist in a virtual space, enclosed by a frame of the edges, and if you stepped into the odd space occupied by an abstraction, I suppose you'd either become abstract yourself of be in a pretty strange mixed space.

Sculpture, as an art form, recreates in a semblance the experience of the bodily traversal of the *lived space of action*, the space of bodily movement. When you look at a sculpture, if it's a good one, it feels as if it has moved into the position it currently holds, and could very well move beyond it. To compensate for the fact that the sculpture really doesn't move, *you* move around it. The artwork exists in a virtual space-time of a history of movements it never actually made, leading to its current pose, and a virtual future of possible actions never to be enacted. The work invites you to furnish in your imagination the movements leading up to the pose, and to finish those actions proceeding from its frozen present. And you *do* that, in your imagination, whether you want to or not. The virtual space and time of physical movement is the sculpture's *world*, and it reminds you of *your* actual world of movement when you see it.

But music, and pay *close* attention here, music creates the *illusion* of what it feels like *living in time's flow*. Nothing in music actually moves or lives, biologically, or has real feeling. Yet, music feels to us as if it's alive. Yes, the musicians are alive and they do move in *actual* time as they play their instruments, but that is not "the music": it's just the physical activity in actual time that *creates* the illusion of virtual time in the virtual movement of the music. Just as the brush strokes are not the painting and the hammer strikes are not the sculpture; they *create* the illusion but are not themselves illusory. This is pretty hard to understand, especially with music, but an example may help.

Imagine that Geddy is working up to singing a sustained high note; his vocal chords are tightening, his throat is constricting, his breath is being forced through a smaller space, and sound issues forth. (I hope he's had a breath mint.) But nothing actually "goes up" when he hits a "high note." There is nothing in the physical activity of singing or playing an instrument that makes one note "higher" (closer to the sky) than another note. Nor does anything *actually move* from "lower" to "higher" notes in an "ascending" scale. Rather, one sequences individual tones in such a way as to produce the *illusion* of rising; it *feels like* something is ascending when you hear it, even though nothing actually rises. What's really altered, in effect, as Geddy sings the high note, is the peaks and troughs of the sound waves, propagating in *actual* space and time. The actual propagation is in actual time and space, with the illusion of "higher" and "lower" pitch, is a part of the *virtual* character of music.

In the same way, music employs the actual passage of time as its physical basis for the sequencing of varied sounds that provide us with an audible series of (oft repeating) virtual markers, called tones, that *remind* us of the actual passage of time. The tones have individual duration, but they don't move. Tones are *made of* sound waves vibrating within a regular frequency of peaks and troughs (with slight variation), but *as tones*, they offer only an illusion of stability for the duration during which they exist. The sounds are actual, but *treating* them as tones is a virtualization of sound, a step from what it actually is (sound) to its virtual temporal relations with other sounds that we will also *treat as* tones. You recognize the difference between music and noise when you hear it, but you may not realize how much of the difference between them lies in your willingness to *treat* the sounds *as tones*. My folks were disinclined to treat my Rush albums as "music" way back when—it was an awful noise they said. My mother, who was a voice teacher, was horrified by what Geddy Lee was doing with his voice. Shrieking, she called it. They weren't willing to virtualize what they were hearing.

Now, if you think about it, you'll agree that the tones do not *make* the actual time any more than the sound does, and neither sound nor tone is *one* with the actual time; rather, unlike mere sounds, which seem to be at the mercy of actual time, the tones *use* the actual time to create an illusion of movement and repeatability within the relentless flow of our experience. The truth is that the flow of our experience renders *real* actions unrepeatable. You cannot genuinely repeat *any* action, in the sense of making one action identical to another action, because the time when any action was first performed is now past, and unrecoverable. The best you can do in actual time is to perform an *analogous act* and then *pretend* the time passage between the first and second enactment *doesn't matter*. This is the basis of virtualizing time, and music does it amazingly well.

Run That by Me One More Time

So we know that tones arranged in various combinations and series use time to create an illusion that reminds us of our own flow of felt experiences: the music *sounds like* what it *feels like* to be alive, to have a rhythmic heartbeat and a breathing pattern, to move our bodies up, down and all around, to be obliged to anticipate the next moment and join it to the last moment by means of our present sensing and feeling. But there are rules about how music has to do this in order to maintain the illusion.

Like so many things, the illusion music creates exists only between two extremes. Too much automatic repetition in rhythms or tones kills the interest: the time is over-virtualized and does not remind us of what it feels like to be alive, but sounds like a machine instead. The musical illusion is broken and becomes mere sound. Too little repetition in the rhythmic or tonal scheme kills the experience of the *illusion* of living (which does incorporate much repetition), and starts to seem like actual, unrepeatable time. *Music*, the illusory semblance of our life of feeling, exists, then, between these extremes; it is virtualized time.

Now I have to report something weird and kind of shocking. If Langer is right, the way humans become *conscious* of actual time is by attending to the ways that music can use actual time to suspend certain moments and contract others; the tension and release of energies in music points us to the otherwise uninterrupted continuity of our flowing experience. Consciousness itself is a virtualization of experience, and we become aware that we are conscious by way of music—not so much its successful semblances, but at the points where semblance breaks down and actual time retakes us. She actually believes that music is the key to our kind of consciousness (a self-reflective kind). If we had nothing that was *like* time, but *not* time, how would we ever become aware of its passage? It's a fair question. So music is virtualized time, and the virtue of it is that it teaches us an awareness of *real* time precisely because music just *is* illusory time.

Now the music of Rush (like all progressive rock) diverges from other rock music in using repetition more sparsely. Most rock music is built on a virtual repetition of four beats, called 4/4 time, or "common time." Whatever syncopation (that is, the violation of the evenness of the pulse created by "early" attacks and the uneven sustaining of tones for rhythmic effect) regular rock music contains is simple variation on the repeating four beats. It is there to punctuate the driving, regular and repeating beat. There are thousands of regular grooves into which ordinary rock music can fall, but all built on the matrix of common time.

Rush in particular and progressive rock in general is partly defined by its habit of hopping from one time signature to another; the rhythms are driven and herded around in community by what seem like almost mystical forces. The gods and demons subtract a beat here, add one there, squeeze two into one, and take us just a bit beyond the predictable recurrent rhythms of ritual dance, or of our living bodies. It feels sort of like being on a rollercoaster. It isn't for everyone. In progressive rock, the regularity of rhythmic order is sacrificed for the sake of a different *way* of virtualizing time. Rhythmic patterns do exist and come back around, but they catch the listener unaware, and the standard AB/AB/CB song structure of verses, choruses, and bridges is totally out the window. Even the concept of a "song" isn't always the basic musical unit. See Yes, *Tales from Topographic Oceans* for some alternatives to the "song" concept. In this regard, progressive rock owes a lot to jazz and even to classical music.

Interlude

So I'm writing this in a bar in Carbondale, Illinois, in December of 2010, and as I just typed that last line, I look over, and the barkeep (a young blonde woman with a two-foot pony tail) is being accused by the owner of playing him "like Tom Sawyer" by convincing him to shine the brass fittings on the beer taps because she "isn't sure how to do it right." From this we learn two things. First, that I'm a lot more familiar with bars at forty-nine than I was at sixteen, and second, that there is a fair case for synchronicity.

The Sign of the Three

Something must be done to make sure the "center holds" when music is being played with little so respect for the repeating latticework of a 4/4 beat. The center of Rush's sound is and always has been a little trick they use. So long as the bass line and the kick drum match exactly, and so long as the actual tempo of the song (the number of beats per minute) does not vary too much, any amount of syncopation (that early and late emphasizing of beats) and violation of time signatures *can* be workable. So Neil and Geddy synch up the bass and kick drum and rehearse it as many times as necessary, until it seems like that pinpoint precision happens *on its own* (which is also an illusion), and then the more melodic elements can move whither they will without the whole thing feeling confusing to the ear and body of a listener. It still *feels* like the passage of time, but with fits and starts, just about where you *want* them. Classical and jazz composers also exploit our desire for more temporal variation in our virtual time, which reminds us of the variations in the succession of our actual feelings, but classical and jazz composers never, ever synch the rhythm of the bass and drum movements as Neil and Geddy do.

I say this is a "trick" because all rock and blues and country musicians draw on the strategy of using the kick drum to reinforce the movement of the bass, below the other instruments, but most of them do it while respecting the regularity of four beats per measure. Of course there's a lot more to the Rush sound than the two characteristics I've mentioned: mixing the bass and kick drum hot with a thin equalization, and synching them precisely. Rush is a three-piece band, and three-piece bands face certain challenges that don't emerge in larger bands. All three-piece bands have to find ways to keep the sound full and fresh with limited hands and voices. There are dozens of ways to accomplish the task.

It's good to remember that having a lot of "empty space" (this is a metaphor of course) in a piece of music is not always a problem. The early recordings of the Police show how three instruments can do the same things Rush does, but in the spacious (as opposed to full) mode. Van Halen (when they were three-piece) synched the bass and kick, kept the drums simple, fattened the bass sound and kept it sustaining, and then let Eddie do the rest. The Who and Led Zeppelin never adopted the strategy of precision synching of bass and kick drum except when it occasionally pleased them, while ZZ Top just made up for its sparse instrumentation with volume and energy.

On the other hand, Rush isn't exactly a three-*piece* band, since Geddy plays so many instruments and sings at the same time, and Alex and Neil kick in the processed sounds as needed. But the music has to be closely arranged so that the ear cannot detect when Geddy has moved off of the bass guitar and is playing the bass line with his left hand on a keyboard or with his feet on the Taurus pedals, which sometimes Alex also does. There are lots of pieces, but just three people, so the name is a bit misleading. And there are three *piece* bands with four people (like The Who), so the point is, that's a lot of music for just a few fellows to be making.

To do all that Geddy does while singing the lead vocal is pretty freaking impressive. Lead singer-bass players are rare enough—count 'em, go ahead. Sting, Geddy, Paul McCartney, Roger Waters, Richard Page, Eric Carmen, and who the hell else? There is a reason for this paucity. Unlike the guitar and the drums, the bass generally plays *against* the melody, even in ordinary rock music, let alone progressive rock. Singing while playing bass requires something quite beyond patting one's head while rubbing one's stomach. To add in keyboards and pedals, and an occasional guitar, is something more than human. It may look relaxed when you see Geddy do it, but that appearance is as illusory as music itself. The boys have rehearsed this stuff into an automatism. They play it exactly the same way every time, and they pretty well *have* to, to get it to work. They have been criticized for this. I'll take that up later.

Saturday Night's Alright, or, Are You Really Up for What You're Up For?

I don't remember the day after J-Wags. I'm pretty sure me and Brice slept in and then probably ate junk food and played board games, in which he probably whipped my ass, as always, and celebrated said ass whipping insufferably. Unfortunately I can't reveal everything about Saturday night (Rush, T-minus twenty-four and counting), even at this late date. Too many of the principals are still alive and haven't given their permission (and they wouldn't give it if I asked them—not for *this* night). Brice probably wouldn't mind, since on the scale of things he did later in life, this night probably doesn't even register a 1 on a scale of 1 to 10, (10 being the most unimaginable bad behavior). But on my personal scale, this was about an 8.

Here's what I *can* say. A lot of young people were celebrating Halloween that night. We actually stayed home, at my folks' (otherwise vacant) place. Brice had somehow procured for our enjoyment a big bottle of Jack Daniels black label, maybe two, I don't rightly remember. It was more than enough in any case. By late afternoon the seals had been broken. We handed out candy to the kids as they came by, rather more cheerily than would be usual. As the night wore on and various other activities began to unfold, we were interrupted in our Bacchanal (which involved Rush albums at extreme volume) by a knock on the front door. This led to a staggered scurrying and stowing of contraband, forbidden literature, and other things that shan't be mentioned.

It was two of my sister's friends at the door—her friend "Carrie" and a fellow named "Bill," whom I barely knew from earlier days when he dated my sister instead of her (very attractive) friend. The friendship survived his transfer of affection, and indeed, the switch led to a marriage of over thirty years duration (and still going), with many kids. Must've been a decent trade. But in 1977 Carrie and Bill were all of seventeen. They were looking for my sister to go driving, or whatever. But she was gone (I still don't remember where). Yet, here we were, Brice and me, and as they peeked in, it was pretty clear to them that, well, we had the "stuff." And they had nothing in particular to do. Let the Bacchanal resume.

What followed I just can't quite describe, except that it probably isn't as bad as you're imagining—and I didn't lose my virginity until some time later, after I got my own car, so get your mind out of *that* particular gutter. Another word to parents: if you want to hasten the loss of your children's virginity, by all means get them cars. This provides a mobile version of precisely what they lack, which is a *place* to do what all of nature is encouraging them to do. Parents who won't leave their kids for *Risky Business* weekends, but who tell themselves it's okay to get the kid a car, well, there is *no* virtual space virtual enough to contain your self-deception. Do the right thing, I say. Get them pills and condoms and tell them to go at it. They're going to anyway. And of course, some won't. *It's up to them.* If you do the right thing, it doesn't matter about the car. None of this is philosophy. It's just a reminder of what you already know.

The only issue is whether you're going to screw up their young minds with guilt. Abstinence my ass. And what is *with* this puritanical culture? We declare wars on weaker peoples and massacre them without reservation or conscience, and then depict it in all its gore in movies and news stories for the public, and you (Republicans) have the audacity to tell me that *sex* is obscene? I'm sorry, but fuck you. (This also is not a philosophical argument, it's just a rant.) And while we're interluding, I notice that the Tom Sawyer routine of the barkeep worked for about five minutes before she ended up polishing the brass by her lonesome. Tom Sawyer ain't what he used to be. It seems that everyone is on to his scam. But he's become mean.

Aftermath: Not Down with What I Was Up For

No more about the proceedings that night, but when I woke up, after daylight, I was in better condition than anyone else. Brice was hanging over the toilet in one bathroom, either unconscious or asleep (who could tell?), and Bill was motionless in a pool of his own upchuckings in the other bathroom, arms crossed over his chest in the attitude of a corpse. Carrie was passed out on the living room couch (I didn't look too close), and I was the only one who made it, part-way at least, to an actual bed. I remember praying that the room would stop spinning. I woke up because, well, my urgent choices were either to move Brice from his perch or to hazard stepping over Bill on my way to transact a similar business in pink porcelain.

I swore to God in heaven (if there is one), as I gave up my insides to the sewer lines of Tennessee, that never, never again would I become that intoxicated. So sincere was I in my repentance that I even swore off all hard liquor then and there. I actually kept that pledge (it still tastes like cough medicine to me). It was one of those deals where you're still drunk when you wake up. I'm no goody good, but I also don't need to cut off a second finger to be absolutely certain I didn't want to lose the first one. If you've been sick-drunk and hung over like that more than once, well, all I have to say is you're not a very quick study.

My folks were to be home in the early afternoon, and one can't take chances, so with much groaning, general bleariness, and a bit of blaspheming, there was the gathering and dispatching of Bill and Carrie, and then there was some serious cleaning, airing, and stowing to do. In our condition, it took quite a while. My first hangover. Remember with me now, brothers and sisters, *your* first hangover. Where were you? And how old? Yes, that's it, let it all out. I'm here to heal your memories. And Jesus protect us from the next hangover. And the one after that too. I now understand the magical power of water and need Jesus less than before, but everybody needs a little Jesus now and then, so I'm not abandoning the faith.

Processed Processes

Rush has been criticized for the full duration of its long career for mixing processed sounds with sounds being played at that moment, on stage. It is actually pretty hard to tell sometimes what is being played and what is being triggered by one of the band members that has been sampled or recorded or sequenced in advance. But it is a fact of technology, up to the present (and this will change eventually), that the processed sounds do not respond to the band's musical activities; so the band has to play along with the processed sounds.

That, friends and neighbors, is not easy to do. Not only must the processed sounds be triggered at the precise moment needed, but the band has to be playing at the right tempo, or at least, they must adapt to what they know the processed sounds will do. If a chord change has been sequenced, for example, the band has to change chords with the sequence, and to know the precise moment. Only mathematical precision on the part of the live players makes possible the mixing of processed sound with live sound, at least if those sounds go beyond mere "sound effects."

Armed with Langer's ideas about virtual space and time, this endless debate takes on a new dimension, so to speak. Given that music is already an illusion that reminds us of the flowing life of our feelings, and given that this illusion is maintained within limits, we confront here the issue of whether the processed sounds, which are illusions of illusions, or second order virtualizations, do or don't belong in live performance, and if so, whether they belong in the genre of progressive rock, and in the music of Rush particularly. You are all aware of how Rush maintains its artistic integrity by recording only what it can reproduce in live concerts without depending on extra musicians (and that would include allowing sound engineers to trigger the processed sounds).

Clearly the band wants to maintain aesthetic and artistic integrity with regard to the limits of processed sounds. They clearly realize that once you begin messing around with processed sounds, there is always a danger that the first order virtualization will be swallowed by the second, and if that were to happen, well, they might as well lip-synch the whole thing, and we won't want to pay the price for the tickets to see *that*. On the other hand, Rush made it clear from the outset that they intended to use processed sounds to create their music. There is no chance that they can be accused of shifting their ground, but as the technology has progressed, so has the sound (at least until they decided to do just a bass, drums, and guitar thing with *Vapor Trails* in 2002).

If you think about this, from Langer's point of view, all music is in some sense "processed sound," because the jump from actual sounds to virtual tones is, itself, a kind of processing. Indeed, that is the *crucial step* because it is the move from actual to virtual time. Simply amplifying the music is another step away from mere sound, but not as radical a step as from sound to music. So the issue is not really *whether* the music is processed but *how* and *how much*. And this, like any other question in the criticism of art, actually comes down to whether the art is *good*. The use of new technologies in any art may or may not lead to better art. Usually the first attempts to accentuate an art form with a new technology are quickly surpassed by later efforts, when the possibilities have been better understood and mistakes have been made.

Once in a while some artist will really just know what to do with an innovation. For instance, the 1939 *Wizard of Oz* was the first feature-length film in "Technicolor," which required quite a lot of adaptation of sets and costumes so that the final film would look right—did you know that the ruby slippers actually had to be orange in order to appear red in Technicolor? And so with Rush. Those Moog Taurus pedals were only the beginning. Consistently Rush has been on the cutting edge of technology and has also occasionally reminded fans and critics that they don't really need all that technological support to do what they do.

So I take myself to have settled a long standing question. Asking whether Rush should use all those processors to make their music is closely akin to asking whether they should make *any* music. They have communicated their aesthetic standards and the principles that maintain the integrity of their art and their live performance. Everyone agrees that they can execute their music in concert, flawlessly. The only appropriate question, then, is whether the music is good. To this question I will offer a short answer. It is not all equally good, and there are times when the mathematical precision, from kick-drum/bass matching up through processed sound, does kill the life in it. (In Langer's terms, the music sometimes becomes "discursive.") But some of it is so very good that life bursts out of it, and here I would mention my two favorite Rush songs. I hate to be predictable, but I never tire of "Tom Sawyer" and "Limelight." Great music. Even if I never can remember all the words.

Houston, We Have a Problem, or, What Goes Up Must Come Down

It was concert time. Brice and I had finished our Rush "homework," and oh so much more. My parents had returned on schedule, and of course, as far as they were concerned, we had arrived only shortly before. I didn't lie. We went to the store and arrived back at the house shortly before the parents, which makes it technically true to say "we got here just a few minutes ago." Parents, it is good to be aware when your children have achieved "sophistication" with language. As with all human achievements, this cuts both ways. If they've come to have a fair command of "nice distinctions," and if you think that niceness won't be used in the service of narrow self-interest, then I suggest you buy your kids cars and trust them to remain chaste and sober in the operation of those machines. You'll get what you deserve down the line.

I had never had such tickets, but sort of suffered through the first two bands, knowing nothing of their music and being quite ready for the main event. And then, there they were, within a few feet, doing, well, God knows what, in order to create all that sound. What did they play? Well, I wouldn't have been able to tell you exactly, except for the invention of the Internet and millions of people with too much spare time. The list was:

- **"Bastille Day"**
- **"Lakeside Park"**
- **"By-Tor and the Snow Dog"** (abbreviated)
- **"Xanadu"**
- **"A Farewell to Kings"**
- **"Something for Nothing"**
- **"Cygnus X-1"**
- **"Anthem"** (Arrggh—but I had never heard of Ayn Rand back then and couldn't understand the words anyway)

- **"Closer to the Heart"**
- **"2112"** (minus "Oracle")
- **"Working Man"**
- **"Fly by Night"**
- **"In the Mood"**
- **Drum Solo**
- **Encore: "Cinderella Man"**

That's how it went, I'm pretty sure. It's a pretty awesome list. I'd pay a lot to see that show again, and in fact, to have back the night (if not the morning that followed). Me and Brice and Jim and about half a million other people saw that show in the course of that year. Maybe you're one of them. I was certainly hooked. Glorious show, definitely in the top ten I've ever seen.

But there was a problem. We arrived at my house euphoric from music (and the contact high we'd managed), only to hear "Brice, call your parents." I could tell by the tone that we were screwed. There was something we hadn't figured on. His mother called *during the concert*. My mother said, "Oh, they're at the concert." I hadn't lied to my parents about that part. I mean, they never would have denied me permission to go to a concert, so why lie? Shit. Double shit. You can see how it unraveled from there . . . "Oh, *we* thought Randy was over there" . . . "no, he wasn't *here*, we thought they were there" . . . "No, we went to Nashville" . . . Screwed. Totally.

But there was a difference. When you start listing and assessing the (known) crimes, you'll see why I wasn't in nearly as much trouble as Brice. He disobeyed a direct order and created an elaborate ruse to do it. I just did a Tom Sawyer *meets* Tom Cruise kind of thing. I was grounded for a week or two, and still got my first car a month later as a Christmas present. And you know what cars lead to. But in order to prevent themselves from killing him, Brice's folks blamed the awfulness of it all on *my* bad influence, and that was it for me and Brice. Never allowed to visit or communicate again. The next time I saw him we were juniors in college, and well, we *really* had nothing in common by that time. Except we still loved Zeppelin and Yes, and Rush, and our memories.

2

Barenaked Death Metal Trip-Hopping on Industrial Strings

DURRELL BOWMAN

A complex ideological field of "musicians' music" explains how artists from an extremely wide range of genres have created tribute versions of the music of the Canadian progressive/hard rock band Rush. From 1996 to 2005, recorded versions of Rush's music comprised fifty-four adaptations of thirty of the band's 167 songs on four tribute albums and in a number of additional tracks. Forty-nine (91 percent) of the fifty-four tribute recordings of Rush songs come from the band's "classic" period of 1975 to 1982. The most frequently covered Rush songs are "The Spirit of Radio" (with four versions), which is the opening song of the first album released in the 1980s (*Permanent Waves*, 1980), and "Tom Sawyer" (with six versions), which is the opening song of Rush's best-selling album (*Moving Pictures*, 1981).

Selected features from within Rush's original recordings of "The Spirit of Radio" and "Tom Sawyer" contextualize the manner in which specific tribute projects have later reworked these elements into vastly different genres of music, such as by the Barenaked Ladies (pop-rock), DJ Z-Trip (trip-hop), Disarray (death metal), Deadsy (alternative/industrial), the String Quartet Tribute to Rush (classical chamber music), and my own "scholarly meta-remix" that interleaves these versions alongside Rush's original into yet a further version of "Tom Sawyer." As Robert Walser reminds us, "musical meanings are always grounded socially and historically, and they operate on an ideological field of conflicting interests, institutions, and memories."[1] Rush

---

[1] Robert Walser, *Running with the Devil: Power, Gender, and Madness in Heavy Metal Music* (Wesleyan University Press, 1993), p. 29.

tribute projects have explored a peculiarly-grounded, social/histor-
ical context for meaning (the band is an "acquired taste"), but the
actual results certainly also conflict in terms of their specific genre
interests, institutions, and memories.

Rush's continuing, "adaptive/evolutionary" interest in fusing
progressive rock with hard rock, heavy metal, and other genres has
conflicted with the "reactive/revolutionary" interests of rock critics,
who have presented an assortment of negative evaluations concerning the band and its music, such as:

> Rush's music is one gigantic mistake. It has absolutely nothing to do
> with rock'n'roll, or even crossing the street against the light. . . . Alpo
> [dog food] . . . pretentious boredom . . . about as dangerous as getting
> shampoo in your eye.[2]

Many rock fans, however, disagreed[3] and described the band's
music as, for example:

> food for ears, heart, mind, and soul. (male, 35, motorcycle shop
> worker, multi-instrumentalist and songwriter)

> thought-provoking lyrics sung with intensity. (female, 39, homemaker,
> poet)

Others referred to Rush's:

> professional image, work ethic, good role model. (male, 34, consult-
> ing engineer)

> sensibility of not conforming only to popular trends. (male, 22, college
> student, drummer)

> ability to reproduce studio sound live. (male, 32, truck driver, guitarist-
> singer)

In 1999, Rush first met the criteria for induction into the
Rock'n'Roll Hall of Fame, but *Rolling Stone* senior editor, rock critic,
and Hall of Fame adviser David Wild said (in the summer of 2000):

---

[2] J. Kordosh, "Rush," *Creem*, June 1981, p. 32.
[3] All fan responses appearing in excerpts here are from my surveys taken in
1996 in Los Angeles, 2000 in Toronto, and 2001 in St. Catharines, Ontario.

> It ain't ever going to happen. Regardless of their success, Rush has never achieved critical acclaim and no one will ever vote for them. . . . most of it gives me a headache. . . . Technical proficiency is not a valid reason to induct an artist, and Rush really hasn't done anything unique.[4]

The problem with Wild's opinion is that Rush *has* achieved "critical acclaim" (but among other musicians, not rock critics), the band's music is quite diverse stylistically (by no means entirely technical and "headache"-inducing), and it is decidedly "unique" (at least by 1976 it was).

Rush charted only one moderately successful US Hot 100 hit, 1982's "New World Man" (at #21), and it's telling that not one of the fifty-four recorded Rush tributes engaged with that song. The song focuses stylistically on music technology and other influences from early-1980s new wave, and it contains no unusual time signatures, no guitar solo, and no virtuosic instrumental segments. It was written very quickly (in the studio) as a "toss-off," and Rush did not include the song on its "anthologizing" live albums of 1989 and 1998, although it does appear on 2003's *Rush in Rio*. Thus, I find it very strange that Katherine Charlton chose this song to represent Rush in *Rock Music Styles: A History*.[5] In any case, a Top Forty hit is certainly not always the best choice to indicate the most important aspects of an artist's work.

In the 1980s, 1990s, and 2000s, a wide variety of professional musicians musically, verbally, or visually acknowledged an interest in Rush's music. Such artists have included the Canadian rock bands Barenaked Ladies and Rheostatics; alternative rock musicians Beck and Kim Deal (the latter of the Pixies and the Breeders); members of the eclectic alternative rock bands Living Colour, Primus, the Red Hot Chili Peppers, Smashing Pumpkins, Pavement, and Deadsy; the heavy metal and hard alternative artists Dream Theater, Korn, Marilyn Manson, Metallica, Soundgarden, and Death Organ; the progressive- and thrash-metal bands Slayer, Sepultura (from Brazil), and Meshuggah (from Sweden); and even piano-based songwriters, such as Billy Joel and Randy Newman.

---

[4] Quoted at <http://inthe00s.com/archive/inthe90s/bbs0/webBBS_450.shtml>.

[5] Katherine Charlton, *Rock Music Styles: A History*, fourth edition (McGraw Hill, 2003), pp. 248–49.

Presumably, many of these artists would generally foster mutu-
ally exclusive ("conflicting") fan communities. For example, most
Randy Newman fans probably dislike Marilyn Manson's music, and
most Beck fans probably don't much care for Meshuggah.
Seemingly even further afield, classical string players (such as violinist Rachel Barton and cellist Todd Mark Rubenstein, the latter of
the diverse "String Tribute" series), a number of death metal bands
(including Disarray), and at least one trip-hop artist (DJ Z-Trip)
have also engaged with Rush's music. The band's music appeals
across these diverse genres partly because of the esteem in which
various types of musicians hold Lee, Lifeson, and Peart as musicians' music "role models." This type of admiration has partly
derived from the band's songwriting, performing, recording, and
touring "work ethic" and partly from its enduring ability to distill
elements of hard rock, heavy metal, progressive rock, and various
secondary styles into something that keeps sounding like Rush.

The Pair of Most-Often-Covered Rush Songs

Rush's first song of the 1980s opens the album *Permanent Waves*,
which was released on January 1st, 1980. "The Spirit of Radio" (see
Table 2.1) inscribes an open-minded approach both to modern rock
radio and to music technology. Many of the song's recurring gestures
display a raw, backbeat energy that fits with the aesthetic of late-
1970s post-punk, such as music by the Police. In this song, Rush consistently combines such energy with the band's ongoing progressive/
hard rock tendencies. 1970s hard rock tends towards modal constructions, whereas post-punk tends towards major/minor diatoni-
cism. In this song, Rush combines these contrasting tendencies.

Table 2.1. "The Spirit of Radio" (*Permanent Waves*, 1980)

energy riff, circular, mixolydian (0–0:17)	unison ascent (3:32–3:49)
unison ascent, semi-chromatic (0:17–0:27)	reggae insert 1, major (3:49–3:58)
verse 1 and verse 2, major (0:27–1:24)	unison ascent (3:58–4:05)
chorus, synth-laden, hybrid (1:24–1:52)	reggae insert 2, ". . . salesmen" (4:05–4:11)
verse 3, hard rock, major (1:52–2:27)	unison ascent (4:11–4:18)
chorus (2:27–2:53)	guitar solo, "chattering" (4:18–4:36)
middle section, modal, 7/4 (2:53–3:18)	ascent (+ piano), riff, cadence (4:36–4:56)
verse interlude, instrumental (3:18–3:32)	

The song's circular energy riff and its repeated, syncopated, semi-chromatic, unison ascent (see Example 2.1) inscribe minor/modal and minor constructions, though with thirds "weakened."

Example 2.1. Rush, "The Spirit of Radio," ending

The ascending passage rises through a chromatically-inflected E-based mode, but flexibly including elements of Aeolian, Dorian, and Mixolydian. By comparison, the song's verses (see Example 2.2) inscribe major-mode constructions (though with prominent suspended pitches), including IV and V chords and prominent thirds-of-chords within the vocal melody.

Example 2.2. Rush, "The Spirit of Radio," beginning of Verse 2

The lyrics of the first two verses recount one's favorite modern rock disc jockey being an "unobtrusive companion" who plays "magic music" to "make your morning mood." Verse 2 encourages you to go "off on your way" in the "happy solitude" of your car. The music's rhythmic anticipations provide a lilting joy, as though driving while listening to the "modern rock" radio of 1979–80 (such as post-punk and the Police) is a ritual to be anxiously savored.

After Verse 2, Lee adds a simple, staccato gesture on a synthesizer, and Lifeson reprises the song's energy riff. Lee's synthesizer parts, which include slow-moving string-like elements, build in intensity as the accompaniment for the song's chorus. Peart's lyrics enthuse about: "invisible airwaves," "antennas," "bristling energy," and "emotional feedback." The following verse, exclusively in hard rock style, then explains the stylistic compromise: "All this machinery making modern music can still be openhearted." However, the lyrics also provide the caveat that "glittering prizes and endless compromises shatter the illusion of integrity." Indeed, by using 7/4 time and 1970s-style cross-relations, flat-VII "hard rock" chords (instead of V chords), and a return to the modal energy riff, the song's later middle section seems to remind the listener that this really still is Rush. The band then follows the song's recurring energy riff "marker" with a reprise of its earlier virtuosic ensemble music. This middle section does not sound very much like the early 1980s, and the band might very well have ended the song after it. However, Rush wished to further its point about not compromising its integrity despite its simultaneous interest in exploring certain new approaches.

The peculiar ending of "The Spirit of Radio" functions as a conflicted meditation on the necessity of musical and cultural change, and the band included this meditation within the opening song on the first album of the 1980s. Rush twice shifts the song's ending into an unexpected, out-of-character musical style. In his lyrics, Neil Peart parodies part of the lyrics of Simon and Garfunkel's 1965 song "The Sounds of Silence." Peart accuses the music industry of focusing too narrowly on "the words of the prof*its*." Thus, according to Rush, music industry executives certainly fail to live up to Paul Simon's subway/tenement "proph*ets*." Geddy Lee sings in his baritone (natural chest) voice, thus contrasting his normal (at the time), higher, countertenor style. This contributes a laid-back vocal quality, coded as complacent or inevitable.

In its music, the band conforms more to a "stripped down" (less busy) aesthetic, featuring stylized back-beats and including pseudo-reggae/post-punk steel-drum sounds. The band quickly inserts a hard rock "concert hall moment," with clapping, whistling, and ascending instrumental music from earlier in the song. Then, as the pseudo-reggae returns and reminds us of the music industry, Lee sarcastically spits out the word "salesmen" and Lifeson's bluesy, angry guitar solo emerges over aggressive hard rock elements. The solo, in its use of voice-like, wah-wah guitar pedal effects, evokes a chattering argument about an artist's apparent stylistic misdirection.

After this fast/active/angry caricature, the band incorporates a more substantial reprise of the song's main unison, hard rock ascent. However, a comparatively simple "rock'n'roll" piano part joins in to further heighten the stylistic ambiguity. Rush *did* sometimes use keyboards in the mid- to late-1970s, but almost always for occasional melodic, timbral, or textural reasons, as in the chorus of this song. "The Spirit of Radio" ends with Lifeson restating the energy riff and with an energetic cadence featuring Peart's virtuosic drumming. These closing gestures may suggest that Rush wishes to assert a hard rock victory over the other styles with which it just engaged. However, it seems just as likely, given Rush's stylistic direction after 1980, that the band meant to suggest that post-punk, hard rock, progressive rock, and other elements should be combined.

In "Tom Sawyer" (see Table 2.2) from *Moving Pictures* (1981), Rush wishes to position itself as a kind of musical updating of Mark Twain's famous young misfit.

Table 2.2. "Tom Sawyer" (*Moving Pictures*, 1981)

synth & drums (0:00–0:05)	instrumental section, 7/4 (1:33–2:32)
vocal introduction (0:05–0:11)	expanded main "swagger" intro (2:32–2:43)
main "swagger" introduction (0:11–0:22)	Verse 2 (2:43–2:56)
Verse 1, with "swagger" (0:22–0:36)	instrumental verse (2:56–3:08)
instrumental verse (0:36–0:47)	bridge (3:08–3:29)
bridge (0:47–1:08)	"chorus" (3:29–3:48)
"chorus" (1:08–1:28)	expanded vocal introduction (3:48–3:57)
new vocal introduction (1:28–1:33)	coda, faded (3:57–4:33)

The song's instrumental section (see Example 2.3) again features the band's characteristic, asymmetrical time signature: 7/4, including a descending chain of thirds on a Minimoog synthesizer.

Example 2.3: Rush, "Tom Sawyer," 7/4 instrumental pattern

The section, however, soon becomes "traditional Rush," with Lee taking over his own synthesizer patterns on bass guitar in order to support Lifeson's guitar solo. The solo ends with Lifeson re-joining the pattern in one of the band's characteristic virtuosic unisons. To get back to the song's earlier music, the band restates the eight-bar, four-chord "swagger" riff that also underscores the song's verses. This returns the time signature to "cut time" (with a half-note pulse), although the music in this case now also features Peart's drumming prowess more prominently, as a substitute for a drum solo. Verse 2 (see Example 2.4) then refers to the libertarian, "post-countercultural" notion of neither god nor government being worthy of one's mind.

Example 2.4. Rush, "Tom Sawyer," Verses 1 and 2

The same verse also refers self-reflexively to change as a permanent strategy. The underlying swagger riff revolves around a "short-long-short-long" gesture that reaches fully-voiced chords from previously-established low pitches.

Tribute Versions of "The Spirit of Radio" and "Tom Sawyer"

Eventually, new versions of Rush's "musicians' rock" appeared within tribute activities by other artists. For example, in "Grade 9" (*Gordon*, 1992), the band's Toronto compatriots the Barenaked Ladies include "mini tributes" not only to the swagger riff of Rush's "Tom Sawyer" but also to the energy riff of "The Spirit of Radio." In addition, the song musically references Vince Guaraldi's piano-based theme music for the 1960s–1970s "Peanuts" TV specials and lyrically references Led Zeppelin's "Stairway to Heaven" (1971).

The Barenaked Ladies include such references to address the socially awkward early years of high school for "geeky" aspiring musicians such as themselves. Thus, the references function not as broad comedic parody (as in "Weird" Al Yankovic) or as critical/destructive parody (as in Frank Zappa) but, rather, to acknowledge and celebrate selected aspects—even geeky, teenaged ones—of one's background as a musician. Perhaps to prove his commitment to this background, during early 2005's post-tsunami TV charity concert *Canada for Asia*, Ed Robertson of the Barenaked Ladies joined Rush (and "Bubbles," from the Canadian TV comedy series *Trailer Park Boys*) in a five-person performance of the trio's 1977 song "Closer to the Heart." Similarly, Rush's "The Spirit of Radio" had appeared on 1990's *The Earthquake Album: Rock Aid Armenia*, a fundraising album.

In 1998, Rush's "Tom Sawyer" appeared in three major motion pictures. *The Waterboy* (an Adam Sandler comedy) uses it to underscore a football game, *Whatever* (a suburban, teenaged "pothead" film, set in the year of the song's release) uses it to introduce a party scene, and *Small Soldiers* (an action-adventure film) includes a scene in which a teenaged girl (played by Kirsten Dunst) listens to it. The song also appears in Rob Zombie's 2007 version of *Halloween* (and on its CD soundtrack), in 2009's *Fanboys* and *I Love You, Man*, and on such TV shows as *Chuck, Family Guy, Freaks and Geeks*, and *Futurama*. Rush also played the song live on a July 2008 episode of *The Colbert Report*.

The CD soundtrack of *Small Soldiers* includes DJ Z-Trip's trip-hop remix of "Tom Sawyer." The remix leaves out many of the original song's more overt progressive rock elements, especially most of Peart's more elaborate drumming. Instead, it incorporates various sectional and chord re-sequencings, turntable scratching and other percussion elements, studio effects on Lee's voice, overt panning effects, and new spoken material. For his version of the original's 7/4 middle section, Z-Trip considerably abbreviates it and also erases its guitar solo in favour of more extensive synthesizer-based sounds. Notably, he also gives the 7/4 Minimoog pattern two extra 8th-notes in order to make it conform to the much more normal time signature 4/4. Disarray's death metal adaptation of "Tom Sawyer" appears on *Red Star: Tribute to Rush* (Dwell, 1999), and it includes the sub-genre's characteristic "demonic," grunted vocals. Although Disarray's version is quite different stylistically from the slightly earlier trip-hop remix, it also modifies Rush's instrumental section by adding two 8th-notes to the repeating pattern and by removing the guitar solo. Moreover, although Disarray generally takes the song at a somewhat faster tempo than Rush's original, it also slows down the instrumental section considerably.

Oddly, the original Rush tribute album, *Working Man* (Magna Carta, 1996), excludes versions of "The Spirit of Radio" and "Tom Sawyer." The album changes Rush's original songs rather little, but it does include minor modifications to certain bass lines, as well as other relatively "cosmetic" differences. The project, led by Dream Theater drummer Mike Portnoy and mixed by former Rush co-producer Terry Brown, for the most part treats selected 1974–87 Rush songs as canonic precursors of late-1980s and 1990s progressive metal. Musicians within this particular sub-genre venerate Rush as the godfathers of such music, but they also seem content to make the band's songs slightly more virtuosic within their original idiom, rather than finding anything new about them. *Red Star: Tribute to Rush* (Dwell, 1999), including Disarray's version of "Tom Sawyer," also treats selected 1974–82 Rush songs as canonic precursors, but within the much-less-expected sub-genre of late-1990s hardcore and death metal. The third Rush tribute album, *Exit . . . Stage Right: The String Quartet Tribute to Rush* (Vitamin, 2002) similarly takes the band's music into a rather unexpected genre area: classical chamber music. The fourth Rush tribute album, *Subdivisions: A Tribute to the Music of Rush* (Magna Carta, 2005), then returns to the progressive heavy metal aesthetic of the same record company's *Working Man*, but it does not duplicate any of the songs already adapted on the earlier album.

Billy Joel suggested, in a 1980 appropriation of and homage to post-punk music, that "It's Still Rock'n'Roll to Me." Rush's musical undercoding, or at least ambiguous coding, in "The Spirit of Radio" and "Tom Sawyer" led to an ongoing engagement with those songs long after Billy Joel's genre-overcoded, new wave-influenced, pop song (US Top 40 #1) ceased to appeal to many of its original mainstream, casual fans. Rush's "The Spirit of Radio" (US Hot 100 #51) and "Tom Sawyer" (US Hot 100 #44) quickly became staples of album-oriented rock and remained so nearly thirty years later. Regarding "The Spirit of Radio," other than the Barenaked Ladies' reference to the song's energy riff, from 1994 to 2002 Catherine Wheel (British, alternative rock), Rachel Barton (US, classical violinist), Premonition (US, heavy metal, also on *Red Star*), St. Etienne (British, alternative rock), Rosetta Stone (British, industrial-goth), and additional US classical string musicians (on 2002's *Exit . . . Stage Right*) also engaged with that song. Regarding "Tom Sawyer," other than the Barenaked Ladies' reference to the song's swagger riff and the trip-hop remix and death metal versions just discussed, in the early 2000s instrumental variations of "Tom Sawyer" underscored a Nissan Maxima TV ad and Deadsy released an alternative/industrial version. The tribute album *Subdivisions* (2005) also includes progressive metal versions of both songs. By comparison, I could only find information about one non-Billy Joel recording of "It's Still Rock'n'Roll to Me," a 1997 punk version by 30 Foot Tall.

David Brackett discusses a similar dichotomy between Gary Lewis and the Playboys' hit song "This Diamond Ring" (1965, US Top 40 #1) and Wilson Pickett's rhythm-and-blues/soul song "In the Midnight Hour" (also 1965, US Top 40 #21). The latter song, although it did not chart especially high as a pop song on its release, quickly became a widely acknowledged classic. The former song, although ridiculously popular on its release, is much less highly thought of in retrospect, at least by rock historians and critics. Brackett cautions, however, that applying Mikhail Bakhtin's preference for polyvocal/dialogic texts (arguably, the Pickett and Rush songs) over univocal/monologic texts (arguably, the Lewis and Joel songs) "runs the risk of oversimplification."[6] As had been

---

[6] David Brackett, *Interpreting Popular Music* (Cambridge University Press, 1995), p. 17.

the case fifteen years earlier vis-à-vis Lewis and Pickett, many young rock fans in 1980–81 found Billy Joel's music at least as meaningful as Rush's. Like Paul McCartney and Joe Jackson in the 1990s, Billy Joel dabbled in the world of "light classical music" in the early 2000s. By comparison, Rush continued to make new *rock* music throughout the 1990s and early 2000s. The band used relatively subtle classical elements in a few songs in 1985, 1987, and 1993, including a wordless choir, a brass section, and several string sections. However, Rush's more elaborate, progressive-oriented music from 1975 to 1981 then lent itself to wholesale classical treatments by others.

In the late 1990s and early 2000s, the Finnish four-cello ensemble Apocalyptica spearheaded the trend of fully translating hard rock songs into something more like classical music. This produces something quite different, stylistically *and* ideologically, from incorporating classical instruments or classical music *into* rock music. From 1965 to 1977, various British rock bands sometimes attempted fusions of classical instruments or actual classical music along with rock instruments and rock music. Procol Harum recorded its 1972 US #5 live album with the Edmonton Symphony Orchestra and Da Camera Singers. After that early period, however, it took quite a while until mainstream rock musicians revisited the large-scale fusion of classical instruments with rock instrumentation. Metallica's *S&M* ("Symphony and Metallica," 1999) features performances by the band with the San Francisco Symphony, arranged and conducted by Michael Kamen, a film composer and former contributor to music by David Bowie, Kate Bush, and (on 1993's *Counterparts*) Rush.

As far as I know, the first recorded instance of translating a Rush song entirely into classical instrumentation appears on Chicago-based classical violinist Rachel Barton's Stringendo album *Storming the Citadel* (1997–98). In her liner notes, Barton raises the question:

> Crossover is hot. . . . As our tastes become increasingly multi-cultural and eclectic, the lines between high art and pop art are becoming increasingly blurred. But isn't playing heavy metal on an acoustic violin going a bit too far?
>
> From a historical perspective, I would have to say no. Classical music through the centuries has always drawn heavily upon the rhythmic and harmonic elements of the folk and popular music of its day .

. . . In turn, the great violin soloists have been known to arrange some of their favorite non-classical tunes. . . . This project continues in that tradition.

. . . the structures of tunes like [Rush's] "The Spirit of Radio" and [Metallica's] "One" are quite sophisticated, much more so than in a typical pop tune.

Barton wishes to hedge her bets by historicizing her project in these terms. Unlike Procol Harum and Metallica's symphonic albums—and most of her own examples—this is not about "crossover" exactly. Toronto's Flying Bulgar Klezmer Band aside, klezmer is hardly "popular music," exactly, and Paganini presumably never had to contend with commercial mediation in quite the same way as popular musicians have in the twentieth and early twenty-first centuries. Barton's project also has nothing to do with newly-composed classical music drawing on elements from popular music. The real truth of it must be that she grew up listening to rock music, still liked some of it, and wanted to play it.

In her string trio translation of "The Spirit of Radio," Barton effectively uses pizzicato technique to convey the stripped-down, reggae-influenced elements of the original song's ending. She aborts Lifeson's guitar solo, however, and goes directly into the song's originally pseudo-rock'n'roll ending, including textural variations of the percussive piano part. Barton recorded the album live at a radio station, and she incorporates additional bet-hedging by including her solo violin version of "The Star-Spangled Banner" as well as classical works by Paganini and Handel. Tellingly, she picked difficult classical works that sometimes sound like aspects of the complex rock songs she selected, *not* classical works based on folk songs.

Exit . . . Stage Right: The String Quartet Tribute to Rush (Vitamin, 2002) references the title, cover, and song order of Rush's second live album, *Exit . . . Stage Left* (1981). Nashville-based producer-musician Todd Mark Rubenstein initiated the arduous task of translating almost an entire album's worth of Rush's music into something quite far removed from the band's "native tongue" of electric guitars, effects pedals, electric bass guitars, electronic bass pedals, a large array of drums and percussion, electronic keyboards, lyrics, and vocals. According to the album's liner notes, Rubenstein began by entering suitable tracks for each song into a keyboard music sequencer. Next, he produced MIDI files and converted them into traditional musical notation using the computer program Finale. Copyists then prepared string parts. Rubenstein (cello/bass), Patricia and Paul Tobias (who both play violin and viola on all tracks), and cellist Andre Janovich used multi-track recording, sampling technology, and so on to create versions of the original guitar, bass, keyboard, and vocal elements. The opening track provides a classical version of "The Spirit of Radio" to compete with Barton's. Unlike Barton's version, it includes an approximation of Lifeson's chattering guitar solo, but electric guitars facilitate many things that acoustic violins cannot. Barton's version of "The Spirit of Radio" also succeeds better than the one on *Exit . . . Stage Right* for the reason that she arranged for live string trio what Rush plays with a live rock trio. In a related vein, the version of "Tom Sawyer" that ends *Exit . . . Stage Right* also incorporates sampled sounds obviously played by a sequencer. Indeed, Rubenstein's website later somewhat guiltily referred to the album as a "string tribute" and to a "10-piece orchestra." Ironically, the album also excludes the closing work of Rush's *Exit . . . Stage Left*, the large-scale instrumental "La Villa Strangiato," much of which (largely because it is lacking lyrics and vocals) one can certainly imagine working very well "transliterated" for classical strings. The US Academy of Recording Arts and Sciences allowed a first-round nomination of *Exit . . . Stage Right* for a 2002 Grammy for Best Instrumental Pop Album. (It did not make the final round of nominations.) This is somewhat ironic given that Rush itself never won a Grammy, despite five nominations for Best Rock Instrumental from 1982 to 2009.

Unlike all rock-oriented Rush tributes, Barton's arrangement of "The Spirit of Radio" and the dozen Rush arrangements on *Exit . . . Stage Right* present nothing equivalent to Neil Peart's drumming *or* lyrics. However, even without those seemingly central elements, Rush's music from 1975-81 still translates quite well into the classical medium. This results from the band's "classic" period of especially progressive-oriented influences, elaborate solos and instrumental sections, and varied textures, rhythms, time signatures, instrumentations, and dynamics. This also inadvertently expands my contention that aspects of progressive rock functioned as "substitute classical music" for many working class and lower-middle-class rock fans in the 1980s.

Vitamin Records, which released *Exit . . . Stage Right: The String Quartet Tribute to Rush*, has also covered a wide variety of additional popular music artists in this way. Thus, certain types of popular music may still function as substitute classical music for some people, and string tribute albums of rock songs may cater to this. Conversely, it is also slightly possible that fans of classical music who do not otherwise much care for the sounds of "real" rock music may find elements of value within such albums.

A "Meta-Remix" of Rush's "Tom Sawyer"

It occurred to me that it would be a useful exercise to combine several different versions of the same Rush song in order to highlight the diversity of "genre artists" who have engaged with the band's progressive/hard rock music. I have termed this approach the "scholarly meta-remix," and it has proven similarly useful for bringing together different songs by comparable artists in order to show their similarities. My version of "Tom Sawyer" is just slightly shorter than the original (4:26 versus 4:33), and it includes the following six versions of the song (in the order I introduce them):

1. Rush's original recording (1981)

2. the Barenaked Ladies' incorporation of its swagger riff into their pop-rock song "Grade 9" (1992)

3. aspects of the versions by DJ Z-Trip (trip-hop, 1998)

4. Todd Mark Rubenstein ("string quartet," 2002)

5. Disarray (death metal, 1999)

6. Deadsy (alternative/industrial, 2002)

Table 2.3. "Toms Sawyer" (Meta-Remix, Durrell Bowman, 2003 at <http://durrellbowman.com/recordings.php>

synth & drums (0:00–0:05) vocal introduction (0:05–0:11) main "swagger" introduction (0:11–0:22) Verse 1, with "swagger" (0:22–0:36) instrumental verse (0:36–0:47) bridge (0:47–1:08) "chorus" (1:08–1:28) new vocal introduction (1:28–1:33)	Rush 0:34, a cut to the Barenaked Ladies reference 0:47–0:50, a cross-fade back to Rush 0:57, a combination of Rush with DJ Z-Trip

Table 2.3. (cont'd.)

instrumental section, 7/4 (1:33–2:30)	1:11, Rush with strings added
	1:33, just strings, then just Rush,
expanded "swagger" intro (2:30–2:42)	1:45, the onset of "chaos:"
Verse 2 (2:42–2:53)	Rush +Disarray (in D) +DJ Z-Trip +strings
instrumental verse (2:53–3:02)	Disarray gradually takes over the texture
bridge (3:02–3:22)	Disarray
"chorus" (3:22–3:36)	
expanded vocal introduction (3:36–3:49)	3:07, cross-fade to Deadsy (in B)
coda, faded (3:49–4:26)	Deadsy
	Deadsy + strings (in E)

I begin (see Table 2.3) with the Rush (in the key of E), but right at
the end of Verse 1 (at 0:34), I cut directly to the Barenaked Ladies'
version of the swagger riff (also in E, with hard-rock drumming
actually more similar to Peart's elaborate drumming later in the
original song), and one can also hear the "Grade 9" words: "this is
me" and, at the end of the reference (at 0:46), a transition back to
the ska-like drumming and the vocal line of the Barenaked Ladies'
own chorus: "This is me in Grade 9, baby, yeah, this is me." During
that, I cross-fade (at 0:50) back to Rush's "instrumental verse," and
in the second half of the sung bridge (at 0:58), I combine Rush's
original version with the vocal effects, "urban"-sounding drumming, and guitar-chord re-sequencings of Z-Trip's remix. At the
beginning of the instrumental section (originally in 7/4, see
Example 3), I start with the strings (1:33), but then switch to the
original (1:38).

At 1:45, "chaos" ensues, as I add Disarray's instrumental section
(which is slower, including a noticeable hi-hat pattern, in 4/4, and
a tone lower, in D), and one can also hear the string version of the
guitar solo and Z-Trip turntable-scratching effects and vocal samples ("he's kind of lost his mind") near the beginning of the peak
section of Lifeson's original solo. During the post-solo return to the
original song's unison statement of the 7/4 pattern and Peart's original "mini drum solo" (at 2:25) I allow Disarray's death metal version (in D) to emerge, and that version alone (with its grunted,
"demonic" vocals) provides Verse 2. During the bridge (at 3:07), I
cross-fade to Deadsy's version (in B), and that version alone pro-

vides the instrumental ending of the bridge and the chorus. For the transition to the final vocal "introduction" (at 3:38), I add the strings (in the song's original key of E) to the Deadsy, and the contrasting keys (a perfect fourth apart) provide an oddly "medieval" sound, with the 7/4 synthesizer pattern temporally spaced in order to highlight its positioning within two different key areas.

Coda

Musicians' magazines and related pedagogical contexts cater to musician-fans by providing article-interviews, technique columns, song transcriptions, and equipment reviews instead of album/concert reviews and opinion pieces. In the 1980s, 1990s, and 2000s magazines such as *Modern Drummer, Guitar for the Practicing Musician,* and *Bass Player* regularly featured one or more members of Rush, placing Neil Peart, Alex Lifeson, and Geddy Lee in "Honor Rolls" or "Halls of Fame." In a related development concerning amateur and semi-professional musicians, dozens of Rush tribute bands performed the group's music for small, local audiences in a number of countries. In addition, numerous future professional musicians learned to play some of Rush's songs. Not surprisingly, for most of Rush's own first five years (1968–73, at ages fifteen to twenty), the band mainly functioned as a hard-working, part-time cover band, playing British and North American psychedelic rock and blues-rock by other groups. Neil Peart similarly played in the mainly cover band Hush, in between an early career attempt in London, England around 1970–72 and replacing John Rutsey in Rush in the late summer of 1974.

Rush's music demonstrates that individualist musicians can pursue a successful career path that continuously problematizes ideology, genre, style, technology, the music industry, *and* fan communities. Robert Walser, in discussing the appropriations of classical music by heavy metal musicians, suggests:

> Heavy metal musicians . . . draw upon the resources of the past that have been made available to them through mass mediation and their own historical study. But it is precisely such predations that the musical academy is supposed to prevent. Bach's contemporary meanings are produced in tandem by musicologists and the marketing departments of record companies and symphony orchestras, and the Bach they construct has little to do with the dramatic, noisy meanings found

by metal musicians and fans and everything to do with aesthetics, order, and cultural hegemony . . . . The drive to enforce preferred ideological meanings is . . . "nondialogic." It is oppressive, authoritative, and absolute.[7]

Rock tribute artists similarly draw upon mass-mediated resources and their own historical study to find variable, refractive, distorted, and disruptive meaning in the much more recent past. In an unexpected breadth of dialogue, Rush tribute artists hail from a field of activities that itself inscribes considerable ideological—and literal—noise. As we have seen, this includes the electronic sounds and digital manipulations of trip-hop, the demonic vocals of death metal, and even the bows-on-strings noise of classical chamber music.

---

[7] Robert Walser, *Running with the Devil: Power, Gender, and Madness in Heavy Metal Music* (Wesleyan University Press: Hanover, NH, 1993), 105.

3

The Groove of Rush's Complex Rhythms

JOHN J. SHEINBAUM

In the Heat of the Beat and the Lights

From the opening notes of the show to its closing moments, Rush rocks. Well-seasoned pros, they display the famous iconography of guitar heroes. Geddy Lee and Alex Lifeson bob the necks of their instruments up and down. Neil Peart throws a drumstick into the air at opportune moments, catching it in time for the next downbeat. Their faces are ecstatic for each whammy bar dive, each driving accent. On the arena stage, a compact studio recording like "Closer to the Heart" can open up into an extended jam, with Lifeson employing Pete Townshend-like guitar windmills, and Lee trying out a Chuck Berry chicken walk. The band is loose, visibly joking around with each other, even through the (very) occasional miscue.

They're in no self-contained bubble up on stage; they actively court the audience's participation in the festivities. I've been caught up by all this myself on numerous occasions, and the evidence is right there for the newcomer—or the old fan who wants to relive the experience—on Rush's concert videos. On the *A Show of Hands* DVD, for example, largely recorded during the tour supporting 1988's *Hold Your Fire*, Lee eggs on the crowd to clap along with the opening electronic textures of "Red Sector A." He gestures with alternating arms, then with his right hand alone, palm down, bent at the wrist, pulsing with the beat.

At the climax of "Marathon" the large screens behind the band show animated film clips of mouths moving, inviting a singalong for the final choruses. In the encore set, he holds his hand up to his ear during the slow-building textures near the top of the instrumental "La Villa Strangiato," asking the crowd for more. As Lee puts it in a voiceover near the top of the *Exit. . . Stage Left* video, recorded on the *Moving Pictures* tour in 1981, "your basic job as a musician is to entertain people, and I really believe that." And the audience responds in kind. The fans move their bodies forward and back while waving their arms. The crowd grooves along, bouncing their heads, playing air drums, shouting to fill well-timed silences. As can be seen on the 2003 *Rush in Rio* DVD, even an audience large enough to fill a stadium is immersed in the performance in a profound, infectious way.

Many of the passages that engage the band and their fans are not filled with the stereotypical sounds of three-chord rock, which might allow participation by someone who's never heard Rush before. Instead they often show striking examples of the rhythmic complexities for which Rush is famous. In the *Exit . . . Stage Left* performance of "By-Tor and the Snow Dog," Lee and Lifeson's fooling around heightens at the very moment that might be most challenging to keep together: they're playing an unpredictable series of accents at shorter and shorter intervals, each time removing one chord from the pattern. During the performance of "Strangiato" on the *Show of Hands* DVD, their playful gestures abound in a middle section built around an unstable and fast-moving 7/8 meter. On "Turn the Page" the audience is shown grooving along for the bass vamp, even though it fitfully alternates groups of four and two beats. On *Exit . . . Stage Left*, the audience cheering is perhaps at its loudest during the heavily syncopated instrumental stop-time passage in "Red Barchetta." The band and the crowd groove not in spite of these difficulties, but perhaps *because* of them.[14] Unlike what we might expect, given conventional assumptions about rock music, notions of "complexity" and "groove" are not opposed in Rush's musical language.

Philosophies of Musical Time

Complex passages of the types found in "Strangiato" and "Barchetta" attracted me to Rush as I was developing my own

---

[1] Adapting Jonathan Pieslak's thoughts on "progressive/math metal"—a subgenre for which Rush served as an inspiration—"the technical aspects" of the music may represent "a source, if not *the* source, of [fan] attraction." "Re-casting Metal: Rhythm and Meter in the Music of Meshuggah," *Music Theory Spectrum* 29 (2007), p. 244.

teenage musical tastes. As a student musician I found myself some-what dissatisfied with the pop and rock surrounding me on MTV and the radio, and it wasn't until a bit later in my life that I was introduced to the wild styles and sounds of twentieth-century classical music and experimental jazz. Many of my musician friends and I were particularly drawn to 1970s "progressive" rock, though the heights of "prog" may have been a few years before our time. The unpredictable chord progressions, the extended song structures, the odd time signatures and mixing of meters: we felt challenged to listen over and over, to grab our instruments and try to figure out how the music was put together without the crutch of published (and not very accurate) sheet music. The harder edge of Rush's music was all the better, since that helped lend an additional air of seriousness and intensity to the whole endeavor.

Focusing on the organization of musical time was especially important in the absence of written music. A note is a note: if you matched a sound from the recording on your guitar then you knew you got the right pitch. But rhythm and meter had to be experienced, actively created, interacted with. Without rhythms to read on the page, inflections in the performance itself were the only guideline as to how the flow of time might be organized.[2] To lock in mentally with the band—to understand how a Peart beat worked, or why Lifeson changed the chord just there, or to predict correctly where Lee's next bass accent would attack—felt supremely satisfying, and musically rewarding. My assumption, though I would argue somewhat differently today, was that something about these rhythmic complexities made Rush's music *better*, while the standard sorts of structures were boringly, well, standard.

The conventional philosophy of musical time asserts that humans understand rhythms and their groupings against a baseline of regularity and symmetry. We use the actual rhythms of the music to abstract a stream of evenly spaced pulses, and these pulses tend to organize into alternating "stronger" and "weaker" beats. This is why so much music from various Western traditions works around a "duple" meter of two or four beats to the bar. The sense of regular meter then serves as a background structure, and

---

[2] For reasons like these, while previous generations of music theorists focused primarily on pitch-based aspects of music, which are reasonably well captured in notated music, a fair amount of recent work in the field explores the temporal aspects of music.

allows the rhythms in the music to be heard as functioning within that structure.

Recent work in the field of music perception largely bears this out. Scientists have recorded electrophysiological data from subjects listening with varying levels of attention to variations of a regular 4/4 rock beat. Even when we're somewhat distracted from careful listening, and even when we're not trained musicians, we're measurably aroused when an accent strikes in a place where the metrical structure doesn't predict it, such as between two beats, and we're similarly aroused when silence occurs on what should be a "strong" beat—the two core experiences of syncopation.[3]

A related concept that has engaged music theorists over the last generation or so is the notion of "hypermeter." Simply put, hypermeter extends the idea of a hierarchy of "strong" and "weak" beats to the function of full bars within longer musical phrases.[4] Thus, whole measures can also be thought of as "strong" and "weak," and alternations of them on even higher levels lead to phrases that last two, four, eight, or sixteen bars. This is often as significant an experience as the feeling of meter itself. If I'm playing guitar in a rock band, and we're performing a cover version of "Fly By Night," while I'm improvising my way through the guitar solo I don't have to count carefully to begin the following chorus correctly; I simply need to *feel* the phrases. Confronted with the sixteen-measure solo, which uses the four-bar chord progression of the opening riff and verses but lasts longer than any of those sections, I simply need to keep track of four phrases, rather than diligently counting through sixty-four beats, or trying to keep track of sixteen bars.

Taken all together, the standard assumption—especially when approaching presumably simple rock music—is that, first, each bar will have four beats alternating "strong" and "weak," with the downbeat even stronger than beat three, the other relatively strong beat. Each of the beats can be further subdivided into faster-moving groups divisible by two. Each "quarter-note" beat can contain

---

[3] Olivia Ladinig, Henkian Honing, Gábor Háden, and István Winkler, "Probing Attentive and Preattentive Emergent Meter in Adult Listeners Without Extensive Music Training," *Music Perception* 26 (2009), pp. 377–386.

[4] Fairly accessible overviews and applications of the concept of hypermeter can be found in William Rothstein, *Phrase Rhythm in Tonal Music* (Longman, 1989), and Jonathan Kramer, *The Time of Music* (Schirmer, 1988).

two faster "eighth notes," or four even faster "sixteenth notes," and so on, in any combination that follows mathematically. Second, the bars, in turn, will combine for phrases that grow out of multiples of two—eight-bar phrases are perhaps the most common—and the phrases will group themselves symmetrically into the various different sections of the piece. Deviations on any level are noteworthy. Syncopations disrupt where we expect strong accents to be heard. Waltzes seem special because they have three beats to a bar instead of four. Phrase lengths can be altered from the model for dramatic effect: a normally eight-bar phrase might be elided against the next phrase, leaving only seven bars before the new arrival, or such a phrase might be extended to nine bars or more in order to increase the tension before the next section begins.

In "Red Barchetta," for instance (the studio version is found on *Moving Pictures*), consider the effect of the phrase beginning with "Down in his barn" (1:43–1:58). The arrival of the final word "dream" functions simultaneously as the eighth bar of the phrase *and* the first bar of Lifeson's two measures of quiet harmonics. The excitement of seeing the well-preserved old car is reflected in a phrase structure that refuses to take its time before hurtling forward. In fact, the seventh bar of the phrase, just before "dream," even has a beat removed from its standard 4/4 structure to increase yet further the effect of the new phrase seeming to arrive too soon. Compare this to the comparable phrase near the song's conclusion, beginning with "At the one-lane bridge" (4:52–5:05). Now, to suit the repose of the protagonist finally back with his uncle at the farm, the final syllable "side" (of "fireside") enjoys a full measure of its own to end the eight-bar phrase comfortably before the next phrase begins.

Without even being consciously aware of the temporal construction of most music we hear, we nevertheless bring a host of expectations to the table. As we might guess, these background assumptions are not universals, but can be seen as bound by place and time.[5] The very perception of meter and hypermeter as I've described it here is likely symbolic of Western modes of organization in general. Sounds are placed within bars similar to the ways

---

[5] See Amatzia Bar-Yosef, "Musical Time Organization and Space Concept: A Model of Cross-Cultural Analogy, *Ethnomusicology* 45 (2001), pp. 423–442; and Roger Mathew Grant, "Epistemologies of Time and Meter in the Long Eighteenth Century," *Eighteenth-Century Music* 6 (2009), pp. 59–75.

a grid delineates a city's downtown, or how a frame affects the painting within, or how a stage orders the space for a performance. The frames impose orientation on the objects within; rhythms make sense only against our perception of the underlying meter. And this basic conception of musical time in the West is itself an idea that only took hold during the eighteenth century.

The way we tend to feel musical time is no less real or powerful because the concepts are social and cultural constructions. Peart's lyrics can easily evoke the stultifying standardization of the suburbs, or reference Shakespeare by suggesting that "we are merely players" upon a metaphorical stage, because Rush's audience is well ensconced within such modes of organizing our experiences.

Musical Time and Individualism

To counter our limited roles in the world, a marked trope of individualism often plays out in Rush's music. In Chris McDonald's words, "Rush presents a vision of society that is divided between a pessimistic portrayal of it as a conformist social order which the individual should resist and an optimistic view of it as an environment in which the exceptional individual stands out and flourishes."[6] Thus, Rush's musical textures tend toward a whole-band virtuosity, where all three members act as "lead" players, and each individual voice is clear within the musical fabric. The tendency towards long and intricate structures helps particular songs develop strong individual profiles, and makes Rush's output as a whole seem the result of remarkable hard work.

Rush's rhythmic and metrical constructions also play an emphatic role in our perception of individualism in the band's music. The copious and complex deviations from rock rhythmic norms can be taken as signs that their music is progressive, and can be interpreted as a push for agency against the numbing effects of contemporary society. Regular rhythms, meters, and phrase constructions can be thought of as evoking the "conformist social order," while intense syncopations, asymmetrical meters, and surprising phrase lengths "resist" the easy paths, and construct musical identities that can speak against the conventions.

---

[6] Chris McDonald, "Open Secrets: Individualism and Middle-Class Identity in the Songs of Rush," *Popular Music and Society* 31 (2008), p. 319.

Consider "Subdivisions," the opening song and one of the singles from *Signals* (1982).[7] The lyrics, about the harsh realities of life within a conventional suburban subdivision, place the song in the routine lives of Rush's main fan base of white, suburban, male teenagers. Thus much of the music similarly focuses on the humdrum and everyday. Synthesizers, a staple of early 1980s pop, are used as the lead instrument for almost the entire song, grounding it in the sounds of the here-and-now. The synthesizer solo appears twice, in virtually identical fashion; such repetition of an entire instrumental solo does not occur on any other track by the band before or after this album. And much of the song is based around a flat-VI-flat–VII–I chord progression in B minor, a rock chord progression so common it borders on the mundane.

However, the band's use of difficult time signatures and mixing meters also comes to the fore in "Subdivisions." The opening phrases of the introduction are built around a 7/8 time signature, where the timeline of fast eighth notes is grouped in a repeating 2 + 2 + 3 pattern. At other points, as during some phrases of the verse, conventional 4/4 bars are placed within tricky three- and six-measure groups. These sections, from phrase to phrase, move quite freely from complex meters to simple ones and back again, and from simple to complex phrase structures and back again. The overall effect is a feeling of constant restlessness. The unending pushing and pulling between and within time signatures evokes the imaginary protagonist's struggle with synthetic life in MTV-watching suburbia at the end of the twentieth century, a struggle with which the core of Rush's fans could have easily identified.

Thinking about Rush's music from such a point of view is complex and contradictory, however, as McDonald also points out. Individualism is a common enough value that when a mass of people assert individuality, a potentially ironic effect is that each person can seem *less* individual. Though Rush is no Top 40 mainstay, it would be a stretch to call Rush fandom subcultural. Listening to the band's recordings and attending concerts are activities enjoyed by millions. Further, the sort of individualism surrounding Rush tends to be valued particularly highly by the Western "hegemonic center," hardly a model—indeed, the polar opposite—of cultural resistance. Like the Ayn Rand novels that provided inspiration,

---

[7] This discussion is based on a passage in my article "Periods in Progressive Rock and the Problem of Authenticity," *Current Musicology* 85 (2008), pp. 41–43.

much of Rush's music "made common middle-class values such as
self-reliance, social mobility, and the Protestant work ethic seem
Romantic, exciting, and urgent."[8]

Rush Grooves

At the same time, it's not quite enough to argue that Rush presents a
baseline of the "simple" background of rock music to evoke convention, and then resists that background by employing "complex"
and "individual" musical features to contradict it. Instead, there's
often a synthesis of opposites at play, a sense of dialectical poles
often operating simultaneously in Rush's musical gestures. My interpretation of Rush's use of rhythm and meter focuses on the fact that
such intricate structures are often employed in ways that seem smooth,
balanced, and regular. In short, Rush's complex rhythms *groove*.

In "Subdivisions," for example, those 7/8 passages, while irregular and somewhat difficult to read in musical notation, also exhibit
essential characteristics of groove. The rhythms are used in a "per-
sistently repeated pattern" that "somehow compels the body to
move," as the *New Grove Dictionary of Jazz* defines the term.[9] A
time signature like 7/8, though not common in any style of music,
let alone rock, practically insists on one's bodily absorption in the
music. The pulses fly by—in the case of "Subdivisions." over and
over again throbbing in a 1–2 / 1–2 / 1–2–3 pattern—at a speed
that needs to be felt, but felt in a way that combines the conscious
mind with unconscious reflexes and muscle memory. Any distraction, however momentary, might disrupt the flow. One's surround-
ings melt away; there's nothing but the pattern. Entering this music
as a player or listener resonates with Simon Zagorski-Thomas's discussion of groove in general: "the timelessness, state of well-being,
heightened awareness of the music and reduced sense of consciousness of the rest of the world do seem to have a good deal in
common with religious trance and meditation."[10]

The 7/8 meter in particular is something of a Rush specialty,
employed in extended passages across their long output, for precisely these reasons. As I've written in an essay from the book

---

[8] The quotes are from McDonald, "Open Secrets," pp. 315, 317.

[9] Barry Kernfeld, "Groove," in *The New Grove Dictionary of Jazz*, second edition, edited by Barry Kernfeld (Macmillan, 2002), Volume 2, p. 100.

[10] Simon Zagorski-Thomas, "The Study of Groove," *Ethnomusicology Forum* 16
(2007), p. 331.

Progressive Rock Reconsidered, such "structures are fairly intricate, especially compared to rock music in general. But the marvel of these sections, to my ears, is that the groove remains paramount throughout. . . . The frequent use of 7/8 time in Rush's music, for example, is fascinating not because such a meter is 'complex,' but because the admittedly complex meter is used as the backdrop of grooves."[11] Perhaps no other time signature in rock quite captures the sense of music that must be both thought and felt at once.

Considering standard rock elements as purely belonging to the "body," while "progressive" elements like complex meters interact with the realm of the "mind," then, does not do justice to how Rush's music works. The band's use of musical time instead resonates strongly with recent scholarship, such as Anne Danielsen's work on the funk of James Brown and George Clinton, that considers groove from the perspective of a non-dualistic framework.[12] The usual mind-body binary resonates too easily with racial overtones, with the assumption that African-based music is purely rhythmic and thus supposedly primitive, while European-based music is thought to emanate from more intellectual pitch-based sources. Instead, grooves can be approached as hybrids of "Western" conceptions of rhythm, focused on the events within individual bars, and "African" rhythmic attention to repetition. Heterogenous asymmetric structures, built on additive combinations of two and three pulses, predominate. The "standard pattern" in a funk groove, for example, employs the eight fast pulses of a conventional 4/4 bar in 3 + 3 + 2 fashion, not all that different from a Rush 2 + 2 + 3 groove in 7/8. Repetitive patterns don't lead to a lack of attention, but rather to an inward focus where small inflections of microtiming loom large, and listeners are submerged in the here and now. In these ways musical grooves, intuitively essential for our reactions to so much popular music, can also be appreciated for their complexity and sophistication.

Close Listening and Move-Your-Body Rock

To illustrate this dialectical approach to Rush's use of musical time, where the complexities of rhythms and meters are not opposed to

---

[11] "Progressive Rock and the Inversion of Musical Values," *Progressive Rock Reconsidered*, edited by Kevin Holm-Hudson (Routledge, 2002), pp. 33, 42.

[12] See Anne Danielsen, *Presence and Pleasure: The Funk Grooves of James Brown and Parliament* (Wesleyan University Press, 2006).

the feeling of groove, I'd like to explore passages drawn from some of the band's most prominent songs, appearing on studio albums released between 1978 and 1982. A number of characteristic categories emerge through close listening. We're invited to move along with the music while simultaneously processing what's compelling us to move in the first place.

1. Complex Meters Used in Conventional Patterns

As in the opening passages of "Subdivisions," where a 7/8 meter is set within four-measure phrases, some of Rush's most distinctive music keeps complex meters comprehensible and groovable by operating within standard phrase lengths.

During "La Villa Strangiato" from *Hemispheres* (1978), for example, an extended mysterious middle section (Part IV, "A Lerxst in Wonderland," from 3:15 to 5:49) is built exclusively around a 7/8 meter. During this passage the energy of the "Strangiato theme" dissipates, and a slowly building guitar solo follows. At the climax (5:14) the band drops off for a sudden lowering of volume, and Lifeson's solo shifts to a repeated arpeggio pattern. The last phrase builds again, finally leading to the next passage of the long instrumental, "Monsters!" But through all these shifts of texture and long-lasting unsettling meter, the phrases all proceed in perfectly neat eight-bar groups. (This is matched by the predictable alternation of harmonies throughout, each phrase built on four bars of F followed by four of A minor.) The initial lowering of energy takes two phrases (eight bars + eight bars), the final arpeggio texture lasts for three phrases (eight + eight + eight), and these passages frame the center guitar solo, built around a perfectly rounded eight phrases of eight bars each.

2. Conventional Meters Used in Complex Ways

Conversely, Rush also characteristically constructs passages where more conventional meters, such as 4/4 and 3/4, are used unpredictably. "Limelight" (*Moving Pictures*, 1981), though one of Rush's catchiest songs, keeps the listener constantly guessing. As Durrell Bowman puts it, "the song's frequent meter shifts also underscore the discomfort and mixed feelings experienced by the protagonist."[13] The tune begins with a pickup figure leading to Lifeson's opening riff, a two-measure idea in 4/4 that's played a somewhat

---

[13] Durrell Bowman, *Permanent Change: Rush, Musicians' Rock, and the*

unbalanced three times. Peart and Lee champ at the bit the final time through, filling in the guitar's spaces, and the band finally enters in earnest. With this full texture the two-bar riff sounds a natural four times, but somewhere along the way it's lost a beat. Now 4/4 bars alternate with 3/4 bars, creating a seven-beat unit for the riff. The introduction thus employs an "easy" meter (4/4) within a "strange" phrase pattern (the guitar-alone riff lasts for six bars), and "strange" metrical play (4/4 + 3/4) is used within an "easy" phrase (the full-band version lasts for a normative eight bars).

The verse (beginning at 0:24) continues in this vein. The first two measures imply three beats in a bar, most easily heard in the changes of harmony and the stressed syllables ("LIV-ing on a LIGHT-ed stage") on the first and fourth beats of the six-beat line. But the same factors imply that the next two lines of lyrics alternate 4/4 and 2/4 bars, such as in "ap-PROACH-es the un-REAL," taking the same timeline of six beats per line, but organizing them differently. For the following phrase, "In touch with some reality" returns to two bars of 3/4, and the next line is set with a single 4/4 measure. A short interlude goes back to the seven-beat riff, which sounds twice. The rest of the verse repeats the metrical structure of the first half, but when the riff idea returns to conclude the section, this time it sounds only once before giving way to the chorus (beginning at 1:00).

Befitting the hook of a pop song, the chorus is a bit smoother, yet it's still not entirely stable. A 3/4 meter is used for the entire first phrase, but it lasts for only seven bars. Then, at "Those who wish to be," the meter shifts to a more straightforward 4/4, and the phrase now lasts a normative eight measures. The chorus concludes with a Lifeson arpeggio idea that shifts back to 3/4 for three measures, followed by the return of the seven-beat full-band riff.

3. Complex Patterns Repeated to Create Groove

Other categories mix and match somewhat freely between these variables of what sort of meter is used, and how the meters combine over multiple bars to construct phrases. One of my favorite devices is where Rush alternates between two different—and often complex—meters, but they repeat the thought over and over such that an irresistible groove is created nevertheless.

Progressive Post-Counterculture (Ph.D. dissertation, University of California, Los Angeles, 2003), p. 191.

"Jacob's Ladder" (*Permanent Waves*, 1980) is a locus for this sort of action. In this case, individual beats keep getting added to the initial idea. For the first minute and a quarter, for example, the throbbing bass alternates 5/4 and 6/4 bars. We can count "one-and-two-and-three - four - five" on the odd-numbered bars, but must shift to counting "one-and-two-and-three - four - five - six" for the even bars.

After a middle section that seems to have no regular pulse at all, a long instrumental passage returns to this notion of unpredictable rhythm within a predictable pattern (3:31–4:53). Here, a rising guitar figure repeats, but with a subtle variation. Six fast pulses (which can be thought of as eighth notes within a 3/4 bar) state the initial idea. But the figure immediately repeats, this time adding one extra fast pulse to the end, making for a 7/8 bar. 3/4 and 7/8 continue to alternate like this—or, we can imagine the entire figure as a single, highly unusual 13/8 bar—for the entirety of the passage.

4. Different Instruments with Different Metric Layers

At times one can interpret Rush's music as incorporating multiple metric streams simultaneously. One of those streams tends to imply a conventional temporal organization, keeping some strand of the musical texture moving predictably, even while the entire texture shifts in and out of phase.

Continuing with "Jacob's Ladder," for instance, once the vocals enter (at 0:46) the bass and guitar continue their odd pattern alternating 5/4 and 6/4 bars, yet if we instead shift our focus to the lyrics and chord changes in the keyboards, more straightforward 4/4 bars are implied. Even more characteristic in cases like these is for Peart's drumming to imply a standard 4/4 rock beat, where snare drum hits accent the "backbeat" second and fourth beats in a measure, while other parts of the texture imply other meters. Both choruses of "Subdivisions" work in this way, as 3/4 organization in the vocals and harmonies coexists with a 4/4 background beat. In "Limelight" the effect is reserved for the final chorus only (beginning at 3:19). As the band comes out of the guitar solo (3:11) the harmonic pattern from the 3/4-based phrase of the chorus sounds, but underneath this, Peart's drumming is notably in 4/4. This brings the strands of the texture out of phase and back in phase with each other every few beats, and this continues deep into the section.

Though the above examples have been drawn from Rush's "classic" output, such active shaping of our perceptions of musical time functions similarly across the band's catalog. "Driven," from 1996's *Test for Echo*, for example, represents a striking case of constant metric play within a relentless hard-edged groove. During the opening of "Far Cry," from *Snakes and Arrows* (2007), standard 4/4 bars are given accents at such surprising moments that even measures that would be relatively unassuming on paper can sound noticeably weird. While the temporal norms almost always function as background expectations within rock music, Rush creates a dialogue with these boundaries, and this play represents one of the most noteworthy aspects of the band's musical style.

The Heart and Mind United

Rush's music is also filled with passages of more straightforward rock rhythms through and through, where 4/4 meters are combined into phrases of standard lengths. Like the rock-'n'-roll fantasy dramatized in "Red Barchetta"—the car on the open road, freedom from "the system" finally possible—moments of glory, victory, and inner peace can enjoy standard musical time without the dark edge of feeling beholden to the conventions.

Thus, "Red Barchetta" itself repeatedly "fixes" its temporal complications at the ends of many sections. In the exciting passage that most closely approximates the feeling of speeding, unhindered, down an empty road (when the protagonist "commits his weekly crime," 2:28–2:58), the music is filled with syncopated accents that keep thrusting us forward. In addition, each phrase takes away two beats from normative four-measure groups in 4/4; we're moving faster than can be contained within standard phrases. But the last group, punctuated with Lee's "adrenalin surge," brings back those two beats—we're entering a new zone, where time can now flow freely. And indeed, in the next section (2:58–3:18), while changing harmonies take us on a bit of a journey, the phrases lock comfortably into relaxed four-bar groups in 4/4.

The following guitar solo (3:18–3:41) introduces further metric complications, alternating 4/4 and 3/4 bars for eight units of seven beats each. But again the last unit brings back the "missing" beat, making for a satisfying conclusion of eight beats before we head back into the main song. And for the final, peaceful phrases built around Lifeson's guitar harmonics (from 5:10), while the initial groups imply 4/4 phrases lasting a somewhat unexpected two, six, and again six bars, from 5:32 to the song's fade normative eight-bar groups sound the rest of the way.

Rush is sometimes given a hard time for its note-perfect renditions in concert. The relative lack of improvization makes the music seem as if it's striving towards a classical music ideal, thereby betraying deeply-held notions of rock authenticity. Yet as this discussion shows, there's little reason to think in such stark black-and-white terms. The band's playing—Peart's performances perhaps representing the shining example—is exceptional in that they present technically hypervirtuosic passages without appearing gratuitously flashy or deflecting undue attention away from the overall composition. The balancing act is achieved as all three members serve as integral parts of the songwriting team. No one is "just the drummer" or "just the bass player." All components are carefully thought out, and each musician brings the song to hard-driving, grooving life. Rush's music, in all its complexity, functions not so much as a fixed text akin to a classical-music score, but as an active performance that moves listeners to engage—both intellectually and bodily—with how time is shaped.[15]

---

[15] I thank Sarah Betz for compiling the initial research for this chapter, Becky Sheinbaum for her thoughtful comments, and Jeremy Wallach for framing the initial point in this paragraph so effectively.

4
Nailed It!

JOHN T. REULAND

Please be kind with criticism. I'm a musician though, so I've heard criticism before.

So a YouTube user appeals to potentially-critical viewers of his video, a drum cover played along to Rush's "The Body Electric." The drummer sits at a black drum kit with a single bass drum, three floor toms, and multiple mounted toms and crash cymbals of varying diameters. Visible on the wall of his practice room are what appear to be Ludwig drum posters from the 1980s that feature Neil Peart and the mammoth double-bass drum kits he played during the era.

As the drummer in the video plays along, it becomes clear that his technical execution and mastery of the song are far from perfect. He compresses and rushes the tune's opening snare drum eighth-notes, speeding ahead of the recorded track, he misses Peart's subtle tom variations, and his overall style is rather stiff, heavy, and grooveless on a track where Peart's own playing is graceful, dexterous, and light

The few comments that appear below the clip are generally helpful and encouraging: "Nice job. I would tighten the grip on the left stick and loosen the tension on the China Type [a kind of cymbal] slightly." Each of the comments about the performance appears to come from a fellow drummer, as they do in other YouTube clips of drummers playing along to Rush. In these clips, an audience of fellow musicians praises, blames, and dissects different aspects of the performance, posts questions and comments about matters of technique and equipment, and regularly pronounces admiration for Neil Peart.

Musician fans of Rush know that playing along can be a rigorous method of musical autodidacticism. You may practice a song section by section until you think it is right, then play along to the recording until the recorded notes disappear, replaced by the sound of one's own precise replication. YouTube transforms this once private musical activity into a potentially public one, a kind of virtual master class where an audience witnesses and dispenses musical instruction. As hybrids of practice and performance, YouTube Rush covers show how Rush's musician-fans assess, interpret, and emulate the band's repertoire in alternating roles as performers, teachers, and critics. YouTube, furthermore, is a performance space particularly suited to, perhaps even ideal for, Rush's musical aesthetic, which, by and large, emphasizes the virtuosity of compositional precision and measured figuration over the type of virtuosity displayed in spontaneous jamming.

Rush's Aesthetic of Replicability

Highlighted in YouTube cover videos are the aspects of Rush's music that traffic in an aesthetic of replicability, an aesthetic in which songs—or more precisely perhaps, the individual instrumental performances that comprise each song—are constructed as artifacts that, importantly, are meant to sound as if they can be reproduced exactly. The exactitude of the band's instrumental performance practice gestures at a musical aesthetics that aspires to effects other than human expressiveness, a quality that seems to be lauded above all others in so much writing about popular music. Rush songs, one could say, are designed to be replicable artifacts, designed to be taken literally by musician fans—to be studied and reproduced note for note on a drum set, guitar, or even a page of transcription.

For many musicians, the exacting technical demands of Rush's music have made playing along with the band something of a rite of passage. As their prominence in music magazines suggests, Lee, Lifeson, and Peart represent a standard of musicianship to which fans aspire and, in playing along, measure themselves against. Although other bands' songs and other styles of music demand a level of proficiency equal to that displayed by the trio, Rush's repertoire interprets the meaning of virtuosity so as to be particularly suited to the process of learning exactitude in execution. A Rush song is a severe pedagogue. There is no room to fudge a style of music in which technique is on display as much for its own sake as for an ulterior expressive purpose—or better perhaps, a style in which technique is its own display of musical excess, a display of virtuosity running away with itself, as in one of Peart's explosive 32nd-note tom fills in that crucible of time signature changes, "YYZ."

A YouTube video allows a musician to verify the quality of his or her execution by subjecting a performance to the criticism of other musician fans. In response to a drum cover of the difficult "Subdivisions," a song that snakes through alternating 7/8, 4/4, and 6/4 time signatures, viewer comments are generally constructive and very positive "this is another tough song man . . . good job." Another viewer also chimes in with praise but with some specific technical advice as well:

> hey there, first of all, i would like to say great job. this is a great song, and a tough one to play well. after watching the video, i am a little surprised that the only thing i see could use just a few minutes worth of work is the phrase that neil uses at 1:34 and 1:37 and many times throughout the song. all that pattern is is eighth note triplets, i feel like you compress them a little bit. give them some room to breathe! you obviously have the skill to play it!

Although some comments are cutting, most are supportive, and strikingly, users generally agree on the criteria for praising play-along performances, namely, the amount of technical skill possessed by the musicians as displayed by their success in replicating the covered song.

While it's certainly true that musician fans assess the quality of YouTube covers of other bands' repertoire, the kinds of critical responses elicited by Rush covers tend to be evaluations of technical prowess. It goes almost without saying that technical virtuosity and exactitude of execution are central both to Rush's aesthetic and to the appeal that such an aesthetic has for its hard-core fans, two thirds of whom, as indicated by Durrell Bowman, are at least amateur musicians.[1]

In their playing styles, Lee, Lifeson, and Peart test the technical horizons of their instruments; they are, in other words, musicians'

---

[1] Durrell Bowman, "Permanent Change: Rush, Musicians' Rock, and the Progressive Post-Counterculture" (PhD dissertation in Musicology, 2003) <http://durrellbowman.com/PDFS/DBowman_dissertation.pdf>, p. 50.

musicians. Covers of this "musicians' band," then, are especially suited to the modes of display, evaluation, and pedagogy that the musical community created by YouTube makes possible. Importantly, the criteria fans use to evaluate play-along performances are derived from values inherent in Rush's own musical aesthetics. The band's recorded performances, for the most part, are meant to be taken note for note, to be read at the level of the letter. A nod to such stylistic literalness is found in the song title, "YYZ," which Rush fans know to be the letters for the Toronto Pearson International Airport, and we should note as well that Peart's 5/4 crotale introduction telegraphs those letters in Morse code. Both Morse Code and airport call letters are codes with a one-to-one, conventionally fixed correspondence between signifier and signified. Unlike everyday language where metaphor demands that one choose from a range of interpretations, these codes are fixed to have only one possible meaning. Rush's aesthetic is likewise an aesthetic of the musically literal, something created to invite duplication as its best interpretation.

As a site where fan instrumental performances are evaluated by other fans, YouTube offers musicological access into the meanings of Rush's aesthetic of virtuosity for the many aspiring musicians who make up the band's audience. It is a medium that enables us to begin to address questions such as: What does it mean for a musician to aspire to play along to Rush in particular? In what ways does Rush's music constitute a form of instrumental pedagogy? Does the appeal of this type of pedagogy and of Rush's brand of literal, anti-expressive virtuosity to its musician fans indicate anything about their socio-cultural positioning? How do the ways in which Rush fans read the meaning of virtuosity differ from the ways it is read by critics? YouTube allows a mode of access into fans' musical practices and aesthetic values that helps understand more deeply how they imagine their relationships to Rush's music, to their own musical instruments, and to the meaning of musical merit.

Dealt a Losing Hand

Within pop music discourse of both the journalistic and academic kinds, Rush is usually disparaged when it is not altogether left out of the conversation. The reasons for its exclusion are the same reasons the band has had such an enduring appeal to its musician fans—namely, its celebration of instrumental virtuosity of a particularly literal, replicable kind. In pop criticism, by contrast, music is assessed more on its expressive qualities—to which virtuosity, when unobtrusive, can be a legitimate means—and less on the instrumental virtuosity that so appeals to Rush's musician fans.

Within the history of pop music's critical values, debates about the meaning of virtuosity have also been, at a deeper level, debates about how music is coded racially. The fact that the band's fans and detractors are split about the value of virtuosity leads into a discussion of some of the racial dimensions of Rush's music.

There is a pair of unstated assumptions in both journalistic and academic music criticism that popular music is expressive, and that expressiveness is a quality to be praised. What is often left unstated about these assumptions, either because it is obvious or because it is no longer seen to be remarkable, is their origin in commentary and criticism on African American-influenced musical practice. In *Blues People: Negro Music in White America*, Amiri Baraka offers a genealogy of the racial connotations of technique and virtuosity. He differentiates African American and white musical practices by pointing out the priority of the artifact in Western aesthetics:

> In the West, only the artifact can be beautiful, mere expression cannot be thought to be. It is only in the twentieth century that Western art has moved away from this concept and toward the non-Western modes of art-making, but the principle of the beautiful thing as opposed to the natural thing still makes itself felt. The tendency of white jazz musicians to play "softer" or with "cleaner, rounder tones" than their Negro counterparts is, I think, an insistence on the same Western artifact. Thus an alto saxophonist like Paul Desmond, who is white, produces a sound on his instrument that can almost be called legitimate, or classical, and the finest Negro alto saxophonist, Charlie Parker, produced a sound on the same instrument that was called by some "raucous and uncultivated."[2]

Even if we cannot entirely accept Baraka's somewhat too binary analysis, it is nonetheless true that much of rock criticism operates according to a dichotomy similar to the one Baraka sees at work in a strain of American jazz criticism that gave higher praise to white musicians than to their African American counterparts. However, in

---

[2] Amiri Baraka (formerly LeRoi Jones), *Blues People: Negro Music in White America* (Morrow, 1963), p. 30.

rock criticism the terms of praise are generally reversed—qualities such as roughness and expressiveness are valued. These are the traits that critics have come to expect from pop and rock music, which was originally positioned as a "countercultural" art against the assumed inauthenticity of classical values.

Rush works according to a different set of musical values. Their affinity for an artifactual style has earned Rush their portion of critical opprobrium. In a review of *Grace under Pressure*, rock critic Kurt Loder showed his impatience with this aspect of Rush's sound: "the lack of melody and any but the most rudimentary harmonic development soon becomes oppressive. In addition, Alex Lifeson is not a particularly interesting lead guitarist, and the strictures of the trio format still result in more splattery drum bashing than you'll ever care to hear." Loder's complaint about Lifeson's playing reveals an expectation that the lead guitar will somehow be the listener's hook into the music, as it is in more blues-based styles. His complaints about melody also indicate expectations of lyricism and expressiveness at odds with Rush's aesthetic.

Taking Individualism to Extremes

Critics also deride Rush because of the social and political connotations supposedly entailed by its aesthetic values. "Taking individualism to Ayn Rand-inspired extremes, Peart's most pessimistic screeds suggest that in the upcoming apocalypse, every-man-for-himself will turn into stomp-the-other-guy," pronounced Jon Parales of *Exit . . . Stage Left*. "Just about everything Rush do can be found, more compactly, in Yes's "Roundabout,'" with the remainder in Genesis's "Watcher of the Skies." Everything except the philosophy—and stage left is, of course, to the audience's far right."

According to Bowman, post-1960s rock critics disparaged Rush because its music appeared to be insufficiently countercultural and, in lyrics that championed a left-libertarian ideology of individualism, politically suspect (p. 74). Throughout the 1970s, however, critics would begin to lose touch with fans, whose values and tastes adapted to a new political and economic climate even as rock's establishment remained committed to 1960s critical values that were institutionalized in organs such as *Rolling Stone*. As one fan complained in a 1982 letter to the magazine, "*Rolling Stone* seems intent on casting Rush's albums into the two-star void. You frown upon any band that doesn't acknowledge any influence from the

Sixties, either verbally or musically." Critics continued to value music for its level of authenticity and political commitment while many fans' tastes changed as they struggled to come to grips with post-1960s political and economic realities.

Bowman argues that "the world-views of many rock fans changed during the 1970s/'80s *post*-counterculture to embrace technique, professionalism, entrepreneurialism, and technology, and rock criticism thus represented a smaller portion of its former constituency" (p. 71). Bowman claims that a post-counterculture arose during the 1970s as dreams of collectivist liberation gave way to the more mundane realities of 1970s deindustrialization, and various forms of "knowledge work" replaced traditional blue collar labor. In this new order a post-counterculture embraced liberatory possibilities that were more individualist, more oriented toward technology, and even more entrepreneurial.

Technical Display Is Primary

In analyzing the difference of opinion between critics and fans, Rush's virtuosity and technical complexity are of particular significance, for it's the band's over-the-top instrumental display that so often earns it the disdain of the critical class and the awe and loyalty of fans, who throughout the 1980s and 1990s consistently propelled Lee, Lifeson, and Peart to the top spots of readers' polls in musician-oriented publications such as *Bass Player*, *Guitar Player*, and *Modern Drummer*. In mainstream criticism, virtuosity is seen as a means to emotional expression, or is hailed as the spontaneous eruption of musical genius and artistic inventiveness.

Again, we return to jazz, from which rock criticism would seem to derive its assumptions about the priority of expression over virtuosity. Critic Scott Saul writes that John Coltrane's virtuosity "puts the quest for self-expression above the demands of professional competence," and "allows for—and perhaps even rewards—awkwardness" (*Freedom Is, Freedom Ain't*, p. 223). For Rush's autodidact musician fans, however, technical display is primary. Refusing to pass itself off as natural, Rush's presentation of virtuosity does not attempt to conceal the labor behind it. Explicitly presented as available for emulation, Rush's music has no pretenses about being anything other than a fiction in the etymological sense of the word, anything more than a made object, an artifact. For Rush, technical prowess is sometimes a means to an end, but often it is its own goal.

It's the conspicuous artificiality of so many of the songs, their sometimes seemingly unmotivated changes of time signature and key, that gives Rush what might be called, somewhat paradoxically, its difficult accessibility. Which is to say, Rush's music presents itself as incredibly hard, but also as a repertoire that, with enough patient labor, can be learned. Take the instrumental "YYZ," for example. A composition designed to showcase the talents of Rush's three members, the song obeys more of showpiece logic—an arrangement of different musical modules each designed to show off the trio's virtuosity—than an overarching expressive principle. Transitions between the song's parts occur through displays of virtuosity—guitar riffs or drum fills. These displays link the song's parts, which generally lack a strong organic connection to one another.

The song famously opens with the pattern of the Morse code for "yyz," which falls into a 5/4 rhythm marked in unison by bass, drums, and guitar. At 0:35 there is a pause, which is punctuated by unison fills of sixteenth-notes in five measures of 6/8 that keep the listener alert by beginning off the downbeat. In the next section Lifeson and Lee play the melody as a tight counterpoint that each embellishes with fills until 1:38. At this point, Peart plays a subtle eight-note drum fill as a beat-four pickup to steer the band into the next section, where the trio trades two-bar riffs. We again see virtuosity connecting the song's parts when Peart executes a descending roto-tom fill to lead into a section that showcases Lifeson's guitar. Lifeson plays a sixteen-bar solo that is followed by two transition measures in which he plays a combination of descending sixteenth notes and sixteenth-note triplets to lead into the next section, a sixteen-bar bridge with guitar and heavy synthesizer background. After "YYZ" returns to its initial Lee/Lifeson counterpoint melody, the song concludes with a reprise of the 5/4 Morse code rhythms. While Peart has said that "YYZ" is inspired by the way it feels to come home to Toronto,[3] the underlying theme of the song is virtuosity itself—which in working as the substance of its transitions, keeps the song together.

---

[3] Bowman, "Permanent Change," p. 189.

Class Bias of Rush's Critics

When it comes to understanding the role of this brand of virtuosity in Rush's aesthetics of replicability, class, like race, is another key but somewhat unexamined point of analysis. When Rush began releasing albums in the 1970s, their fans were mainly young white men of working- and middle-class origins who were forced to adapt not only to the decay of the industrial economy, but also to the information economy that would (at least for the lucky ones) come to replace it.

Today Rush's fans are a more diverse lot than the stereotypes or the 2009 film *I Love You, Man* would have it, although not much more. According to Bowman's estimate, about a two-thirds majority is white, male, and (at least in the late 1990s and very early 2000s) in their twenties or thirties. About a third of the audience is female, and about a sixth nonwhite. Of the class positions of fans Bowman writes, "Nearly all of the band's fans came from the post-industrial, post-countercultural working and lower-middle classes. More specifically, two-thirds of the band's hardcore fans—even the third who were not white, male, and/or in their thirties or forties—formed a social class of post-industrial employed people."

Class is central to understanding the social meaning of Rush's aesthetics of replicability, to understanding how and why music that many critics disparage as pretentious, baroque, and mechanical remains so enduringly appealing to musician fans. Why does Rush's brand of anti-expressive virtuosity hold such sway for its white, lower-middle-to-middle class male fans? How do the class origins of Rush's fans inflect what it means to want to become a musician who can play Rush? What does it mean to aspire, through hours of sedulous practice and the risk of Internet humiliation, to play a style of music with so little cultural *cachet*?

The literalness of Rush's performance aesthetic and the pedagogical appeal that such literalness holds for its autodidact musician fans helps to explain Rush's disfavor among critics, but it also begins to illuminate some of the class connotations that being a Rush fan entails in critical discourse. Attention to Rush's literalness highlights a certain unconscious class bias in the critical taste that marginalizes the band. As Pierre Bourdieu contends about the class coding of taste, the social value of appreciation for an art is linked to the way in which the capacity for such appreciation is gained. The less learned it appears—the more it seems a "natural" product of years of unconscious exposure and absorption—the more *cachet* it has:

> Total, early, imperceptible learning, performed within the family from the earliest days of life and extended by a scholastic learning which presupposes and completes it, differs from belated, methodical learning not so much in the depth and durability of its effects—as the ideology of cultural 'veneer' would have it—as in the modality of the relationship to language and culture which it simultaneously tends to inculcate. It confers the self-certainty which accompanies the certainty of possessing cultural legitimacy and the ease which is the touchstone of excellence; it produces the paradoxical relationship to culture made up of self-confidence amid (relative) ignorance and of casualness amid familiarity, which bourgeois families hand down to their offspring as if it were an heirloom.[4]

Bourdieu suggests that what legitimizes cultural learning through early immersion is not that it produces superior knowledge, but that it leads to a more self-confident manner, a sense of "seniority within the bourgeoisie." An arts-enlivened upbringing, in other words, produces the confidence required to maintain a class position. The manners that learning tends to index, then, perpetuate the apparent naturalness of social stratification:

> The ideology of natural taste owes its plausibility and its efficacy to the fact that, like all the ideological strategies generated in the everyday class struggle, it naturalizes real differences, converting differences in the mode of acquisition of culture into differences of nature; it only recognizes as legitimate the relation to culture (or language) which least bears the visible marks of its genesis, which has nothing 'academic', 'scholastic', 'bookish', 'affected', or 'studied' about it, but manifests by its ease and naturalness that true culture is nature—a new mystery of immaculate conception. (p. 68)

---

[4] Pierre Bourdieu, *Distinction: A Social Critique of the Judgment of Taste* (Routledge, 1984), p. 66.

Celebration of Diligent Effort

Clearly marked, then, are the class connotations of "studied," deliberate learning, the kind of painstaking and deliberate musical autodidacticism in which Rush's musician fans engage. Although Bourdieu is talking about a kind of learning that has to do with art appreciation rather than with musicianship, the same distinction between unconscious immersion and assiduous, methodical training applies in a discussion of Rush's critical reception—in no small part because in the very difficulty of its compositions, Rush's music celebrates diligent effort and deliberate study.

With Bourdieu in mind, we can understand more clearly why, given the assumptions that govern discourse about popular music, the band has been so critically marginalized. In analyzing the relationship between social status and modes of cultural acquisition, Bourdieu reminds us that deliberate autodidacticism bears a kind of class stigma which is the substance of what it means to say—as Bowman does proudly—that Rush is music for dorks (p. 50). Even when embraced with pride, to be a dork or a nerd is to be associated with literalness—and possibly, to be confined in such a marginal position because of a reluctance, or even an inability, to display the mannered ease that Bourdieu associates with social power.

In presenting interpretations of virtuosity that are explicitly marked as autodidactic, YouTube performances of Rush are the performances of musical marginality, whatever the performer's actual relation to musical culture. In these videos, we uncover a musical practice eccentric to the values that govern mainstream music criticism.

Non-Mainstream Whiteness

A well-known twist in the story of American music criticism is that its canonical values, the values that confer the highest status in its field of cultural production, originated in the performance practices of an oppressed, marginalized population. The expressiveness features that Baraka argues belong to African American music have been easily assimilated in support of a bourgeois taste for naturalness and ease in the arts. American popular music attains prestige by incorporating aspects of African American dialogical performance style such as improvisation, figuration, and expressiveness.

Positioning itself outside dominant musical aesthetics, Rush makes visible the ways in which whiteness, a racial position that would otherwise seem to pass itself as an unmarked one, can come to be seen instead as marked and, in particular, inflected and varied by class. As a disengagement from more critically prestigious forms of musical performance, the literal aspects of the music of Rush, then—a band whom in 2008 the *Pittsburgh Gazette* called "music dorks' holy trinity"—display a brand of non-mainstream whiteness. Facetiously speaking, one might call those who perform this brand of whiteness "nerds."

Based on field research at a California high school in the mid-1990s, sociolinguist Mary Bucholtz has characterized nerdiness as a racial position marked by hyper-whiteness.[5] Hyper-whiteness is achieved when nerds reject the "coolness" of their white peers, coolness that is based on modulated engagement with African American-influenced youth culture. According to Bucholtz, "cool" white students at the high school appropriated styles of dress and language that had African American origins but had largely shed their African American associations. "To remain both culturally and racially acceptable," she observes, "white students had to maintain a delicate balance between embracing coolness and avoiding cultural practices that were racialized as black by their European American peers." For nerds, however, the situation was different. In the way they presented themselves, "African American culture and language did not play even a covert role." White nerds' rejection of African American-influenced youth culture carried over into the way they spoke as well. They chose to speak in a dialect that sociolinguists call "Superstandard English." As Bucholtz explains, "Superstandard English contrasts linguistically with Standard English in its greater use of 'supercorrect' linguistic variables: lexical formality, carefully articulated phonological forms, and prescriptively standard grammar. It may also go beyond traditional norms of prescriptive correctness, to the point of occasionally over-applying prescriptive rules and producing hypercorrect forms." Another important characteristic of Superstandard English is its lack of slang. "Nerdy teenagers' deliberate avoidance of slang . . . displayed their remoteness from the trends not only of white youth culture but of black youth culture

[5] "The Whiteness of Nerds: Superstandard English and Racial Markedness," *Journal of Linguistic Anthropology* 11:1 (2001).

as well, since African American slang was a primary source of European American slang."

No Heart to Lie

Bucholtz's research on nerds and race supports the contention that literalness, be it linguistic or musical, is an ingredient in a marginal, non-hegemonic practice of whiteness. This nerdy literal whiteness rejects modes of social performance that would multiply rather than restrict the possibilities of meaning and interpretation. In complementary ways, Bucholtz and Bourdieu each associate higher social status with a linguistic or social performance somehow moves beyond the literal—in Bucholtz's analysis, by incorporating African-American cultural elements and, for Bourdieu, by operating through a natural ease whose principles are ineffable. Given the association of literalness, then, with low status, why would anyone want to go through the trouble and labor necessary to learn a Rush cover? What is the attraction to a virtuosity that would seem to earn such a limited quantity of respect?

For the musician fans that cover their songs in videos, Rush's aesthetics of replicability literalizes the idea of meritocracy by imagining that success is identical to skill. The YouTube performances of its musician fans embody a hope that the criteria for musical excellence are clear, and that such excellence is a matter of technical execution alone, attainable by anyone with enough patience to practice. If in addition to pure luck certain unteachable, ineffable qualities are often necessary to succeed in life, on a strictly meritocratic view of the world intangible qualities such as manner ought not to play a role in determining one's fortunes. As a species of aspiration, the musical autodidacticism of Rush fans offers a critique of the meritocratic ideology tendered by the post-industrial information economy, for it takes literally the promise that technical mastery is directly convertible into success. If the ideology of meritocracy promises that success is like a code to which skill is the cipher, an aesthetics that sets up an exact correspondence between technical perfection and convincing performance parodies that ideology by literalizing it.

It is on the plane of sociopolitical desire and aspiration that Rush's post-countercultural ethos and politics and its aesthetics of replicability converge with its thematic interest in literal statements like codes. The story of "an android on the run / seeking freedom beneath the lonely desert sun," the song "The Body Electric" depicts a humanoid protagonist's quest for human selfhood, which depends on the outcome of his struggle to "change his program," to "change the mode" and "crack the code." The chorus contains two codes—"SOS" and "1–0–0"—and is infused with the urgency that "SOS" is meant to telegraph, with Peart's snare drum punctuating the "zero"-"zero" sung on the second and third beats of each measure. In binary code the numbers "1001001" stand for the capital letter "I,"[6] which in the context of the song refers to the human identity the android is trying to achieve.

In "The Body Electric," code cracking is thematically linked to aspiration and desire, to an ambition to transform oneself. Like the android, musician fans who aspire to replicate Rush's instrumental parts on YouTube struggle to crack a code and in so doing, to attain a more highly developed musical identity, that of the virtuoso. Such virtuosity is marginal, confined to the practice room because of its literalness, because its main purpose is not to engage in expressive musical dialogue with either an audience or with other musicians in a live performance. It is slightly unsociable, slightly nerdy.

YouTube, however, injects a new type of sociability into the traditional practice of playing along; it complicates any easy distinction between practice and performance, between playing alone and playing for others. While YouTube performances solicit audience responses, they do not do so in a mode in which an audience reacts to a band and spurs it on with its applause and cheers. A YouTube performance is thus perhaps the medium most suited to Rush fans, for its alternative sociability takes into account a skepticism of performance thematized in the band's repertoire.

The song "Limelight," we know, critiques performance as a "gilded cage" inside of which authentic existence cannot be found. For Rush, performance falsifies relationships—"I can't pretend a stranger is a long awaited friend"—and so one must avoid such inauthenticity by putting up "barriers to keep oneself intact." Performance does not augment or enhance but indeed attenuates the self; preserving the self requires that performance be undertaken with an ironic, skeptical distance.

---

[6] <http://www.songfacts.com/detail.php?id=3308>

Rush's aesthetics of replicability thus erects a barrier against fal-
sification and inauthenticity by subordinating dialogism to musical
exactitude. As Rush's musician fans know, the replication of the
trio's difficult music cannot be faked. Used mainly for musical pedagogy and homage, play along videos of Rush recode performance as an act of autodidactic self-improvement, an act that is
not a dissemblance but an invitation to criticism and an effort to
improve.

5
Can't Hear the Forest for the Cave?

ANDREW COLE

A man of genius makes no mistakes. His errors are volitional and are the portals of discovery.

—JAMES JOYCE

If it's been a while, and you have all day, watch the concert film, *Rush: Exit . . . Stage Left* (1981). When the closing credits roll, stay seated and realize that, while you're at it, you might as well put in the live Rush vids, such as *Grace under Pressure Tour* (1984) or *A Show of Hands* (1988). Finish and reflect.

You'll notice that the band went through some changes over those years, 1980–88, replacing their gauzy spirographic light shows with pulsing laser displays, their Moogs with MIDI pads, their obviously glam-inspired rock'n'roll haircuts with new-wave 'dos verging on mullets (let's be honest). The fans have changed right along with the band. That flannel-clad audience welcomed into their ranks, front and center, squads of air-drumming murgatroyds (having been one myself). What the *Grace under Pressure* tour video documents is the birth of an experience, a new way of listening to Rush and getting into the band. This is the experience of playing along, in your very own way.

Since 1984, the opportunities for playing along with Rush have only multiplied. Exponentially, too. There are video games such as Rock Band and Guitar Hero. Music editing programs allow you to stand in for Alex, Geddy, or Neil. The Internet is chock full of Rush tributes, and other examples of fans playing Rush: you can behold the twelve-year old "ameri" playing all—yes, all—of the instrumental parts to "YYZ" practically flawlessly on a Yamaha Electone

Organ (Elc-01c), or "Pauliewanna" supplying a birds' eye view of his drum kit while playing Rush songs, again, quite impeccably, enabling listeners to visualize Peart's drum parts and play along themselves.

What's next? A philosophical essay on playing to Rush? Why not? After all, this amazing mimicry cannot be dismissed as just so much geeking out, like the redonkulous antics of Peter and Sydney in the film *I Love You, Man*—two dudes who are soooo into Rush, wagging out the riffs to "Limelight" with their tongues. Nay, I propose here that philosophy itself needs to "get into" Rush by philosophizing about the experience of imitating the Canadian troika. I here present two philosophers on the subject of imitation and will ask them to play with the band, adapting their philosophies to account for the sundry performances of Rush music, by the band and fans alike.

On stage right is the ancient philosopher Plato (429–347 B.C.E.), whom we can thank for giving "playing along" and other imitation a bad name. Plato was ever the lover of originals, finding nothing to commend in copies and imitations, as we will soon see. Stage left is the modern thinker Walter Benjamin (1892–1940), who gives bad imitations a good name (no joke). He was ever the lover of copies, finding originals to be commendable but expendable.

These two philosophers play different roles in the history of philosophy, much less music. But together they offer a conceptual framework for thinking about what it means to imitate Rush. To say this in another way, a philosophical appreciation of Rush requires that we embrace imitation, warts and all. Whether the imitation is perfect or imperfect doesn't matter, because these two qualities, perfection and imperfection, are sides of the same coin. What is that coin? It is aesthetic experience itself. Musical imitation will here be construed as original thinking.

I Have Not Left This Cave for Days Now

Plato's theory of imitation is simple, even if huge. It boils down to claiming that all experience is imitation.

How can he say this? Well, he doesn't say it. Socrates says it, as Plato tells us in his *Republic*, which is a long dialogue between Socrates and his student Glaucon. These two, master and pupil, get around to discussing the nature of perception, the truth of our experiences, and the reliability of our knowledge—you know, those small topics you resolve over the course of a lazy sunny afternoon. It makes great sense, therefore, that Socrates at some point in the discussion pauses and blurts out what seems to be a headline: "Behold! human beings living in a underground den!"[1] The fine print of this headline bears more depressing news: we are those human beings. Or we might as well be them, given that our view of reality, our understanding of the natural and cosmic order, is about as thin and dim as the shadows cast on the wall of a dank cave.

There's more to the story. In this cave, we're prisoners, chained to the ground, with our heads unpleasantly fixed in one position, so that we can only look at the wall in front of us. And as if that's not enough, there's also a huge fire roaring behind us. Far be it from a place like this to feature shadow shows, but there they are: between us and the fire, people are carrying stuff, "all sorts of vessels, and statues and figures of animals made of wood and stone and various materials." All of these items cast shadows on the wall, thanks to the light of the fire, and we see only these shadows.

And the moral of the story? As Socrates sums it up: to the prisoners, "the truth would be literally nothing but the shadows of the images." Likewise, for us in the here and now, the truth is equally provisional. What seems real are but shadows, phantoms of real things we cannot see. So where are these real things? They are outside of the cave, and on the intellectual or, better, metaphysical plane of perfect "forms" and infallible ideas. Real things are, in other words, ideal things—things that are perfect, true, archetypal, and universal.

It requires a heavy dose of idealism—the belief that ideas put the "real" in reality—to take this all in. The point is that, in Plato's world, art fares no better than the shadows, and in fact, it may fare worse. As Socrates teaches, an artist is but a "creator of appearances." A painter is an "imitator" who is "a long way off of the truth." And a "poet is like a painter," weaving likenesses that are not even remotely real.

We Are Merely Players

So, are imitations all that bad? Not according a band that began as a four-piece playing covers at the Coff-In in Toronto in

---

[1] Plato, *The Republic* (Vintage, 1991). All references are from pages 321–26.

1969,[2] emerging some eleven years later to write "Limelight" for the *Moving Pictures* album. While our bromancers Peter and Sydney hear in this song "I Love You Man," a philosopher hears in it a challenge to Platonism and a defense of imitation. Take it away:

> Living on a lighted stage
> Approaches the unreal
> For those who think and feel
> In touch with some reality
> Beyond the gilded cage. ("Limelight," *Moving Pictures*, 1981)

Peart has said on numerous occasions that he feels ill at ease with his stardom and the concomitant fanfare, but there's more to his story in these lyrics. For Peart and Plato tell much the same tale. After all, a "gilded cage" is just a prettified cave.

Yet, yet: whereas Plato would suggest that art and music are exercises in self-deception, drawing you deeper into the cave, Peart proposes that "we are merely players, / performers and portrayers"—words he takes from the master of the stage himself, William Shakespeare: "All the world's a stage, / And all the men and women merely players" (*As You Like It*, Act 2, Scene 7). As Peart sees it, by performing and playing, we leave the cave, we step outside the gilded cage, and "put aside the alienation." On stage, we pursue the "real relation":

> Those who wish to be
> Must put aside the alienation,
> Get on with the fascination,
> The real relation,
> The underlying theme. ("Limelight," *Moving Pictures*, 1981)

On stage, the experience is "unreal" not because it's false but rather because, frankly, it's awesome, authentic, and a way of relating, "each another's audience" in the good sense. These "real relations" can be experienced in your suburban bedroom or, for half the world, your "man cave."

---

[2] See Bill Banasiewicz, *Rush Visions: The Official Biography* (Omnibus Press, 1990), Chapter 1.

Test for Echo

So what of these "performers and portrayers." Like, really, what about them? Enough of caves and puppets!

So, you're a musician, maybe even casually, but you often play to Rush, or warm up with their riffs. I would bet the farm you've said the following on more than one occasion, "I need to try this again to get it right." As many know, there are a lot of variables when it comes to playing Rush, and here, you can take "variables" to be a euphemism for "mistakes" and "errors." We do not always get it right nor does anyone else.

So, I ask: Is there room for error in Rush music? Can a good philosophy of imitation give variation a pass? In other words, whenever we talk about imitation, do we always have to talk about error in that bad sense of the term? I answer no, for this reason: we would be thinking too Platonically if we insisted that imitations must be perfect or they must not be at all. But not only that, we would be thinking contradictorily because an imitation that is perfect is no imitation. Rather, it is the real thing, according to Plato.

I raise these questions with the culture of Rush in mind. Fans, for example, are fond of identifying and analyzing errors by the band or their imitators, and in so doing reveal a microscopic attention to the detail of Rush music. The audience even holds the band up to the same standards they have set for themselves and the tributes. On those rare occasions when, say, Geddy flubs the lyrics to "Closer to the Heart," Alex breaks the high-e string in his intro to "The Spirit of Radio," and Neil breaks a stick or goes off time (or not?) on the studio cut of "Limbo" (0:48–9) on *Test for Echo*, the fans talk, analyze, and compare versions, often disputing that an error was even an error but just an intended variation. The examples of errors and potential errors could be multiplied depending on how hungry for detailed analysis you are. Just visit <www.musicintheabstract.org> to get into the weeds of errors and versions, pre-releases, live cuts of equipment gone wild, and studio tracks that separate the guitar, vocals, or drums from the main mix, enabling a level of analysis never before possible. Errors offer fans a new way to look at the music and to reflect on questions of value, what kinds of arrangements, parts and "rearrangements" we like best.[3]

---

[3] Just look at the comment thread for the 2007 version of "Between the Wheels": http://www.youtube.com/watch?v=UDeVQJok3B0.

Errors are part of the fun. They are a facet of imitation. They are pathways to understanding.

He's Adept at Adaptation

So thinks Walter Benjamin, whose philosophy of imitation lights the way forward on this topic of mistakes, variations, and versions. Benjamin was a translator, among other things, and desperately wanted imitation to involve something more, something else besides copying the original with mechanical exactitude. His commitment to that position derived from his experience translating the work of the poet Charles Baudelaire (1821–1867), and his eureka moment comes from the difficulties of his task. Namely, there's no way he could write like Baudelaire, so how can he translate him or make a translation that is as great as the original?

It's an epiphany many of us have had in trying to play like any of the three members of Rush. And therein, I propose, lies the connection between Benjamin and Rush: imitation or, if we can use Benjamin's word here and call it "translation," cannot be perfect or Platonically ideal, and so it must embrace improvisation and variation. Passages in literature or moments in music may be translated with a bit more texture and emphasis than what's in the original, as long as the "effect" of the original is conveyed.

It's all about effects, in fact. Being a literary man, Benjamin predictably makes this point about translation by way of a metaphor, what he calls the "language forest"—an environment far more inviting than Plato's lugubrious cave:

---

observes: "I notice Neil is stopping (hitting the ride bell) a bit before the fills during the chorus. Look at 2:59 and all points during? the ride groove. Hhmm...sign of age?" To which Toolshed76 says: "Well, he is almost 60." Or check out this comment on the tempo of a 2007 version of "Spirit of Radio" played in Atlanta (a show I had seen with my wife): http://www.youtube.com/watch?v=KTOAR9mSGBk. RustyIShacklefurd remarks: "Interestingly enough, if you play the studio recording over top of the sound in this video the two of them sync up almost perfectly. Actually, being the anal person I am, I found this song to be only about 1/2 beat per minute slower. Definitely not significant enough to pick up on just by memory." (Unfortunately, as this essay went to press, YouTube's annoying "use violation" bots removed my examples, which were obviously not said violations. I retain, however, the note just as I had written it, as the comments by the users remain valid.)

translation does not find itself in the center of the language forest but on the outside facing the wooded ridge; it calls into it without entering, aiming at a single spot where the echo is able to give, in its own language, the reverberation of the world in the alien one.[4]

Call into the forest and it answers back with an echo, a copy of your call returning in altered form, as if the sound absorbs the ambient noise of the trees, the wind, the calls of fauna, the chirking of insects. This is translation, an imitation that contains a difference: the echo copies the original call but changes it. It takes great imagination to hear the forest answer back in all its rich sonority. And when it answers back, it speaks a "pure language."

By "pure language," Benjamin means that combination of elements—the original, the copy, and "the totality of . . . intentions" between the two. In music, for instance, we frequently listen to a cover song while also knowing the original very well. But it's not that we only "know" the original. Rather, we also hear the original. The original raises expectations or, better, provides an aural frame for listening, for hearing the two versions pulling in different directions in their variations of instrumentation, tempo, and all the rest.

This is that "pure language," spoken and heard only in the mind, where versions jostle to produce new meanings and intentions.

"Pure language," in other words, bespeaks an experience that traditional philosophy and logic cannot properly describe. Why? Because philosophers since Aristotle (Plato's greatest student) have asserted that you cannot hear, much less think about or see, two things in the same place at the same time. Why? Because one thing can never be two things. It can never be itself and something else at the same time. This is the principle of "non-contradiction of identity." As Aristotle defined it: "The same thing cannot at the same time both belong and not belong to the same object and in the same respect."[5] In other words, something can't be itself yet different from itself. Either something is, or it isn't. It is never two things at once, ten pounds yet four hundred tons. The later Platonist, Pseudo-Dionysius, expands the idea to speak of

---

[4] "The Task of the Translator," *Illuminations*, trans. Harry Zohn and ed. Hannah Arendt (Schocken Books, 1968). All references are from pages 73–78.

[5] *Aristotle's Metaphysics*, trans. Hippocrates G. Apostle (Peripatetic Press, 1979), 58–59.

experience in general: "One cannot participate in contradictory realities at one and the same time."[6]

But in "pure language," you can.

Respond, Vibrate, Feedback, and Resonate

Rush's 2004 album, *Feedback*, is a perfect example of "pure language," because it's Rush covering the classic hits that influenced them. Go no farther than the title. "Feedback" is like the noise of Benjamin's "language forest," an echo of the original sound amplified and looped, and amplified and looped yet again, until it translates into a screech or roar that is somehow gutturally satisfying. After all, in rock'n'roll, you want feedback, and the right dynamic between feedback and original tone make for an intense live experience. It's probably no surprise, then, that the first track on *Feedback* starts with feedback. "Summertime Blues" features feedback unmistakably reminiscent of Jimi Hendrix's "Foxy Lady." As the song continues, however, we move from Hendrix to Blue Cheer, whose version of "Summertime Blues" is loud and clear in the unique intro Blue Cheer added to Eddie Cochran and Jerry Capehart's original joint. After that part, we hear the now signature chords (E, A, B7, E) of "Summertime Blues," from which point we hear the band channeling the Who, with Entwistle flourishes at 1:42 and the distinct "Live at Leeds" key change at 2:16. By the time the song winds down at 3:01, we hear once more the unique Blue Cheer intro as an extro, which fades into Rush's closing jam.

There's a lot going on here, and probably more than I'm able to notice. But suffice it to say that in Rush's cover of "Summertime Blues," we are hearing two, maybe three versions of the song simultaneously. And from there more layers are revealed, because if the Who are the inspiration for the main parts of the tune, then Rush is covering the Who covering a song live, which is always how their predecessor played this number. In hearing the Rush version, then, you are experiencing multiple horizons of possibility as you observe the variations and hear the versions together as one. This unique mental object, this "pure song" that is not one particular version but multiple renditions, qualifies as "pure language." In hearing it, you have entered the language forest, in which experi-

---

[6] *Pseudo-Dionysius: The Complete Works*, trans. Colm Luibheid (Paulist Press, 1987), 206.

ence of different realities, different songs, different sounds, are combined into one aesthesis, one perception.

We can see why, then, Benjamin says that "the original undergoes a change" in translation. This principle also applies to Rush's translation of its own music for live shows. For the band, the live version can become the new original and overtake it. Think about "Witch Hunt" from *Moving Pictures*. On the *Grace under Pressure* tour video, you can hear one of the earliest, if not the earliest, versions of the extended solo that's now a regular feature of that song. Alex plays this part in the final thirty-five seconds or so of "Witch Hunt." He is embellishing, nay, translating Geddy's flangey breakout bass part from the studio cut. You can hear it again, in more elaborate form, on the final forty-five seconds of the live album, *A Show of Hands*. Ever since, Alex has played this part with some variation on the variation, as you might have heard on the *Snakes & Arrows* tour. Rush practices Benjaminian translation in homage to its own originals, plausibly knowing that interest can lie as much in variation as in fidelity.

The song never remains the same. Granted, Rush has always been lauded for its near pristine reproductions of its music on stage. But make no mistake. Or, rather, make one. For error just may be a part of Rush's process of translation. Consider "Turn the Page" off of *Hold Your Fire*. On *A Show of Hands*, both the video and live album, at 2:52 Lifeson arpeggiates a chord prematurely, stops, waits for the right moment, and resumes. Is this a mistake? It sure sounds like one, if you compare it to the version on the studio album, which has no such half-start. Perhaps Lifeson at some point committed an error in a live show, starting the chord too soon, but liked what he heard and went with it. (After all, Rush constantly speaks of their accidental discoveries, riffs from noodling around in warmups making it to the studio cut, like the opening bass part in "Force Ten.") If this is the case, then, we have yet another example of translation as Benjamin saw it, whereby erratic copying overtakes the original. The "mistake" or variation becomes the new authorized version for all subsequent live performances.[7] It is even adapted by at least one tribute band (Atlantis1001) in their cover of the song.[8]

---

[7] Here is a very earlier version of the "mistake" or variation I'm discussing (New Haven, CT, November 8, 1987): http://www.youtube.com/watch?v=qiywWlA25Lg. Accessed on November 30, 2009, with thanks to XanaduRush for posting.

[8] http://www.youtube.com/watch?v=eBOJWzqZXU0. Accessed on November 30, 2009, with my gratitude to wiiild.

On their "Time Machine" tour in 2010, Rush had real fun with musical translation in the concert's opening video—a skit involving the band members in a diner called "Gershon's Haus of Sausage."[9] Alex and Neil are customers, while Geddy runs the place. There is also a haus band, named "Rash," featuring actors vaguely resembling Rush from the 1970s, with "Alex" on accordion, "Geddy" on tuba, and "Neil" on drums, playing "Spirit of Radio" as a polka number. When Alex, the sausage-eating customer, activates his time machine, the haus band renders the same tune as a disco number; repeat the pattern, and the band does a country version. These comical translations of "Spirit of Radio" offer nothing particularly profound apart from the real pleasure of hearing the song done differently before hearing it done right by Rush themselves.

He's Got to Make His Own Mistakes

It's hard to deny that, with Rush, the entire venture of imitation wobbles on a fulcrum, tilting from "getting it right" to "getting it wrong," and back again. Common sense may tell you that Rush's technically complicated music is the worst case for translation— making it difficult, if not impossible, to achieve that ideal, that universal, Platonic perfection. And that's the point. Rush is, in fact, the best case for translation, because there are so many opportunities for imitation to morph into improvisation to morph into error to morph into variation, and so on. What Baudelaire is to Benjamin, Rush is to us. Just ask anyone who has tried to render into tablature Lifeson's solos on "Freewill" or "Analog Kid." I've tried, and there are parts that can only be "approximated," never duplicated, not even by Lifeson, who in his faster solos (like these) tends not to reproduce the studio cut note-for-note in his live performances but always manages to resolve the solo on perfect time with the band.

Video games have especially broadened our access to the challenges of imitating Rush and the joys of tarrying with the Platonic universal that demands perfection. The video game Rock Band 2, for instance, includes (to date) nine Rush songs for any fan wanting to play Rush music on instrument controllers in a fashion some parts real, some parts imaginative. Players are awarded points for

---

[9] http://www.youtube.com/watch?v=E1ZUdF9Q-3M. Accessed on October 10, 2010, with props to toddvernon.

getting it right; for getting it wrong their "star power" depletes. On Guitar Hero 5, a competing game, fans can play a live version of "The Spirit of Radio" recorded on the *Permanent Waves* tour at the Apollo in Manchester on June 17th, 1980.[10] Commenting on a demo vid, one message board member wrote, "Wow! That sounds sweet! Even with the dude's mistakes!" Like Rush copying a live track by the Who, fans can translate live music into their own "live" performance, their mistakes becoming part of the pleasure of playing, watching, and laughing.

Speaking of laughable mistakes, the boys in South Park have also contributed to this culture of imitation. They made it to the stage, via screen projection, during the *Snakes & Arrows* tour (2007) in the so-called "*South Park* intro." Here, the band "Lil' Rush" attempts to play "Tom Sawyer" but gets it wrong, causing the frustrated Stan Marsh to say, "Just start the song again and this time do it right!" at which point Rush returns to the stage to play the popular song the right way. The pleasure of this moment is not solely in laughing at a funny cartoon usually seen on basic cable. Rather, the "joke" cuts both ways, at the boys for sucking so much and at Rush for being almost too awesome—as if the point is that perfection and, by deduction, Platonic universals are funny for seeming so unreal, so unrealizable.

Rick Mercer, on the CBC's *The Mercer Report* (7th November, 2006), capitalized on this idea of unreal perfection during his "drum lesson" with Neil Peart in "the Rush bat cave," as Mercer calls Peart's practice space.[11] Yes, we're back in the cave, where the two men get behind their respective kits. Peart does a roll with the usual punch and speed that quickly resolves into the opening part of "One Little Victory" off of *Vapor Trails*. And Mercer plays, admittedly self-mockingly, in 4/4 time. Obviously, the "you're a better drummer than I am" routine doubles as a "your kit is bigger than mine" scenario. As Mercer says, "Okay, this is my drum kit. . . . I'm feeling slightly inadequate. It's not what you got, it's how you use it, kids, though I don't really know how to use it. . . . Small is beautiful!" The joke here is that one cannot measure up to Rush, as was amply demonstrated when both Mercer and Peart set about playing the famous drum crescendo in "Tom Sawyer." Mercer's contribution is

[10] http://www.rushisaband.com/display.php?id=1943.
[11] http://www.youtube.com/watch?v=mNFz74nHw4Y. Accessed on November 30, 2009, kudos to nathan7007.

not even audible, whereas Peart's performance morphed into a mini-concert. In the "cave" Peart mounts the stage, for all intents and purposes: his drums rotate in both directions as explosions, fore and aft, punctuate the awesomeness of the whole scene. The audience breaks out into laughter, not at Peart, so much as at the entire, overblown staging of this scene. Explosions? In a garage? No, in a cave!

These moments are all a variation on the order of the "Wayne's World" theme of "We're not worthy, we're not worthy"—reverential laughter, celebratory mocking. We can acknowledge a certain truth about Rush as a technically proficient band without having to be self-righteously serious or Platonically metaphysical and, of course, without having to be a Wayne or Garth, not that there's anything wrong with that. (I once worked at the Fox Valley Mall just miles from their basement in Aurora, Illinois). When we laugh in response to virtuosity, we close the distance between the "inimitable" band and admiring fan. What's ideal is made real, brought down to earth.

Rush, too, laugh at their musicianship. Take that 2008 episode of *The Colbert Report*, when Rush tried their hand at Rock Band, playing their own music on flimsy plastic instruments they clearly could not handle, though Peart's "drums" seemed familiar to him, as they would to any drummer who taketh stick and striketh object. When all was said and done, the band earned the score of "Song Failed. Tom Sawyer. Thirty-two percent Complete."

In the long run, then, even Rush can't measure up to "Rush," that Platonic ideal, that universal dream shared by so many but practically realized by very few, if any, at all times, in all performances. When Benjamin says that "the original and the translation" are "recognizable as fragments of a greater language, just as fragments are part of a vessel," he is saying that the imitations by fans complete the experience of Rush, and help the band itself speak a "pure language" across a variety of music histories, media, and even national languages from, as the familiar saying goes, "Nome to Rome."

Benjamin could never have known that Rush and its audience substantiate his ideas—probably because he didn't know what an audience could do when given the means to imitate, embellish, and analyze master works through continuously generative acts of translation.

PART II

The Ebb and Flow of Tidal Fortune

6
Rush's Revolutionary Psychology

MITCH EARLEYWINE

Any fan can detail extensive, delighted experiences spent crank-ing favorite tunes from this band. Why all the joy? Queries reveal the usual responses: "Because they rock!" and "Virtuoso music with stellar lyrics!" and best of all, "Just listen!" My academic friends start riffing on various brain structures squirting happy chemicals to explain Rush-induced thrills.

But with Rush, there's also something else. Rush pairs music and words in a way that trains listeners in some of the key ideas in modern psychology, leading us to think clearly, responsibly, and happily. Rush lyrics frequently offer ideal examples of adaptive ways to view the world, communicate difficult emotions, or rally resources to motivate action.

A mountain of research now supports the idea that the way we think and behave has a tremendous impact on how we feel, and vice versa. The idea goes back to the ancient Greek philosopher Epictetus, but we lose it and find it again across generations. It hardly sounds like rocket science now, but in the years before the band formed, most of clinical psychology and psychotherapy had lost touch with the idea. The simple impact of thought was masked in the manufactured mystery of Freudian notions. There were still a lot of folks floating in a sea of weird, impractical, psychodynamic sewage. A few giants (especially Albert Ellis and Aaron Beck) had already climbed out of this sludge with clearer, more sensible, more realistic models of human functioning that centered on rational, adaptive, responsible approaches to life. What we now call the cognitive-behavioral revolution had begun.

These new approaches helped minimize misery left and right. Suddenly the anxious, depressed, and traumatized had new ways to see the world, inspiring them to take action calmly and rationally. I'll leave the fact that some of these ideas overlap with popular philosophical notions attributed by the band to other thinkers. Some psychologists and philosophers emphasized independence, rationality, and personal responsibility, and Rush took these ideas from wherever they could find them. What I want to underscore is that just as a revolutionary new breed of psychotherapy was helping people think straight and feel better, Rush was doing the same.

Archaic Looks at Thought and Mood

A lot of this work in psychology began with studies of depression. Depressed people thought that these long bouts of horrid moods and paralysis simply 'happened' to them—a conviction that left them essentially powerless to intervene. Reductionist notions of deviant neurotransmitters and wounded brains were popular at the time. We had some chemical mood elevators that seemed to help briefly, but many had bad side-effects or didn't work after awhile. Amphetamine was prescribed for depression, for example.

There was also a long, arduous, strange treatment known as psychoanalysis. I'm parodying a bit, but psychoanalysis essentially involved lying on a couch and free-associating. Ideally, whatever came into your head popped out your mouth during a sort of unleashed Dionysian hour. If you happened to construct a narrative about one of your dreams, that was supposed to be prime material, too. An analyst, an authority so powerful that he (and it was always a "he" at the time) took your money hand over fist, provided interpretations that were supposed to lead to insight. These insights purportedly uncovered unconscious material, resolved repressed conflicts, and ended guilt-ridden punishments of the self.

If you're scratching your head, join the club. I'm not sure what all that means either. The treatment burned tons of time and cash. The few successful clients spent years and thousands, and then left the ranks of the depressed to the glories of everyday unhappiness. Even Freud said that this was the goal. Other clients just spent years and thousands—begging hands and bleeding hearts crying out for more.

But we learned one thing: insight alone is not enough. It doesn't bring long-lasting changes in action or emotion. Dwelling on ancient slights or mistakes from days long ago tends to increase rumination and bad moods. We can't deny that these things happened, no matter how nasty or rare they were. As "Turn the Page" emphasizes, "Every day we're standing in a time capsule racing down a river from the past." Of course we take our past with us, even if it's only in memory. The problem with insights into the past, though, is that the past does not lend itself to change. Learning from the past is only good if we can apply it to the present and future. See the phrase in "Bastille Day": "Guide the future by the past." The line in "Time Stand Still," "I'm not looking back" also comes to mind. And "Let the pain remain behind you" from "Carve Away the Stone" gets the point across too.

In fact, what we tell ourselves about the past may be more story than reality. Our memories are filled with vagaries, tainted by our mood at the time events happened and at the time when we recall them. "Totem" mentions the idea: "I believe that what I'm feeling changes how the world appears." Psychologists ran a few studies for confirmation. Data on this selective memory usually requires getting folks into a mood, having them read a story with an equal number of happy, sad, and neutral events, and then asking them to recall the tale. Almost invariably, the recalled events match the mood. How we feel not only contributes to what we think, it even alters what we remember.[1] As "Vital Signs" recommends, we could "leave out the fiction". But when someone else provides the interpretations (psychoanalysts in this case), no matter how well-trained or well paid the alleged experts might be, we should check our own experience. No one is a better authority about our own lives than we are. If this all sounds familiar, perhaps we should thank "2112." This wading through the past is less efficient than examining the thoughts we have right now. As "Heresy" mentions, we do have to say goodbye to the past.

Thoughts Alter Perception

Better theorists who escaped the psychoanalytic death star noticed some key thoughts common to all of their clients. The distressed

---

[1] Joseph P. Forgas, "Affect, Cognition, and Social Behavior: The Effects of Mood on Memory, Social Judgments, and Social Action," in *Memory and Mind* (Erlbaum, 2008), edited by Mark A. Gluck, John R. Anderson, and Stephen M. Kosslyn.

tended to have a negative view of themselves, the world, and the future. They believed they were awful, the world was awful, and it would always be this way. They felt so rotten that they couldn't even put a positive spin on anything they saw. As we learned in "Vital Signs," a tired mind becomes a shape shifter; the distressed mind alters all it perceives. Research on the fact is crafty and intriguing. Distressed minds really do shift shapes. One study asked anxious folks and others to explain ambiguous sentences. They read the words "The Doctor was impressed by Mary's growth." Happy campers said, "Sounds like a little girl used to be short but now she's taller." The anxious said "Oh no! She's got a tumor."[2]

As the pantoum "The Larger Bowl" mentions, some only see the worst. In fact, they see it so badly and it frightens them so much that they can hardly think. In another set of studies, when asked "What color ink is this word written in?" distressed folks took longer to name the color if the word was negative (such as 'agony'). Clearly, they were battling their own minds, as if difficult feelings slowed their reactions in even a simple task like naming a color. That's no way to begin the day with a friendly voice. Research also revealed that these distressed people believed tons of completely irrational, subjective, maladaptive thoughts that would bum out Mother Theresa. These thoughts appeared to lead to the bad mood, insomnia, inactivity, and irritability so rampant in the distressed. They also lead people to interpret the whole world as threatening when only parts of it are, creating over-reactions and wasted efforts that perpetuate fear or hatred. See "Witch Hunt." Better yet, listen to the pairing of its hypnotic rhythm with the repetition of the dichotomous labels people apply to each other as the lyrics warn just how destructive this habit can be.

Recognize the Real Thing

So what did this new breed of psychologists recommend instead of hours on the couch every week for years and years? Take a look at our own thoughts for ourselves. Examine the evidence for them. Acknowledge the truth. Let the maladaptive half-truths and distortions fall away. Then get to work doing what we love, not what someone else told us to do. And enjoy those moments for all that

---

[2] Michael W. Eysenck and others, "Bias in Interpretation of Ambiguous Sentences Related to Threat in Anxiety," *Journal of Abnormal Psychology* 100 (1991).

they're worth. Part of examining thoughts requires recognizing that they are thoughts and not necessarily reality. (Dare I call this "catching the witness" in the tradition of "Tom Sawyer"?)

If we can get above the battlefield in our own heads and witness our own minds, we can see these beliefs, opinions, and attitudes for what they sometimes are—interpretations of facts rather than facts themselves. (If the opening strains of "Cygnus X-1" are appearing in your mind's ear, you're in good company.) Catching these thoughts as we witness them is the key. As "Vital Signs" mentions, internal incoherence can make mood run amuck. Thoughts will come and go. It's just part of being human. Recognizing them for what they are, before they lead us to behave in ways counter to our real values, can make the difference between delight and despair. Confusing what we think or how we feel for The Truth with two capital T's, particularly in environments where our beliefs or moods are manipulated, can create genuine disadvantages. And as "Witch Hunt" warns, mistaking our thoughts for truth can be downright dangerous.

The next part of examining thoughts requires a taxonomy of the maladaptive ones, a list of tell-tale signs that whatever's buzzing in our heads probably isn't reality. If we had categories of maladaptive or distress-inducing thoughts, we could probably recognize them better when we thought them. It's sort of like that myth about Eskimos having fine distinctions among types of snow, except that this time it's true. Once we know the types of thoughts that drive us crazy, we can catch them better. Note that none of this means that thinking is itself bad. The line in "Fly by Night," "Clear head, new life ahead" emphasizes that accurate cognitions have great potential. A clear head is a key to happiness. As alluded to in "Between the Wheels," thoughts can take you around or cut you down. I've struggled with distorted cognitions so much myself, and had clients, students, and friends resist this idea with such enthusiastic fervor that I feel a need to elaborate.

What happens and what we say to ourselves about what happens are not the same. More often than not, we upset ourselves because of our own opinions, beliefs, and interpretations of events, not because of the events themselves. Sure, some events are truly tragic. The goal of examining thoughts is not to eliminate negative emotions, only to turn them into tolerable and motivating feelings instead of paralyzing, unbearable ones. As Rush has emphasized time and again, there's plenty in the world that justifies righteous anger and concerted, rapid change. There's no need for absurd denial of situations that sincerely stink. This is not some Pollyanna put-on-a-happy-face approach to life. Adaptive thoughts might still lead to bad moods, but they're endurable ones. Rational cognitions can transform clinical depression into common sadness, disabling guilt into tolerable remorse, debilitating anxiety into motivating concern. This is a big opportunity for Rush fans as well as the unenlightened.

One of the most common of these maladaptive thoughts, identified by Beck and Rush, is a ubiquitous invitation to misery, is dichotomous thinking.[3] (Yes, one of the most prominent researchers on cognitive therapy is named Rush!) That all-or-none, black-or-white misperception of a world in glorious but messy color, can stymie anyone. Rarely is the world completely one thing or its opposite. "Between Sun and Moon" alludes to this idea, and the line in "Distant Early Warning," "black and whites of youth," underline how this simplistic thinking does not reflect reality. A personal favorite lyric that disputes this kind of dichotomizing comes from "Bravest Faces": "In the shakiest will there's a core of steel." Dichotomous thoughts usually include words like 'always', 'never', 'every', and 'none'. Thoughts with words like 'best' and 'worst' can lean this way, too. Lots of bad moods and troublesome acts rest on dichotomous thinking.

I'm not sure where to point fingers first, but institutions that seek to control others often rest on manufactured dichotomous distinctions like black/white, evil/good, and right/wrong. I have to be careful with healthy/unhealthy, adaptive/maladaptive, and even correct/incorrect, as these distinctions may be more manufactured than real, too. Artificial dichotomies like these distort our minds to the point where personal preferences get confused with demanded duty. These thoughts lead us to think in "musts" instead of "coulds"—a process Albert Ellis dubbed 'musturbation'.[4] Suddenly actions we could take become actions we must take, because of some manufactured 'always' or 'never'. Even the attempt to challenge them can get sucked into the same distortion (for instance, "I must never have dichotomous thoughts").

[3] A.J. Rush and Aaron T. Beck, "Cognitive Therapy of Depression and Suicide," *American Journal of Psychotherapy* 32 (1978).

[4] Albert Ellis, "Must Musturbation and Demandingness Lead to Emotional Disorders?" *Psychotherapy* 34 (1997).

Perhaps these ideas seem minor at first, or deceptively self-evident, until they inspire something as dramatic as a suicide bombing or something as insidious as a life spent in thoughtless toil. Throw a rock in government, religion, or academia and you're bound to hit the result of a must, should, or ought that arose from some dichotomous thought. And do me a favor—throw it hard. Note that even the idea of dichotomous thinking can't be thought about dichotomously. Some always and nevers are true. We can't uniformly dismiss every single one. We can examine the evidence before we decide. But the odds are high that there's some grey in between the black and white, some silver lining, some in-between way to see each event that will make it less debilitating.

Another common, popular, but potentially maladaptive distortion in thinking involves reasoning from emotion alone. Of course, the entire *Hemispheres* album sends this message with varying ranges of subtlety. But the more specific confusion of feelings and truth is an important subset of the more complicated idea that the heart and head need to work together. "I feel it, therefore it must be true," is the kind of emotional reasoning that can perpetuate sorrow. "I feel sad, therefore I am sad," is completely accurate. "I feel sad because this is a disaster, therefore it is a disaster," need not be. Note the leap from a thought about one's feelings to a thought about something more. "Emotion Detector" emphasizes that our feelings are essential, but "sometimes our big splashes" aren't the overwhelming proof we might think that they are. Bad moods are infallible indicators of one thing and one thing only: bad moods. They're important for letting us know when things are awry. "Double Agent" repeatedly refers to "My precious sense of . . ." in an effort to let us know that these beliefs and emotions don't often align with the truth. Holding on to them blindly, rather than seeing how they relate to the data we can gather, can lead us down a sad path. The bottom line for any of these thoughts requires that we identify them as thoughts and then check them with reality before we decide what to do with them. By this I mean that we have to get evidence from the real world, as best we can.

Counterexamples

Discussions of how Rush's lyrics and music fit modern recommendations from cognitive therapy invariably lead my informed but unconvinced friends to make arguments filled with counterexamples.

Depending on how the evening has progressed, these can digress to repeated shouts of "Be cool or be cast out!" First, few bands with this much enduring success can stick to only a handful of themes for their work. Variety is part of the appeal that has helped this trio remain popular for three decades. Nevertheless, some of the counterarguments grab lyrics out of context. Others ignore the jocular aspects of the music that coincide with the lyrics in a way that reveals that they are meant sarcastically.

The examples from "Subdivisions," including the line above as well as "Conform or be cast out" are, of course, completely the opposite of any healthy, adaptive way to think. But citing these lines as evidence that Rush has encouraged this kind of maladaptive thinking is complete nonsense. "Subdivisions" critiques suburban life for its potential to be stifling, conventional, and sterile. The repetition of the title word in a deep, superbly un-Geddy voice emphasizes the darkness that anyone longing for liberty could perceive in a cookie-cutter environment filled with demands for compliance and orthodoxy. It seems a realistic assessment of a troubling situation, inviting recognition and action. The suburbs are not for everybody. Those who grew up there would benefit from seeing somewhere else. For those of us who moved from our parents' homes the year this album was released, the song became an anthem, not an invitation to depression.

Nevertheless, other tunes do not fit this model. I will be the first to admit that the lyrics to "Losing It" will never be a pick-me-up. The song details the tribulations of artists who have passed their proverbial prime, exerting effort that seems doomed to never pay off while showing no appreciation for the process of creation or the joy in discovery. The description of the blocked writer could horrify anyone who has ever put a pen to paper. The line "sadder still to watch it die than never to have known it" could undermine the most motivated. Why attain goals if watching skills deteriorate is worse than never developing them? But the deviant rhythm, rich instrumentation, and fun interplay between electric violin and drums have a way about them that's hard to describe on paper.

There's something peaceful, a sort of letting go, which says that all of our attachments have an illusory feel. I don't think it's too much of a leap to say it encourages us to examine our thoughts about the big issues, including the giant dichotomy behind the bells tolling for us. It also certainly feels like a warning about where we place our efforts. A grave reminder that achievements fade can certainly help us set our priorities. Of course, the fact that even twenty years later the band would record the celebratory "One Little Victory" and the optimistic "Earthshine" seems quite the message about not taking momentary moods too seriously. Again, if we take the band's (and cognitive therapy's) recommendations to examine the evidence for our thoughts, dispute the less healthy ones, get to work doing what we value, and enjoy each moment, things are bound to improve.

Show Don't Tell

Examining the evidence may sound completely rational, like something done by the head alone, but it rests almost invariably on attending to our own emotions. (If this all sounds familiar, perhaps we should thank *Hemispheres* after all.) Is this thought true? We have to look around. If we've come across a fact, what are we going to make it mean? If "I Think I'm Going Bald," I need only look in the mirror now and glance at pictures from days that passed long ago. In my case, it's true. I can sit and curse my genetics and a society that I think values youth over all else. Woe is me! Why does it happen? As "Roll the Bones" explains, it happens because it happens. Must I comb over, shell out for implants, accept it and move on? The decision should be mine, based on my own values established from attending to my own feelings. I need not mention what happens if I choose not to decide. But the important thing is that I check out the truth first. Yes, I'm going bald. What do I want to make this mean? Is going bald a tragedy, or am I only thinking so? If I feel that going bald is a tragedy, does that make it so?

Acknowledging the truth doesn't always tickle. The frequently misheard and misquoted lyrics of "Entre Nous" contain several lines that encourage us to uncover "differences we sometimes fear to show." We are not all alike. We don't always agree. We all have aspects of ourselves we'd sincerely like to improve. But this is no disaster. Hiding these facts takes more energy than recognizing them. As the song emphasizes, these differences leave us room for growth, a chance to identify ourselves and interact with each other in genuine ways rather than presenting false fronts in hope of avoiding conflicts. Candor about our foibles and disagreements may be tough, but it beats being loved for who we are not. The declaration in "Limelight" that I "cannot pretend a stranger is a long awaited friend" seems to allude to the point.

The lesson of "Resist," a hard truth to acknowledge in its own right, emphasizes that we "never ever win without a fight." This fight may not require left hooks and atom bombs so much as the discomfort we create within ourselves by confessing that our own preferences may not be the ones we thought that we were supposed to have. We have to decide not only what we think, but whether or not we still want to think it based on reality. "Animate" can be interpreted this way, with its allusions to parts of ourselves we need to relish and cherish rather than deny. Interpersonally, these out-and-out arguments about how we truly feel and think, these fights we cannot win without, may not mean every day is moonlight and roses, but they beat a life spent throwing barbs at each other while avoiding honest disagreement.

Let It Go

With this kind of approach to identifying and examining our own cognitions, the next step may be easier said than done: Letting the maladaptive thoughts fall away. As "Vital Signs" suggests, hold the ones you need. But as "Distant Early Warning" asks, "Who can face the knowledge that the truth is not the truth?" Sometimes it seems that we can't help believing what we believe, even as evidence mounts to the contrary. These changes in beliefs, moving from maladaptive to adaptive thoughts, may not be a dichotomous, categorical enlightenment. The gradual transition, a sort of splintering off of irrational aspects of the depressing thoughts to leave the realistic, rational ones, may be more common. Like the process described in "Carve Away the Stone," we can make the sum of small movements turn into big ones over time. The vigilance required can be daunting. The band's whole career is a lesson in perseverance. But "We Hold On." A lot of this process is more about losing illusions than finding new truths.

The band's advice to lay down false beliefs is often more memorable in the stories they tell than in any direct urgings. The disobedient tale "Red Barchetta" comes to mind. This description of a tire-squealing ride in a forbidden vehicle in a future that has outlawed the gasoline engine details the genuine pleasure inherent in defying rules that go unexamined. The fact that the narrator's old uncle has saved the sporty speedster for him sends a nice message about the beauty of interpersonal care and close relationships as a nice aside. The rhythmic tune echoes the sound of a zooming hot rod at times. The narrator's success at eluding those who would deny him this freedom is a celebrated triumph. Chipping away at archaic, maladaptive beliefs, or even good ideas that have gone too far, can be its own source of glee. The fact that these beliefs may arise from government, family, education, or religion should not make them too sacred to challenge. The song goes well beyond the realm of an attractive auto and encourages an independence of mind. (I have rarely laughed harder than the first time I heard Geddy's deadpan introduction of this tune as "a song about a car.") Of course, this tale also emphasizes the import of action, any action, no matter how small.

Do What You Love

The next step in the process concerns translating thoughts to deeds. "What you do is your own glory," from "Something for Nothing," makes this point nicely. Rather than leaving us all spinning in thought, both cognitive behavioral therapists and Rush recommend concerted action. A whole philosophy and treatment program has developed around the intuitive idea that the key to improved moods is a dynamic life filled with behaviors consistent with your values. It works as well or better than Big Pharma's favorite anti-depressants, too. See Kantor, Busch and Rusch's (I kid you not!) 2009 book for an accessible review of this behavioral activation therapy.[5] The treatment is more than doing fun stuff, though there's plenty of that, and there are few better ways to lift mood. The therapy is all about choosing the acts that are consistent with what we think is most important, and, most importantly, doing them.

"Days of barefoot freedom racing with the waves," from "Lakeside Park," certainly describes the kind of enjoyable activity that's guaranteed to cultivate happiness. Increasing positive events increases positive mood. "We just need a break," from "Between Sun and Moon," illustrates how time away from the grind is essential. Other tunes emphasize thoughtful leisure's import in a world filled with the mundane or distracting ("The Spirit of Radio," "Afterimage," "Sweet Miracle"). But more than simply having fun, the transition to longer bouts of pleasant emotion requires work that we value. Even the pre-Peart "Working

---

[5] Jonathan W. Kanter, Andrew Busch, and Laura Rusch, *Behavioral Activation: Distinctive Features* (Routledge, 2009).

Man" points out the distinction between living and working when the work seems separate from any meaningful mission. This is what the move of "Tom Sawyer" to the friction of the day is about. "Roll the Bones" mentions "Good work is the key to good fortune," which may include good feelings, too. Even the downers described in "Everyday Glory" end with a call that we're the ones who need to take action to make things better.

Enjoy These Moments

Recent studies in psychology confirm what every Zen meditator has said for centuries: pay attention to the present and delight will follow.[6] "A fortune hunt that's far too fleet," from "Freewill," underscores the import of what little time we have. The whole of "The Camera Eye" certainly stresses a joy in the moment, a calm at the center of things that is available if we only attend to it. The narrator who walks through a bustling city cannot help but wonder if the surrounding hustlers and bustlers notice unique qualities of the moment. Note how this message differs dramatically from the "live for the moment" sorts of lyrics that are quite popular in the genre. This message is distinctly not "Love the One You're With."

"Time Stand Still" could not be more aptly named, its title almost a fruitless command to indifferent planets orbiting an ancient sun as an astute listener's illusions about the inevitability of aging and death slip away. The song emphasizes how attending to the current moment may be our only way to intensify sensations and joy. The description of moments appreciating beauty and nature, from "The Analog Kid," actually creates the kind of moment we can appreciate as we listen, in part because the music itself is so delightful. As "Chain Lightning" states so bluntly: "This moment may be brief, but it can be so bright."

The beauty of all these tunes comes in the way that they are the incarnation of their own recommendations. Though they make splendid background music, they are particularly joyful when we attend to them. And so the best approach from Rush or cognitive therapy may be one of the answers mentioned in the beginning: Just listen!

---

[6] Mark Williams and others, *The Mindful Way through Depression: Freeing Yourself from Chronic Unhappiness* (Guilford Press, 2007).

7
Rush's Metaphysical Revenge

GEORGE A. REISCH

In 1977, as a freshman at Bernards High School in New Jersey, I went to Rush's hometown of Toronto, Ontario, with the marching band for a regional competition. I didn't want to go, because I generally dislike marching-band music. The routine that year included "Brian's Song" and something by Chicago. I was a drummer, so whenever possible I'd pound out the necessary beats, but still imagine in my head that I was playing along to Rush's "Xanadu" or "2112."

All this happened a long time ago, so the details are fuzzy. But one thing I remember vividly: as I arrived at the hotel in Toronto, I turned on the clock radio in my room. My jaw dropped as Rush's song "Fly by Night" came out of the speaker. Back in New Jersey, where all the radio stations were out of New York, Rush was invisible and inaudible. You never heard them on the radio, saw them on TV, or even saw them mentioned in the mainstream music press. I was crazy about Rush and was always on the lookout for some bit of information about them, some mention, some glimmer of recognition from the other human beings that, indeed, this was a great and unique band. You could buy Rush albums at Sam Goody; you could see them at the Capitol Theatre (which I did twice); but they were otherwise invisible. That seemed strange to me.

I ran to the door of my room and yelled down the hall to the room where a few other Rush fans were staying. I thought they'd never believe me if they didn't hear it for themselves. "Hey, they're playing RUSH on the radio. Turn on your radio!" My friend John Croot came out into the hall and looked at me as though I had lost my mind. Now, John was a very cool guy because he played bass and keyboards in the school's stage band (thus steering clear of the geeky marching band), and he clearly thought I was acting like a geek: "We're in Canada," I remember him saying. "Up here Rush is like . . . Led Zeppelin. Of course, they get played on the radio!"

I thought about John's remark over the years, even after Rush's fortunes changed in 1980–81, as *Permanent Waves* and *Moving Pictures* (with "Tom Sawyer") took the world by storm and put them on radios all over the world. How can you make sense of this? Was Rush's marginalization and invisibility in the New York radio market and press just a matter of demographics and marketing? If Led Zeppelin and Rush could get airplay in Toronto, why couldn't Rush get any in the New York markets? It seemed arbitrary, as if Canada and New Jersey were ruled by different councils of high priests who control the words we read and the songs we heard on the radio.

There are surely lots of reasons and circumstances that make a band big in one demographic market and invisible in another. But in Rush's case I think there is also a philosophical prejudice in play. One of these high priests that tend to control our judgments about music is Plato—not the ancient philosopher himself, obviously, but his theory of knowledge which often lurks behind our beliefs about what is "good" or "bad" in music and art. It's especially in play whenever a fan or a critic spells out what is means to be a good band, a good song, or a good album. This is because Plato's theory of knowledge was tightly connected to a theory of what actually exists in the world and what is possible. In a sense, Rush really was invisible in New Jersey in the 1970s because according to the reigning notions of what a "good" rock band was like, they were off the map. And, for some, that even made Rush seem funny or ridiculous. But Rush is getting the last laugh.

Rush Judgments

The role of Plato in judgments about Rush's music became clear to me while watching the 2010 documentary *Rush: Beyond the Lighted Stage.* For if you compare what these Rush-loving fans have to say about the band and its history with what the critics (or just people who didn't 'get' Rush) used to say about the band, you can see Plato's theory in action. It's writ large because the range of opinions about Rush is huge. Fans are as dedicated and respectful as can be. They devote large chunks of their lives to concerts, deciphering and debating the songs, and reading books like this one.

But Rush's critics are often agitated and upset. Take some of the reviews quoted in *Beyond the Lighted Stage*:

"overbearing and pretentious to the point of tears . . ."

"Rush's humorless (and limited) interest in literary themes and meager sense of melody made for one dull, dull concert."

"Smug, hypocritical, pseudo-symbolic drivel. If pop music is a grassroots reflection of our times, I am saddened that our culture prompts Rush to exist, much less flourish."

For these critics, their dislike of Rush is not a simple matter of preference—as in, hmm, yesterday I listened to *Power Windows*, so today I'll pick . . . *A Farewell to Kings*. No, these writers feel violated, as if Rush's music or their performances or the band's very existence were somehow at odds with the metaphysical grain of the universe. Seriously, one of them is crying about it.

Well, if that's the way they feel, the obvious question for them is this: What *is* the metaphysical grain of the universe, and how do you know about it? If Rush somehow doesn't fit into the scheme of things you understand, what is your understanding based on? When pressed, most of them will fall back on a Platonic theory of knowledge. They will say that certain kinds of things legitimately exist and others don't. And, they will insist that their claims are not merely their opinion. Instead, they will say, their claims rest ultimately on deep metaphysical knowledge about the nature of the world and how knowledge of it is possible. This takes us back to Plato . . .

When a Tree Falls in a Forest

Distinguishing between mere opinion and genuine knowledge was the central task of Plato's theory of knowledge. Knowledge, as opposed to mere opinion, was possible, Plato believed, because of the Forms. Forms for Plato are something like pure, perfect ideas that were fashioned by the creator of the world (the "demiurge," Plato called it in his dialogue *Timaeus*) and which function as a kind of template or cosmic blueprint for everything that exists. All trees are different (one classic example) because they have different markings, branches, leaves, sizes, shapes, and so on. (Some, of course, are very "greedy, and they grab up all the light"). Despite all these individual differences, however, they are all trees because they share an imperfect and partial resemblance to the Form of the tree. The existence of the Form, the theory goes, makes the claim "these are all trees" true, objective and not just some person's whim or opinion.

Here's another example: how do we know that "La Villa Strangiato" and "Happy Birthday" are both songs? They don't have much in common. They sound different, they're different in length, they are played on different occasions, one does not have words . . . This list could go on forever, but we presume (as Plato instructed us) that they are essentially the same kind of thing, and that the source of this shared identity is the Form of the song. The same goes for things that are Beautiful, Just, and—the ultimate Form of all, Plato said—the Good.

If you're skeptical about this theory, you should be. Can we really believe in the existence of these things Plato called Forms? What kind of things are they? Where do they exist? Is there one Form for trees, or does each species of tree have its own Form (and, if so, what about sub-species and varieties)? Some of Plato's dialogues (like the *Phaedrus* at lines 245c–257b) imply that the Forms exist outside of our world, up in the heavens; and Platonists through the ages (after Platonism was combined with monotheism in the early Christian era) have supposed that the Forms are ideas in the mind of God. However they are conceived, the Forms must be thought to exist apart from us mortals—otherwise they can't mark the difference between knowledge and mere individual opinion. If I have my Forms and you have yours, then we're back at Square One, with "Forms" being just a name for our different opinions.

If you'd lived centuries ago, these beliefs surrounding the Platonic theory of knowledge might have seemed reasonable. But time has not been kind to Platonism. Now, we know that our Earth is not at the center of anything, that there is no heavenly realm of immaterial ideas floating around us in space, and we take people who claim to be thinking God's thoughts or having God's ideas to be, more or less, insane. We don't know everything about what knowledge is or how it's possible, but we know it involves things like neural networks and biological brains, not ghostly immaterial Forms floating up in space.

Drummers in (Geek) Heaven

Still, the Platonic theory of knowledge surrounds us. You see it at work all the time in rock criticism and debate. Rush's fans and their critics can make use of it equally. Take actor Jack Black, interviewed in *Beyond the Lighted Stage*, who clearly believes that his love of Rush is grounded on something more than just his opinion. With that half-crazed I-am-so-sure-of-this look in his eye, he claims there are objective, scientific measures, that prove how great Rush is. If you analyzed a spectral diagram of Neil Peart's drumming, he says in the interview, you'd probably find that it deviates from perfect mathematical time by, at most, "one atom!" Peart is such a great drummer, he says, that when you listen through headphones you may have come to an eerie conclusion: Peart is so good, "he's not even human!"

You can't get much more Platonic than that: for Plato, mathematics was the highest form of human knowledge available (legend has it that "Let no one ignorant of geometry enter" was inscribed over the door to his school, The Academy) precisely because mathematics abstracts from the sensual world around us and points to the immaterial realms of ideas, concepts, and relationships in the world—including, Black would emphasize, impeccable timing.

But compare this to Greg Kot's comments about Peart in his review of the *Snakes and Arrows* concert tour. You can almost hear Kot snicker when he writes,

> Neil Peart's drumming still sounds like he's working out a calculus formula. This is geek heaven for the band's ardent followers; for the rest of us, it's very much a mixed bag. (*Chicago Tribune*, May 22nd, 2007)

Kot agrees that there's something about Peart's drumming that evokes the precision, perfection, and otherworldliness of mathematics. But that's what wrong with it! Good drummers, Kot thinks, drum from the heart and from the emotions with all their sentiments and surging passions, not from some cold, precise sense of mathematical thinking or timing.

Kot's comment helps us make sense of why some people find Rush funny or ridiculous, too. Progressive rockers, Kot has said elsewhere, display a "willingness to be pompous and ridiculous" (*Sound Opinions*, show number 207). His point seems to be that bands like Yes, Genesis, or Rush are attempting to combine things that do not legitimately belong together. In Peart's case, it's rock-'n'roll and a fascination with mathematical precision. More broadly, it's rock'n'roll and musical virtuosity, lyrical ambition, or philosophical curiosity or sophistication.

Kot is not saying that these things are bad or unworthy; nor is he saying that merely in his opinion they don't mix well with rock and roll. His claim, I suspect, is much stronger and it again depends on Plato. He's saying that real rock'n'roll bands don't concern themselves with topics and values like this. If you were to go up into Plato's heaven and inspect the Form, 'rock'n'roll band', it's mostly about girls, parents, and school. There is no philosophy, no art, and no literature. So when a band tries to inject these things into rock'n'roll, they don't fit. It doesn't work. And it looks funny.

Aristocrats and Critics

It's not just critics that find humor in Rush. In *Beyond the Lighted Stage*, Geddy recalls the way UFO, the British (and German) band they toured with in 1977, made fun of him. They called him "Glee" (for G. Lee, I guess), nailed furry slippers to the stage in front of his mike, and teased him about the lyric "for I have dined on honeydew" from "Xanadu." UFO probably weren't laughing when Rush was actually playing, of course. Alex Lifeson plays circles around UFO's guitar ringer Michael Schenker and Rush's massive and intricate wall of sound has a power and precision that a lesser band like UFO could only wish to create. And they're probably not laughing now, as Rush's popularity continues to increase and UFO is more or less unidentifiable (sorry) on the rock landscape. But you can't deny that UFO's jokesters had their finger on something.

Picture it. The coliseum is buzzing with anticipation. The lights go down. Shadowy figures take the stage. The crowd is ready to explode and Alex rips into the opening of "Bastille Day." The drums, guitars, and lights suddenly explode into life. Then Geddy steps up to the mic. What do you expect to hear, especially if you've never heard Rush before? A growl like Ian Gillan's or Ronnie James Dio's, or a croon like Jack Bruce's? But when Geddy opens his mouth to sing, it is a surprise. In the early years, he really did sound like a guy from a glee club (a soprano, even).

Rush's lyrics pack a surprise, too. Almost from their beginning, when Neil came on board, Rush's songs addressed very unconventional topics—like political revolution ("Bastille Day," from *Caress of Steel*), allegorical heroes, and battles ("By-Tor and the Snowdog" from *Fly by Night*), and philosophical theses like this one:

> It's philosophically indefensible and culturally dangerous for us to believe that there exists a categorical divide between cognition and emotion.

If you stumbled a bit on that, you probably didn't when you first heard "Closer to the Heart." But that's what the lyrics say; that's their point—which is why I imagine Greg Kot laughing right now. Rock music, he'd say, is not supposed to have a point!

Incongruities and surprises like this are probably essential to humor. Take the classic vaudeville joke "The Aristocrats." Penn Jillette and Paul Provenza made a film, released in 2005, dedicated entirely to performances and analysis of this one joke. The joke is a story about a family that auditions for a talent agent. The members of this family do all kinds of raunchy, vulgar, and unprintable things in their performance (which the joke-teller describes in creative, disgusting detail). When it's all over, the talent agent is shocked and nearly speechless. All he can think to ask is, "What do you call your act?" They respond, "The Aristocrats!"—just the opposite of what you'd expect this comedy troupe to call itself.

A Farewell to Kinds

If we press these critics and the guys in UFO to specify why Rush's musical talents and their interests in philosophy and literature don't belong together, they will inevitably appeal to the dubious metaphysics of Plato and the Forms. Great rock singers, they will say— Robert Plant, Mick Jagger, John Lennon, and so on—or classic rock albums, like the Beatles' *Sgt. Pepper's Lonely Hearts Club Band* or Radiohead's *OK Computer*, are great not merely as a matter of collective opinion, but rather because they achieve a standard of greatness or perfection that lesser singers or albums imitate (more or less, usually less) and which we can use as a yardstick in making evaluations. Just as a beautiful tree (in Plato's worldview) is understood to embody more of the pure Form of Tree than its mangled, gnarly neighbors, *OK Computer* towers above the latest from Justin Bieber.

This is fine so far, but there is a temptation once an album or performer has achieved this kind of greatness in the popular imagination to assume that they truly have the same kind of status as Plato's Forms, that they are permanent and immortal, never to be rivaled again by lesser performers, and always the singular yardstick by which others must be measured—as if *Sgt. Pepper's Lonely Hearts Club Band* didn't create a new benchmark in 1967 but instead met a benchmark that had always existed. The difference is crucial, for if you believe that standards and achievements in rock music are eternal and metaphysically real, or that they become eternal and metaphysically real, you will always stack the deck against bands or artists who try to do things differently. You will not just be surprised, or humored, by a band that does things differently, you will make a metaphysical judgment asserting that this band is corrupt, illegitimate, or somehow offensive to the status quo.

Look at the basic argument against Rush from these critics with all the dubious metaphysics in place. As best as I can reconstruct it, it goes like this:

1. **All works of art that combine radically different kinds of topics and interests will fail and seem ridiculous or pretentious.**

2. **Rush's music combines radically different kinds of topics and interests.**

3. **Therefore, Rush's music fails and seems ridiculous or pretentious.**

But once we cease appealing to some immutable and controlling realm of Forms or kinds, the critic can no longer claim that rock and philosophy or political history are independent kinds of things that can't be connected. The best he can do is to point out that no other band he knows combines these interests. However, if that's so the argument collapses:

1. **[Platonic metaphysics of Kinds or Forms removed].**

2. **Rush's music uniquely attempts to combine different interests.**

3. **Therefore, Rush's music fails and seems ridiculous or pretentious.**

Ouch. What's left is not even a valid argument. It's just an insistent claim that Rush's music is bad because it's different or unfamiliar.

No self-respecting rock critic would go in print saying that. But that's what some have been saying about Rush for decades.

Smashing Critics' Pumpkins

All of this is really just an expansion and articulation of what some of Rush's most insightful defenders have been saying for years. One is Kiss's Gene Simmons who, in *Beyond the Lighted Stage*, pointed out that Rush confounds the critics because critics can't put them in any familiar category; they can't say Rush is some definite "kind" of band. "What kind of band is Rush?" Simmons mockingly asks. "It's Rush."

Billy Corgan made a similar point. Corgan grew up listening to Rush albums in his Chicago basement, not far from Mercury Record's old downtown headquarters, and in a Midwest state that was generally more friendly to Rush than the east coast. (Rush first broke in the States in 1974, after a Cleveland radio station started playing "Working Man.") Corgan also sensed that Rush was getting a raw deal, just as I sensed back in New Jersey in the 1970s. "Why was this band marginalized?" Corgan asked. Because "they just don't fit in a neat box."

In so many words, Corgan and Simmons are kicking away the same platonic metaphysics I have been criticizing. It's our platonic inheritance to reflexively reach for Plato's Forms in the guise of "boxes" and "kinds" and pigeonholes that help us organize and label what we know and believe. But this backfires on us when we start to trust our own sense of "boxes" and "kinds" instead of paying attention to the new boxes and new kinds of bands that come along from time to time. It's only because "the people have generally and consistently voted for this band," Corgan explained, that rock critics have been taught an important lesson. Rock belongs to the people, not to the critics.

As the years go by, Rush's popularity has continued to grow, with their 2008 appearance on *The Colbert Report*, the success of Neil Peart's 2002 book *Ghost Rider: Travels on the Healing Road*, and crowds around the world (such as the Brazilian crowds in 2002, documented on *Rush in Rio*). So, will a new generation of rock critics take Rush and their classic albums as the platonic standards that all other bands will have to meet, or else seem "ridiculous" or "pretentious"? I doubt it. Rush fans are too smart for that.

8
Ghost Riding the Razor's Edge

JIM BERTI

No one, especially not Neil Peart himself, could have predicted the unforeseen tragic events following Rush's *Test for Echo* tour. In August of 1997 the Pearts' daughter died in a car accident while on her way to college. Less than a year later, Neil's wife Jackie succumbed to cancer, though death by a broken heart would more accurately describe her fate. Soon after the passing of his loved ones, Peart's best friend Brutus was incarcerated and facing federal drug trafficking charges.

They say that when it rains, it pours. If this is true then Peart's life had become a monsoon. A lifetime's worth of pain and suffering was delivered to him in less than a year. Needing space for his emotional scars to heal, Peart "retired" from Rush to embark upon a fifty five thousand mile motorcycle journey, a trip that would become known as the Ghost Rider travels. Much has been discussed of Peart's tragic events, Peart himself documenting much of his personal turmoil in his book *Ghost Rider: Travels on the Healing Road*.

Seems We'll Never See the Sun

"Dark and gloomy", are the words Peart used to describe the morning of his departure, symbolic of the weather and his emotional state. Armed with two bags of luggage, and the emotional weight of tragedy, Peart set off with no itinerary and no plan or destination. This was not a vacation, but rather an escape from what had become an unbearable living Hell. Peart knew the ramifications of this journey had the potential to end badly, even accepting the fact that he may never again return to what he had known as home.

Just how does one survive an ordeal such as this? And, for that matter, if one does survive, what kind of person emerges? The answers to these questions were to be found somewhere, just not in the Peart family homes in Ontario and Quebec that had become a source of painful reminders, acting like salt to a fresh wound. For Peart, home, just as his physical being, had become nothing more than a ghostly aberration, haunting reminders of what once was, and never to be again. In the song "Face Up" Peart writes of the benefits of getting out of town in order to clear one's head when problems arise. A change of scenery and landscape can provide a comfort for the mind and body, removing one from the habitual routines of everyday living. Life on the road can clear the mind and soul, giving one the space to ponder the answers burning deep within.

A Thinking Man's Band

I still remember the moment "Freewill" came on the radio, my first Rush song. The year was 1993 (I was a late bloomer to the Rush scene, just as I have been for much of the music I listen to now, better late than never). At the time, I had no concept of what free will was, I only felt the connection between the lyrics and my own feeling of teenage rebellion. Although my "rebel stage" would pass, my enthusiasm for Rush has remained. Flash forward sixteen years.

One night while reading Jean-Paul Sartre's *Existentialism and Human Emotions*—prior to reading this book, my experience with philosophy had been nothing beyond my Educational Philosophy courses—I was overcome with this feeling of 'higher' understanding—when complex ideas and concepts synchronize to form a complete picture. Taking a closer look at Peart's journey on the healing road, I could see parallels between existential beliefs of free will and Peart's journey on the healing road. I want to be up front, this chapter is my first attempt at philosophical writing. I may be far off in what I say, or perhaps there is something beyond the surface. Guess we all have to start somewhere.

You Can Choose . . .

Life is like a box of chocolate, to paraphrase the genius of Forrest Gump, and each day we awake there is no guarantee what kind of day, or piece of chocolate for that matter, we will have. Some problems are small and trite, while others can mushroom into great sources of stress and anxiety. Now, we have little control over the events of the day, a point I will come back to, however, we have a choice in how we react to events. We can choose to be the author of the day, so to speak, creating our own story based on our own choices and meaning. Conversely, if we choose to let the events of life get the best of us, we are choosing to let life write our story; we can control how we react to life.

According to the French philosopher Jean-Paul Sartre, the concept of freedom is derived from the belief that individuals bear responsibility for their own existence, free from outside influences or forces. If God does not exist, states Sartre, then there is at least one being whose existence precedes essence, a being that exists before he can be defined by any concept. That being is the individual himself. In other words, if God does not exist, there is no pre-determined plan for our existence. Therefore, it is up to the individual to accept responsibility for creating our own existence.[1]

To illustrate his belief of individual responsibility, Sartre tells the story of a meeting with a student who sought out Sartre's advice. The student's mother—estranged from her husband and mourning the loss of another son in war—had become so dependent on her only son that he became her sole purpose for living. The son wished to join the Free French Forces, however, he feared that leaving his mother would trigger within her a feeling of abandonment; especially in light of his mother's fragile emotional state. If the son were to choose to remain in France to care for his mother, he would be conceding his own goals and visions for the good of his mother; thus, he may come to resent his mother for holding him back. Sartre's advice to the student was simple; it is up to the individual to choose for himself, free from outside influences. Individuals must do what is best for them. We can only worry about ourselves, and we can make ourselves happy by choosing what makes us happy. This is not as easy as it seems. Disappointing others, especially when it is not our intent, can wreak emotional havoc on us. From Sartre's perspective, free will is the ability to listen to our self, using the heart and mind to guide our decision, free from the guilt of doing what others think is best.

---

[1] Jean Paul-Sartre, *Existentialism and Human Emotions* (Wisdom Library, 1957). For helpful follow-up on this, see David Detmer, *Sartre Explained: From Bad Faith to Authenticity* (Open Court, 2008).

Christ, What Have You Done?

We did not have a say in when we were born, just as we will more than likely not have a say in when our time is up. Everything in between, however, is within our power to determine. Scriptures, words, and self-help may provide solace and comfort in times of need, but true change comes from within the person himself. In the song "The Pass," Peart writes of a teenager who is contemplating suicide. The narrator, Geddy Lee, is the guiding voice of reason telling the young man to "turn around and walk the razor's edge" and think about all the available choices rather than settling on the perceived easy way out. The song is empathetic toward the teen's situation, with Lee singing how we have all done time in the gutter of life, however, those who are emotionally strong find a way to pull themselves out. The narrator provides the guidance but does not dictate.

Thoughts of solitude and isolation, especially when our emotional foundation has been rocked, can be stressful; therefore, it is natural to seek guidance and advice from others. The human connection, especially when dealing with an emotional crisis, can have a therapeutic quality, helping us to feel less alone in our situation. However, when we become dependent on outside guidance, we give up the sovereignty of free will. Sartre criticizes the irrationality of calling ourselves free when in reality we are living our lives through the influences of others. The responsibility of choice and action fall on the individual. But this raises the question: how can we set ourselves free from opinion, influence, and blame, especially when faced with tragedy?

Just as the student left Sartre's office alone, to make his own choice, Neil Peart took to the road in solitude, seeking to find some meaning behind the circumstances thrust upon him. As he wrote in "Freewill," the only path one can choose is the one that is clear. But what happens when those paths become clouded and dark; and we becomes alienated and disassembled from ourselves?

I Do Not Know Who I Am

The events of Peart's life had reduced him to a shell of his former self. Besides walking away from the drum set, Peart left behind activities that comprised his previous life—reading, bird watching, writing, traveling—all activities that he had enjoyed. Shortly after leaving home, Peart was stopped for speeding. When asked by the officer if he was a musician, Peart, lowering his head, mumbled, "um . . . not anymore". All sense of identification prior to 1997 had been lost.

Most of us have had a day or two when we wake in a dark depressed funk, sometimes for no reason at all. Those days can trigger a flood of emotional outburst when asked "How is your day"? Such questions reveal our inner most hypersensitive nerves, rendering them as Peart writes in "Scars," sensitive to touch. These are days when we feel so detached from life, almost as if in another dimension. When depressed, seeing people happy can make us envious. Therefore, sometimes the best remedy is to get away for a change of scenery and perspective. Alienation can best be described as a feeling of being cut off from life, as if we're invisible and estranged from the world. Peart's thoughts exemplified such feelings. In order to reconstruct a new sense of Self, we must determine the values and priorities that define how we wish to live our lives. Psychological pain, just as physical pain, can destroy the perception of our being.

Blame Is Better to Give than Receive

How do we react when we are in a depressed state of mind? Speaking from personal experience, there have been times I just want to be alone, avoiding all contact with people, especially those who seem so happy. Other times, I may use a friend or family member for my own venting, rattling off all my problems and watching the other person graciously listen, probably thinking to themselves, "What the hell, I have got problems of my own that are a hundred times worse."

Traumatic events compel some to put up barriers against further pain and suffering. Just as a band-aid covers a wound allowing it time to heal, unconscious thoughts allow emotional scars the time to heal. However, this comfort is only a short-term fix, an escape from the responsibility of dealing with the source of the pain, a task that can be accomplished only through the transformation of one's thoughts.

Brought Up to Believe

Journal entries and letters written by Peart early on in his travels illuminate feelings of anger and hostility. Peart questioned the fairness of life; weren't we brought up to believe that good things happen to good people and bad things happen to bad people? Weren't we brought up to believe that everything in life happens for a reason, and God has a plan for us all? If that were true, then why was Peart experiencing such horror? If we believe that life is "supposed" to be fair to us, we become disappointed when our path is deviated. "It wasn't supposed to be this way." Emotional trappings—the "supposed to," the "could have," the "should have"—distract us from the source of energy we possess to create our own meaning.

After all, sometimes life is just not fair; regardless of who we are or what our secular beliefs are. Good things happen to bad people, just as bad things happen to good people. There are times when it feels as if life ingested an enema and we are standing directly in its path. Like the maples and the oaks in "The Trees," our economic, political, and class standing are irrelevant when it comes to life. Events have a way of humbling us, keeping us all equal by the hatchet, axe, and saw of life. Though we may not be empowered to control life's events, we can control our reactions to events. Again, we have a choice.

Each of Us, a Cell of Awareness

Sartre wrote of the absurdity humans display when complaining of events that are beyond their control. For example, those who wish they could go back and change the course of history. Sartre questioned why humans who have no control over the future or the past become so preoccupied with trying to do so. Those who choose to are missing what is occurring in the present moment. Since it's possible to control our thoughts, according to Sartre, we can change the perception of our circumstances.

I walk into a dark room looking for a pair of keys, I have two choices: I can walk into the room, ignoring the light switch and stumble around the room getting angry each time I bump into something, or stub my foot, and become increasingly more frustrated when I cannot locate them. Or, I can walk over to the light switch, turn on the lights and clearly see where the keys are without risking any destruction to the room or myself. It may take more of an effort on my part to find the light, but it sure as heck beats the anger and frustration of not knowing where I'm going or what I'm looking for. Like light in a darken room, Sartre believes we have the capacity to turn on the light of conscious thoughts—liberating thoughts—that illuminate the circumstances of life.

While in exile, Peart penned over one hundred letters and journal entries. For Peart, writing was cathartic, allowing him to free himself from all pent-up emotions negatively affecting his life. This new sense of awareness presented Peart with the opportunity to gain control over his thoughts, a beam of light in what had become a dark life. Through his writing Peart recognized that his only chance at peace would come if he eliminated the resentment he held for what had happened to him. In a letter to Brutus, Peart expresses his desire to change the events in his life, but is cognizant that as much as he wished he could get his old life back, nothing could bring back his loved ones. All he could do was get up in the morning, and go.[2] As long as he remained alive, Peart clung to the hope that something meaningful in his life would arise.

A Spirit Breaking Free

Following the events of 1997–1998, just who had Neil Peart become? Conventional wisdom tells us he is still Neil Peart, drummer and lyricist of Rush; however, circumstances continually alter and reshape our being. I am Jim Berti and to many of my friends and relatives I'm the same Jim Berti they have known all their lives. My true sense of Self is the same, but many of my physical and mental characteristics and traits have changed. I know that I am not the same person now that I was a year ago.

As the *Ghost Rider* travels continued, Peart began to forge a new sense of his Self. A desire to create meaning out of his life was evident in a letter to Brutus, where Peart writes: "Although I don't think I know where I'm heading, I will know when I get there."[3] This sentiment is a far cry from the man who left his house just hoping to survive another day, a man with no plan or destination. Something was happening, though it was clear to Peart that he was not sure what it was.

An advantage of the open road is the healing sights and sounds of nature, allowing us to reconnect with so much of what we get separated from. As Thoreau wrote,

---

[2] I'm not sure how many Rush fans are also fans of the Grateful Dead, but all I could think of as I wrote this line was the song "He's Gone", "nothing gonna bring him back, he's gone."

[3] Neil Peart, *Ghost Rider: Travels on the Healing Road* (ECW Press, 2002), pp. 304–05.

I went to the woods because I wished to live deliberately, to front only
the essential facts of life and to see if I could not learn what it had to
teach and not when I came to die, discover that I had not lived.

Peart's solitary journey allowed him to reconnect with many of
the activities of his former life; hiking National Parks, snowshoeing,
swimming, and bird watching were once again meaningful activities for Peart. Though the Neil Peart who before had partaken in
these events no longer existed—in the existential sense—what
made up the core of his Self was still intact. What Peart dubbed his
"baby soul" was now fed by a sense of purpose; a reason to awake
each morning. Rather than just survival, Peart was rediscovering a
reason to celebrate the moments of living. The answer to the existential question of "what is my purpose for living" was becoming
clearer each day.

Ask Tom Sawyer and he will tell you changes are not permanent, but change is. The events of life do not last forever. However,
the outcome of those events, and how we react to them, may be
more permanent. Once again, Peart used writing to express his
feelings. Peart outlined his own directives for adapting to life's circumstances: 1. Keep moving; 2. kick your own ass, gently; 3. allow
others the pleasure of helping you; 4. when thoughts want to
replay the unfortunate circumstances, move these thoughts elsewhere; and 5. make peace with others when you can (*Ghost Rider*,
pp. 258–262).

Experience can be our best teacher, if we choose to learn the
lessons. By sharing his experiences with others, Peart was acting as
a voice for those who may face similar circumstances. Peart's lyrics
have frequently conveyed a message much deeper than appears on
the surface. He's nicknamed "The Professor" because of his innate
ability to challenge listeners to discover and interpret their own
meaning. Though at the time he was not on the drum kit, or wearing his lyricist hat, Peart had a pen and paper and continued to
convey this message.

The Time Is Now Again

Since the tragedies, Peart has re-married, moved to California,
fathered a child, authored three books, rejoined his Rush mates to
record three studio albums, and participated in five Rush tours. If
Peart had made the choice to ride away from his life on the morn-

ing of August 20th, 1998, none of this would have happened. Sartre argues that an individual's decision affects not just him, but all of human kind. Whether it's our intent or not, our actions can set an example for others to follow. How many times have we turned on the news to hear of a "suicide epidemic"? The phenomenon called the "copycat syndrome" in which others follow the lead of those before them. It's easy to call Peart a role model for overcoming the tragedies in his life, but what if Peart with a clear conscience had determined his pain was too great, and chosen to end his life? While some may call such an act cowardly, is that a fair assessment? After all, until one walks the edge between life and death we really do not have the credibility to pass judgment on one another. Maybe the most appropriate summary of Peart's experiences can be found in Peart's words, those of a guiding voice, a teacher helping us to discover meaning through thought. Peart's book, *Ghost Rider*, concludes with the following verse from "Bravado," written in 1991— long before the tragedies of 1997–98:

> And if the music stops
> There's only the sound of the rain
> All the hope and glory
> All the sacrifice in vain
> If the love remains
> Though everything is lost
> We will pay the price
> But we will not count the cost. ("Bravado," *Roll the Bones*, 1991)

As Sartre was for his young student, Peart's own words had been a guiding voice through troubled times, and never was that more important than for Neil Peart himself.

Let Your Heart Be the Anchor and the Beat of Your Own Song

For more than half of my thirty-three years Rush has been, and continues to be, my "go-to band" when I need inspiration, or to hear a familiar voice of reason. A few months back, I was experiencing my own personal Hell, a dark period that toed the line of physical and mental breakdown. As I have done so often during rough patches in life, I turned to Rush to help me through. The album *Vapor Trails*, especially the song "How It Is," took on a greater significance. I'm not saying that my problems were the same as Peart's, but I shared the same feelings of despair and pain, and hearing Peart's story told through music was the perfect combination of emotional and physical release for me.

In "Something for Nothing" Peart wrote:

> What you own is your own kingdom,
> What you do is your own glory,
> What you love is your own power,
> What you live is your own story.
> In your head is the answer let it guide you along.
> Let your heart be the anchor and the beat of your own song.

It's always nice to have a friend or confidante to help shed some light when all seems dark, helping us to become aware of the answers that lie within us, creating meaning in our lives.

9

Honey on the Rim of the Larger Bowl

MELISSA BECK

While at a Rush concert on the *Snakes & Arrows* tour at Madison Square Garden (trying not to get my eye poked out by those playing air drums) I overheard an interesting conversation. Two fans were discussing the lyrics of "The Larger Bowl" and the fact that many of Rush's songs contained thought-provoking topics to debate about. One fan said to the other that through their lyrics Rush "really teach me."

I thought that this was the highest compliment that these talented musicians could be paid. Being a "Geddicorn,"[1] I am attentive to the lyrical content of Rush's music. In his book *Roadshow*, Neil Peart points out that this seems to be the general trend with female fans. The band's lyrics are full of thought-provoking topics for anyone, Rush fan or not, to mull over. This combined with the fact that I am a Latin and classics teacher by trade, helped be to discover some similarities between Rush and the Roman Epicurean philosopher Lucretius.

How can we possibly connect a philosophical movement that was created over two thousand years ago with a progressive rock band from the twenty-first century? The bottom line of Epicurean philosophy is: How do I live my life in the best way so that it is free of pain? Life is full of chaos and randomness, and especially pain; how can we best deal with bad circumstances that inevitably come up in our lives and manage to move on from them? Epicurus,

---

[1] According to *Urban Dictionary*, a Geddicorn is a mythical creature similar to a unicorn, a good-looking female that willingly attends a Rush concert without having to be coaxed to do so by a dude.

the founder of this school of philosophy, would give lectures to the vast throng of followers who came to his Athenian Garden to listen to his diatribes on this topic. He lived and studied during the Hellenistic Period, the years following the death of Alexander the Great in 323 B.C.E. His writings were so extensive that they were said to fill three hundred rolls of papyri. The loyalty of his close circle of followers who would meet and discuss philosophy in his garden can only be compared to the devotion of Rush fans who devour every lyric and musical note of the band.

Unfortunately, only three of Epicurus's letters survive: one of the more significant sources for understanding his philosophy is *De Rerum Natura* (*On the Nature of Things*), written by the Roman Philosopher Lucretius during the Late Roman Republic, between 94 and 55 B.C.E.

Lucretius employs the art of music as a didactic or teaching tool in order to instruct Romans about Epicurean philosophy, hypothesizing that he can better teach through his writings. In his book, *On the Nature of Things*, Lucretius writes in the form of a poem. The sweet sounds of his poetic meter distract the reader from even realizing that he is learning something. Similarly, although it is interesting to read Rush's lyrics, it is really the combination of melodies and lyrics that gives life to the sentiment of the words. As Neil Peart writes the lyrics and sends them to his band mates to put to music, his thoughts and ideas are transformed into something that actually teaches people to think about deeper philosophical issues such as life, love, and in the case of *Snakes & Arrows*, philosophy and religion.

Another reason why Lucretius uses epic poetry, in particular, is because of the repetitive nature of this genre. In epic poem epithets, brief descriptive phrases for characters are repeated, with each line having a specific repetitive rhythm. This fit in ideally with the concept of prolepsis, which is a theory of how the Epicureans believed humans learn. Prolepsis is the repeated exposure to certain stimuli that causes a permanent conception of it to exist in your mind. Rush's lyrics are similar in the fact that through their rhythms and choruses thoughts about religion and philosophy seep into the listener's mind.

Lucretius exemplifies the idea of teaching others by telling the story of how to give medicine to a child. He says that when you are going to administer medicine to a child, and the child knows that it's going to taste horrible, just put some honey on the rim of the cup so that he won't even realize what he is ingesting. The honey will entice the child into putting up with the medicine to get to taste the honey. For Ancient Romans, the poetry was like the honey. Similarly, Rush uses their music to entice listeners to think about philosophical issues like morality and religion, therefore putting "honey" on the rim of the Larger Bowl.

Unfortunately, the concepts of Epicureanism have been misinterpreted throughout history. It has been associated with people who engage in excessive behaviors. According to Epicurean readings, the ultimate goal in life is the pursuit of pleasure. The early Christians incorrectly interpreted this as a philosophy that openly encourages people to involve themselves in fleeting pleasures such as food, sex and intoxication. As I came to learn while attending an all-girls' Catholic school, anything associated with the word *pleasure*, had a negative connotation. I saw a recent episode of *The Simpsons* where Maggie ends up in a Catholic daycare and the sisters sing to the children: "If you're happy and you know it, it's a sin."

Such a Lot of Pain on This Earth

So what types of "pleasures," exactly, do the Epicureans believe that we should pursue? Lucretius acknowledges the fact that life is full of fear and pain. However, we all have an opportunity to free ourselves from the unpleasantness of life's circumstances through the teachings of Epicurean philosophy. In Book 2 of *De Rerum Natura*, Lucretius says that when you're standing on the shore and you look out and see another person being tossed by the waves in a shipwreck, your first thought is one of relief because it is not happening to you. It is not that you are taking joy in someone else's misfortune, but you are sure pleased that it is not *your* misfortune. We can become aware of the endless possibilities of liberation from life's pain, thus leading us to feel the same pleasure as the person standing on the shore watching a shipwreck.

The Epicurean idea of pain is common in Rush songs. Lyrically, Peart oftentimes brings up the fact that life is not always pleasant, a theme to which he is no stranger. In the song "Bravest Face," Peart writes, "we could be down and gone but we hold on," a comforting concept knowing that there are others who also suffer, regardless of age or social status. Even someone famous who seemingly has everything is not exempt from pain. It gives us some comfort to hear about it in a song and allows us to reflect from a safe distance, like that person standing on the shore feeling relieved that he is not involved in the shipwreck.

Why Such Different Fortunes and Fates?

The writings of Epicurean philosophy, just as many of the songs of Rush, point out the idea that life is not always fair. There are no exemptions from pain and suffering. According to Epicurean philosophy, the world and everything that is in it is made up of tiny particles called atoms. The word atom is an Ancient Greek word meaning something that cannot be cut or divided. Although their basic substance is the same they differ in shape, size and weight and this is what accounts for all of the variety of things in the universe. These atoms move around with an unpredictable and random swerve. And so all of us suffer different fates according to the way the atoms fall around us.

The song "The Larger Bowl" from *Snakes & Arrows* best illustrates this Epicurean idea of how the arrangement of the universe is random. Peart was inspired to write the lyrics while bicycling through Africa and on many of his motorcycle journey's, witnessing first-hand the enormous disparity between the rich and poor. He writes, "Some are blessed and some are cursed / Some live behind iron gates / While others see only the worst."

As I sat at that concert in Madison Square Garden listening to Rush play "The Larger Bowl," the powerful images that flashed on the screen made me realize at that very moment the important philosophical points that are made in this song. The pictures were ones of grand *prosperity* juxtaposed with those of *horrifying* pain. What struck me as most clever about these images was the fact that they were visually similar but in reality were worlds apart. For example, a gate or a fence can be an innocent enough symbol when it is surrounding a mansion. But then that picture fades to a prison with fences and barbed wires around it which puts this gate in a very different context. What can be seen as a symbol of protection for the wealthy, a fence surrounding an elaborate mansion, is viewed in the next scene as a sign of oppression, or tyranny.

Our Better Natures Seek Elevation

Epicureans believe that atoms are not fixed in place by some divine plan. Therefore, all human beings do have free will and moral responsibility for their own actions. Even though we experience pain, through the contemplation of philosophical ideas we can persevere. This is a topic that Rush has explored many times throughout their career from the songs "Freewill," to "Roll the Bones," to "Ghost of a Chance." While Peart expresses on "Larger Bowl" a sense of finality, "some things can never be changed," I believe that there is a positive, Epicurean, undertone to the lyrics. In the song "Far Cry," for instance, they state that we are all subject to the "ebb and flow of tidal fortune." The song continues with "one day I feel I am ahead of the wheel and the next it's rolling over me." The song's final chorus, "I can get back on," is an inspirational message for the listeners, encouraging them to take charge of their lives and make necessary changes to improve the quality of their lives. The final choice, however, is up to the individuals themselves.

You Can Call Me Faithless

Epicurus and his followers like Lucretius have been accused of being atheists and even enemies of religion. But in fact they are against *false* religion and superstition. Lucretius, in the opening of the *De Rerum Natura*, has a powerful image that illustrates this. The main character in Lucretius's epic is stomping on *religio,* which can be translated as religion or superstition.

In Lucretius's poem, man is crushed beneath the heavy weight of Religion personified and Lucretius's protagonist dares to turn the tables and trample religion under his own foot. This is not to say that all belief systems are to be disposed of, but Lucretius is criticizing the blind following of superstition, religious dogma, and ritual without truly thinking about the spiritual nature of things. Lucretius concludes that this type of blind devotion can cause men to do very destructive things, which is the same conclusion in the Rush song "Armor and Sword." Religion is supposed to be a comfort or a shield to console us from pain. But there are those who turn religion into a "sharp and angry sword."

In the introductory essay that Neil Peart writes for their album, "The Game Snakes and Arrows: A prize every time," he points out that many people are "imprinted with a particular faith, along with their other blessings and scars." This faith can be "good" faith, like armor, or "bad" faith, like a sword. Neil further states in this essay that people who really *choose* their own religion are few and far between these days. Most can only "grow the way the wind blows," as he states in the song "The Way the Wind Blows." Similarly, Lucretius believed that too many Romans blindly followed the conventional polytheistic religion of the day. In his epic he was trying to get people to realize that there are different ways of thinking about spirituality.

Epicureans also argue that one aspect of religion that especially brings people a lot of pain is fear of the gods. This fear causes people to do crazy things in the name of religion. The Ancient Greeks would sacrifice hundreds of animals to the gods in long, elaborate rituals in order to appease these spirits. Especially in recent years, we have witnessed people exhibiting extreme behaviors in the name of religion. The events of 9/11 immediately come to mind. There are also many Christian extremist groups that promote intolerance and violence against groups that are opposed to their beliefs. Rush acknowledges this extremism in their song "Armor and Sword": "Wide-eyed armies of the faithful / From the Middle East to the Middle West / Pray and pass the ammunition." This brings up an important philosophical and religious debate: If I kill in the name of my God or my faith, can I still go to heaven?

But Epicurus believes that the gods are not responsible for creating and influencing the universe. Therefore making sacrifices to influence them becomes a fruitless act. They live in a state of perfection where they are always tranquil and peaceful. The wise man will worship the gods in the hope of gaining insight into this serene world of the divine. The Rush song "Faithless" sums up this Epicurean idea nicely in modern terms. I think that the prevailing thought behind this song is that, although we may have different people preaching in our ears we can still make wise moral judgments based on our own sense of what is right and wrong. Neil Peart writes, "I've got my own spirit level for balance / To tell if my choice is leaning up or down." Although there may be chaos and different opinions around me, "Faithless" ends with the words "I will quietly resist."

. . . The Songs and Stories of Vanished Times

One Epicurean is a man named Philodemus, who, if it weren't for a group of workers in the Italian countryside may never have been known to us. He lived in a Roman town called Herculaneum, which was completely buried by a volcanic eruption in 79 C.E.

Because it was buried in sixty feet of lava, mud, and ash, it was lost for centuries, along with the more famous city of Pompeii, which was also buried by the volcano. One day in 1738, workmen building a house discovered it. Since then both of these towns have been extensively excavated, revealing intact buildings, temples, and libraries. In one of the libraries (originally owned by Julius Caesar's father-in-law) were volumes of papyri with writings from an Epicurean philosopher named Philodemus.

Modern science has allowed us to very carefully unravel these charred scrolls and decipher his writings. The best one that I have come across sums up Epicurean philosophy very nicely. He writes (Paypri, 1005, 4.9–14):

> Don't fear god,
> Don't worry about death;
> What is good is easy to get, and
> What is terrible is easy to endure

If nothing else, the lyrics from *Snakes & Arrows* have taught Rush fans that we all suffer different fates in life, but in the end we can endure.

Hope

On a more personal note, it makes me sad when I encounter a student who is so indoctrinated into a belief system that he or she can only "grow the way the wind blows." Any attempt at introducing some of them to other points of view is met with fear and even hostility. My husband and I are trying to raise our three-year-old daughter with an open mind, despite the best efforts of my family to the contrary. I am hoping that even if she doesn't want to learn Latin or read Lucretius that she will listen to Rush's music.

I think at heart, as Rush fans, we are all Epicureans. Nothing gives us greater pleasure then to be at a concert, no matter what the cost of a ticket or length of the drive. Epicurus would wholeheartedly agree that this is a *pleasure* worth spending our time on.

As I have experienced first-hand, some of Rush's faithful followers still need some work on the whole philosophy thing. At that same concert in Madison Square Garden on this latest tour, I heard some zealous fan yell, "If I have to pee I am going during 'The Larger Bowl.'" I don't think that's the "larger bowl" they had in mind. Apparently he didn't recognize the different nuances of such a thought-provoking song. I guess some people are a work in progress . . .

10
How We Value a Gift Beyond Price

KAYLA KREUGER

To speak of Rush fans is to conjure a particular community comprised of various nationalities, races, ages, and personalities. In bonding over the work of Geddy Lee, Alex Lifeson, and Neil Peart, these fans have come to speak a unique language with specific reference points, a distinctive vocabulary, and a wide array of cultural allusions, largely introduced by lyricist Neil Peart, but also owing something to album art choices and the animation sequences used in Rush's live shows.

The distance between language and value may at first seem too wide a gulf to cross, equivalent to the personality change By-Tor made between his hell-prince appearance on *Fly by Night* and his new role as liberator on *Caress of Steel*. Fortunately, the thoughts about language expressed by French philosopher Jacques Derrida in his 1968 essay "Différance" can be applied to value, helping us to bridge the gap.

Signs and Signals

Derrida wrote his influential essay prior to the release of Rush's self-titled debut, and it's unlikely that he ever considered the possibility of his writings being applied to so unique a vocabulary as the one used by Rush fans wherever they meet. Still, Rush, and especially their cover artist Hugh Syme, are savvy users of one of Derrida's primary concepts: signs. Different periods of their career have been marked out by different symbols: the starman and pentagram in the 1970s, the Presto bunnies, and the dragon from the *Vapor Trails* tour are just a few examples.

To a Rush fan, able to read these signs, meaning is both common-sense and instantaneous. The signs take on the meaning of the band itself and bring Rush, by association, to mind. Or, as Derrida would have it, "every concept is necessarily and essentially inscribed in a chain or system, within which it refers to another and other concepts;" so you can follow the starman to the concept of *All the World's a Stage*, to Rush itself.

For Derrida in "Différance" (the title is a deliberate mis-spelling of the French word for "difference") language does its important work through signs. That is, when you hear the word "bird," you might visualize a bird in your mind. You might even think of the snowy owl from *Fly by Night*. What's important to us is Derrida's notion that meaning gets deferred, or moved farther away, because we all visualize things differently. To test this out, ask your best Rush-fan friend what he or she imagines when you mention the band. Is it the Seventies kimonos and makeup? Alex's outrageous suits and the roadkill hair of the 1980s? Or how the band as they looked on their *Snakes & Arrows* tour?

Obviously these images only stand in for the band in the real world. They act as signs representing the real thing, where the meaning or essence of that thing resides. And the more you try to capture that meaning through other words and images, the more signs you collect, without touching the real thing. Each successive sign moves you farther and farther from the very object or concept you are trying to reach. This is what Derrida is describing when he notes that "the movement of signs defers the movements of encountering the thing itself, the moment at which we could lay hold of it, consume or expend it, touch it, see it." So, your description of Geddy Lee can be spot on, but the real Geddy Lee is not present in your words. For the sake of potential future albums, this is fortunate! For Derrida, the signs we use make thought possible; we can share our ideas without the object we're discussing being with us. His ideas can also be applied to value, specifically how Rush is given or denied value in the music industry and, more importantly, among the fans.

The Big Money

Establishing the value of Rush, or at least their music, is easy enough when surrounded by other Rush fans. However, Rush fans are accustomed to derision being heaped upon their main musical interest by critics, professional and otherwise. The articles calling the band everything from bombastic to humorless outnumber those that contain more positive value judgments, at least for the first half of the band's career. However, to anyone with an eye for the charts, Rush's value in the glittering world of rock'n'roll seems self-evident. With twenty-four gold albums decorating the office walls of Anthem Records, Rush's worldwide sales are considerable. Furthermore, they have been known to sell out an arena or two.

Yet, even though Rush's economic value seems solid, their value remains contested in the mainstream rock world. They lack the status of either a Led Zeppelin, who produced far fewer albums, or a Kiss, who heartily embraced the idea of marketing. If numbers were all that counted, we should at least, when talking to other "knowledgeable" music fans, stop having to answer the question, "Who?" with "The band who plays 'Tom Sawyer'. Sigh." Clearly there is another type of value being assigned to Rush's music.

Value Without a Price Tag

Unlike the objective fact of Rush's enormous sales, another type of value can be recognized by its subjectivity. This definition focuses on qualities like "imagination, genius, and originality." The different experiences we've had with Rush influence how we assign value to their work. Because I am a "younger" Rush fan at twenty-five, I had greater access to the albums produced in the 1990s, and so they resonate more strongly with me than the band's earlier work. Similarly, a drummer might highlight Peart's playing over Lifeson's because drums form a central part of the song for her. Subjective value is a matter of opinion, a way of personally saying "yes" to a particular quality.

In the cultural arena, Rush's value has long been contested. Critics, managers, and rock fans have struggled to assign the band a place in the rock world. Never mainstream, the band has been seen as having a cult following. Rush fans have responded that integrity, the ability to create art without bowing to market demand, makes Rush superior to more heavily marketed bands like The Eagles or Fleetwood Mac. While I agree that the value that Rush finds in the music they make has more to do with "art as expression, not as market campaigns" a fan base, cash in hand, is needed to sustain the continued creation of their music, at least as long as they wish to appear in the public sphere. However, it is this second definition of value that seems to matter the most to Rush fans, so that even as Rush's economic value gets deferred, there remains the possibility to recover their cultural value.

Time Stand Still

Most of us can sympathize with the chorus of *Hold Your Fire*'s "Time Stand Still." We all have moments we wish we could freeze—moments we value. For value can be deferred through the passage of time. Just as the starman sign shifts you one step away from the meaning of Rush, time can also bring you to value, at a remove.

Imagine yourself in the moment of opening a new Rush album (because it's imaginary, you can value whatever you want about it—guitar solos, instrumentals—your choice!). The album was released today. Your copy was pre-ordered and you play it as soon as it arrives. Yet, the moment of recording is long over. The voice, notes, and rhythms you're hearing are ghost echoes: captured, but unable to take you to the actual moment of recording—which is what you paid for.

This concept becomes much more understandable if we look back to older Rush albums. Let's take *2112* for example. Some fans argue for a return to this sound, but though your recording of "A Passage to Bangkok" has not changed, the band who recorded it has.

The original sound (the one valued by fans) cannot be recaptured specifically because of the passage of time. You may have noticed, for instance, how Geddy avoids some of those high notes on tour! And although Rush is in some ways not the same band you hear on *Caress of Steel* or *2112*, the value of these albums continues to increase. With music, we're always being asked to pay for a moment that has already passed, or for a fleeting experience.

Concert Hall

In the case of live concerts, where Rush makes the majority of its money, paying for a fast-disappearing experience is the rule. Being permitted to stand in an open space at the moment when certain notes and rhythms will be performed by Alex Lifeson, Neil Peart, and Geddy Lee carries a price tag from anywhere to twenty-five dollars (for lawn seats) to over eighty dollars. The way fans scream for an encore is a vivid (and loud!) measurement of just how short these shows seem to be, despite a setlist that lasts for nearly three hours. What you're paying for is to be in the moment that these songs are being performed, but you can't take the experience with you (unless you count a t-shirt as a substitute—it does, after all, let people know you were there, on that date, in that moment). Since you can't bring the show home with you, the value slips away, deferred because of the impermanence of the experience. Bootlegs may be created for just this reason, as an attempt to freeze the experience of hearing that song you came to sing along to, to retrigger that feeling you had in the moment when Rush walked on stage and the cheering began.

I Can Hold the Future in My Virtual Hand

Due to recent technological improvements, fans have sought to lessen the time that elapses between an album's creation and their reception of it. Albums frequently "leak" before their release date, as *Vapor Trails* did in 2002. Once albums are released, fans sometimes access them through legal online downloading which guarantees that the album's value increases. These sales "count" and the proceeds make their way back to the band. Illegal downloads are also prevalent, secured through peer-to-peer programs like Bit Torrent. Previously, bootlegs performed this function, but the process was longer. Though today's downloads may provide a fan with an album faster than legal channels, deferral remains the rule, since the studio session is long past. The age-old desire to be part of the music-making process that keeps Rush fans air drumming like mad, remains unfulfilled. As Derrida puts it, because of deferral "desire or will" are carried out in a way that annuls or tempers their effect.

But what about the recent mini-documentaries *The Boys in Brazil* and *The Making of Snakes and Arrows*? Unfortunately, editing and selection increase the distance between the viewer and the event (the making of album, a performance) and we are left with signs of the process, not the process itself.

Infinity, the Star that Would Not Die

Just as the voyager on the *Rocinante* in "Cygnus X-1" was changed by his journey to the heart of a black hole, space changes the nature of value. Distance can cause value to be deferred, just as time can. Music comes to us through a variety of channels. The distance it travels, or fails to travel, affects how value is assigned to it in the market.

One of the primary ways that music crosses distance and gets to its audience is radio play. Prior to the release of *Vapor Trails,* radio play of Rush centered on a few staples: "Tom Sawyer," "Limelight," "New World Man," and "The Spirit of Radio." Much of their catalogue lacked mainstream value because it was distant from radio listeners. For example, songs like "2112" or "The Necromancer" are much too long for radio play. To experience songs like these, listeners would have to go out and find them, rather than having them come to them via the airwaves.

One of the ways Rush initially achieved status and value was through the radio play of "Working Man." Initially championed by Donna Halper of Cleveland's WMMS, the song helped establish the band's value in the States, a formerly distant market. Unfortunately, many listeners mistook the song for a new Zeppelin track, assigning the value to the wrong place!

While its distance may defer the value of music from our lives, we also assign value when we pick up our music and carry it into other spaces. The evolution of music devices from record player to mp3 player has allowed music to become more portable. In this new format, music can be heard and valued in new venues. If you want to interest a friend in Rush, for example, you might pick and choose among albums, creating a compilation meant to appeal to their interests. Imagine how much more 'damage' our *2112* hero could have done with an mp3 player! He might have managed to save the file and transmit it to others—the priests would have had their work cut out for them then!

The Words of the Profits are Written on the Studio Walls

Applying a philosophy to the work of Rush is a fine mental exercise, and may well help us to understand more deeply the forces that underpin the music and the lyrics. Yet, it is ungenerous not to ask, "What does the band think about all of this?" Even as avid a reader as "The Professor," Neil Peart, may never have tangled with Jacques Derrida. Lifeson, upon buying a second house, probably failed to pause and consider that the royalties still being paid to him are the results of moments long past, triggered by songs played all across the world. Geddy Lee may not realize that his signature bass acts as a sign for all of the talent he has as a bass player. Nonetheless, there is evidence in the lyrics of Rush that show that the band members have considered the nature of value before.

The opening track of *Permanent Waves*, "The Spirit of Radio" begins with a "friendly voice," creating an intimacy out of the ghost-voice of someone who recorded these words long ago. The song is called "elusive" and "magic," hearkening back to *2112*'s version of music as a powerful and necessary force. The value here assigned is cultural value, not economic value. This music has value because it can influence your mood, because it acts as a pleasant background tapestry as you "hit the open road." Furthermore, you control just what music has this type of value for you; "there is magic at your fingers." This is the personal choice we talked about earlier. Your value judgments dictate what you listen to.

The "invisible airwaves" show how music travels across time and space, but the wavelength is also called "timeless." It's for this reason, the timelessness of value, that we may expect to hear *2112* for hundreds of years. The "bright antennae" bristling "with the energy" is a literal explanation of how music travels, but "the energy" may also refer to the energy the band put into the song. The song brings Rush to you through its signs and symbols, though the literal band remains out of reach.

Value enters the song more explicitly in the lyric that gave this essay its title, "bearing a gift beyond price, almost free." The notion of music as priceless is a reference back to the second form of value we encountered, cultural value. The words "almost free" reference the deferral of music's value. Listening to the radio is free (except for the electricity). Furthermore, the radio play hopes to get the fan to buy the album. However, even the album price is paid only once, and the songs can be listened to again and again and again. Value, you see, is always being negotiated.

The next stanza engages with the "machinery" of the music system. "All this machinery making modern music," writes Neil, "can still be open-hearted." As *Permanent Waves* was released in 1980, this may be a comment on the amount of equipment (synthesizers and effects pedals for example) being used in the studio. (Lifeson is much documented as being antagonistic toward the band's keyboard phase.) But it also serves as a commentary on the machinery that keeps value being shuttled around: radio play, touring, and the industry itself. The song continues with a criticism for the "coldly-charted" music that gets its value only through its place in *Billboard* charts. As Rush has never been this sort of band, their scorn is understandable. The value they seem to crave has to do with the honesty spoken of in the next lyric. For Rush, this honesty has both to do with themselves and with their fans.

The song continues, "One likes to believe in the freedom of music." This freedom may both be the notion of music as priceless as mentioned earlier and the freedom for the music to find the listeners most suited to it, the freedom of the band to create that which bests suits them without pandering. The song laments the lack of these freedoms, noting that "glittering prizes and endless compromises shatter the illusions of integrity." In a satiric adaptation of Simon and Garfunkel, the song ends with a stab at the music industry, "for the words of the profits are written on the studio walls, and echo with the sounds of salesmen." This section has been appropriated by live Rush audiences who, at the words "concert hall," cheer like mad—they've paid the price for admission, they are ironically cheering for and simultaneously caught up in Rush's defiance of, the larger structure of industry and the value it promotes, measured in T-shirt sales and concert tickets. Thus Rush seems to hear the "sounds of salesmen" echoing even beneath the cultural value. Yet, does "The Spirit of Radio" have to end negatively?

Tallying the Total

Rush covered Buffalo Springfield's "For What It's Worth" on their 2004 EP *Feedback*. We've already noted that value is never fixed, that it changes constantly. In fact, Rush's value has (to the joy of some fans and the chagrin of others) recently increased. They made an appearance on *The Colbert Report* in 2008, and the following year were featured in *I Love You, Man*, after which the band's mainstream appeal seemed to increase. They've also been featured in the popular video game *Rock Band*, garnering them new listeners among a younger crowd. Rush's economic value has, perhaps, never been so secure, and their cultural value seems to be gaining ground too.

So, you may be asking yourself, if it's all a happy ending, why spend so much time on deferral? In the end, deferral is actually a positive thing. Derrida hoped that all of those signs that kept meaning moving along would result in "a weaving or a web, which would allow different threads . . . to separate . . . as well as being ready to bind others together." For him, deferral results in "the condition of possibility." Sure, you say, but what does this have to do with Rush?

For one thing, signs offer us possibilities that the real band could not deliver. You can repeat your recording of "YYZ" on *Moving Pictures* (a sign) one hundred times in a row with no negative effects (as long as you're with other Rush fans). The band itself (the real thing) could probably not perform the song in the same way one hundred times—they'd fall over from exhaustion! Also, signs are portable in a way that what they symbolize is not. After all, Rush likes to travel in style, and few fans have private jets at their disposal. So, instead of trying to cram Geddy, Alex, and Neil into the back seat, you can bring them along via compact disc or mp3 player. In effect, you can recreate Rush for yourself, under almost any condition.

Furthermore, if value is never fixed, that "condition of possibility" applies to our favorite power trio as well. Old reviews and old criticisms, which may have once assigned negative value to the band, may be overturned with time, and the value they deferred may be recovered. We may even be witnessing this right now, with Rush's recent upturn in popularity. We, the fans, will appreciate Rush's gain in cultural currency, and will celebrate the silencing of the naysayers (Father Browns, all). For all that, the value we assign the band is likely to be unchanging. We have always recognized in the band "a state of integrity" and that, to us, is beyond price.[1]

---

[1] With greatest affection to the GedsGals, who hope to circumnavigate deferral through the creation of a GedClone!

11
Free Wills and Sweet Miracles

NEIL A. FLOREK

By the time I noticed the lyrics to Rush's "Freewill" (*Permanent Waves*, 1980) posted on my philosophy professor's office door during my freshman year of college, I already understood that Rush had something important to say about how we should live our lives.

Apparently, my prof knew his stuff and had good taste, because "Freewill" is a tightly composed, driving, spirited, philosophical tour de force. In about five minutes of propulsive beats, melodic guitar figures and utterly inimitable vocalizing, Rush perceptively observe the tendency to blame someone else for our faults, deny that fate is controlled by outside forces, and embrace self-determination. Even as the song champions free will, it also perceives, without pessimism, some shadows cast on the bright field of human autonomy, and on human life in general. (These shadows returned as a personal tragedy for drummer-lyricist Neil Peart in 1997–98 and afterwards led to a remolded, post-tragic ethics.)

In the climactic bridge of "Freewill," Geddy Lee passionately sings in a clear but tortured, impossibly high register that we are "genetic blends with uncertain ends on a fortune hunt that's far too fleet." Choosing to exercise your autonomy is the clear path. But valuing and practicing self-determination does not guarantee a happy result. There is no naïve optimism here. The path that's clear is after all, only a path, not a guaranteed destination; and, in any case, pursuing our projects in a finite, ephemeral human life just goes too fast.

As in so many Rush songs, from this relatively early classic to "Sweet Miracle," human life's fundamental value is affirmed—if it's

"far too fleet," it must be good. There's also a moral model presented. We should be clear thinking, autonomous, free spirits who
make no excuses. We can still play the "air drums" to Rush and simply enjoy the music, but if we don't think about the lyrics, we're
missing a chance to reflect on our own lives. We're also missing a
chance to learn about philosophy. Like the most important, influential philosophers of the Western world, Rush's music expresses a
conception of how best to live to become excellent, happy persons.

Peart Discussing No Small Matter

When philosophers, both ancient and modern, think, talk, and
write about how best to live, they are doing ethics. Ethics is critical reflection about morality, with a strong emphasis on justifying
the moral values and principles that a person believes are right. As
Socrates famously expressed in Plato's *The Republic*, "We are discussing no small matter, but how we ought to live" (Book I, line
352d). In these beautifully brief, pregnant words Socrates indicates
that the real point of ethics is practical—to reflect upon how we
should live. For the ancient Greek philosophers as well as for Peart,
the realm of the "ought" is quite encompassing. Not only are basic
values, principles, and judgments within the realm of the "ought,"
but also, dispositions, personality traits—more precisely, developed
human excellences—what Socrates, Plato, and Aristotle, among
others, called virtues.

Aristotle believed that to progress in our thinking about morality, we must determine the highest good for persons. Aristotle
thought that in order to answer Socrates's question, how we ought
to live, we must figure out what we're aiming for, what the ultimate
goal is. For Aristotle, this goal is eudaimonia or "happiness." Its
equivalents are "living well" or "well being," with a connotation of
an active, rational life, not just a subjective state of feeling good that
might be induced by drugs or just one euphoric event.

In Aristotle's ethics, there are various ingredients to the recipe for
a life well-lived, including degrees of wealth and honor, bodily
health, a few good friends, and a measure of good fortune (such as
avoiding disasters in the prime of your life). These ingredients are
prerequisites for well being, but not good enough to achieve genuine happiness. The individual who really desires eudaimonia must
develop crucial character traits to their peak form. A character trait in

its peak form is known as a virtue. The most important virtues for Aristotle are prudence, justice, courage, temperance (or moderation), and pride; Peart agrees with Aristotle but, as we'll see, adds to the list. For both, however, these virtues bring to reality our distinctive capacities as humans, our rationality and our faculty of choosing.

So, if we can be virtuous, on top of the previously mentioned ingredients, then we can attain eudaimonia. In contemporary English, if we can develop crucial character traits, actually apply them in the real world, then we can be happy! But here's the catch. Even though we have the potential, we're not just born with these virtues in their peak forms. We have to learn them, and develop them until they become second nature for us. We can't just read Aristotle, or Plato, or Peart, and then, armed with that wisdom, consider ourselves fulfilled. For Aristotle, and as we'll see for Peart as well, you have to work for excellence. You have to be actively engaged in building a life and attaining happiness. There is no guru or god who can magically transform us into happy people.

Aristotle's and Peart's critical reflections on how we ought to live, their ethics, do not revolve around gods or supernatural forces. (Recall that Peart won't be the one to choose "a ready guide in some celestial voice.") They agree that how we ought to live is a human matter of profound importance, and human life is valuable enough to pursue the matter with diligence and passion, marshalling all human powers of investigation. But they're operating in a horizontal, here-and-now dimension, not a vertical, transcendental dimension that would aspire to a next-world prosperity at the expense of well-being in this world. In short, these approaches to the good life are humanistic ethics.

Armed with the knowledge gained from our whirlwind tour of ancient Greek ethics, let's inspect some of Rush's songs to detect Peart's values, virtues, and recommendations for living well. We may be pressed into doing our own philosophy, filling in any explanatory gaps in the lyrics. As philosophers themselves, Socrates, Aristotle, and Peart would approve!

Assume Free Will, Choose Autonomy and Responsibility

The key to unlocking a deeper understanding of "Freewill," especially its ethical import, is found in the concluding line of the chorus: "I will choose a path that's clear / I will choose free will."

You might reasonably ask: if you have free will, why would you need to choose free will? And if all people naturally have free will, why encourage people other than yourself to choose it as well? To understand how the line can make sense, consider that in philosophy, whether free will actually exists is a separate, complicated issue about which there is no consensus. Accordingly, Peart is not arguing for the existence of free will in this song. Rather, he assumes its existence and observes the attitudes toward it, including the range of life determinants that people can choose to believe in which would destroy it, from celestial voices, presumably gods, to "venomous fate."

Many popular attitudes would theoretically undercut free will. If this is done, then individuals have a convenient excuse for their own stations in life, and their degrees of success. That excuse amounts to an assertion of incapability and irresponsibility, which in Peart's still quite idealized account of humanity (contrasted, for example, with the sentiments of "The Stars Look Down," *Vapor Trails*, 2002), would be a slap at human dignity, a way of emasculating a very real human power to determine our own fates. In Peart's view, making excuses such as "it just wasn't meant to be" denigrates human potential for self-improvement and self-determination.

So what we're really choosing when we "choose free will" are autonomy and responsibility. We're right back to virtues, which, if not classic in nature, still loom very large in the modern consciousness. In the search and struggle for well being in human terms, we must develop our capacity for rational self-direction (autonomy) and take responsibility for our own faults, strengths, failures, and successes. If you were to fail an important test which is the basis for a promotion at your job, only you are responsible. Your choices have led to this result, and it won't help you to blame someone else. In what we might think of as a developing existentialist ethic originally hinted at in "Anthem," Peart continues to assert our responsibility for our own happiness, but now emphasizes free will as the primary mechanism to secure it.

Drag Your Dreams into Existence

In "Vital Signs" (*Moving Pictures*, 1981), free will is once again assumed, as well as our capacity to choose our dreams based on our basic values. The problem, foreshadowed by the thrust of

"Something for Nothing" (*2112*, 1976) is how to attain those dreams. "Something for Nothing" does forcefully communicate the obvious need to work for your dreams, but "Vital Signs" specifies further virtues which must be developed and fully engaged if our dreams are to be realized. Often overshadowed by the same album's "Tom Sawyer" and "Limelight," at least in popular culture, the quirky, even funky rhythms and relatively spare arrangement of the concluding song of *Moving Pictures* sonically frame a passionate plea to avoid the vice of conformity and actualize our dreams through courage and persistence.

Part of what makes the idealistic, hopeful lessons of "Vital Signs" so relatable and convincing is the challenging, realistic portrait of the human condition that Peart paints as the background for his repeated pleas to deviate and elevate from the norm. What makes it so aesthetically enticing and memorable is the unusual, eclectic musical accompaniment. Following a brief, dynamic musical introduction that begins with a percolating synthesizer figure accented with a fuzzed-out staccato guitar riff, temporary resolution is signaled with a tumble of chords played in unison. Then the real fun begins. Rush, who at times in their career have sounded like a very heavy progressive rock band, almost sounds like Devo as it establishes a funky, new-wave-ish accompaniment to a summation of the human condition:

"Unstable condition: / A symptom of life / In mental / And environmental / Change." As the music continues to pulsate and morphs to yet another inventive accompaniment, we're reminded through electronic metaphors that "sometimes our circuits get shorted, by external interference." Moreover, not only do outside forces unsettle us, but "the balance" is "distorted by internal incoherence." Whatever the precise source and nature of these unsettling forces, which Peart does not literally specify, what's certain is that "everybody need a mood lifter," and without a doubt, "Everybody got to deviate from the norm."

To this point in the song, the only virtues implied are authenticity and perhaps self-determination (autonomy), with a correlation to the desirable state of non-conformity. So far, this is nothing new. These are already well established in Peart's table of virtues. But as this brief song—brief by Rush standards—nears its climax, we're finally given the missing ingredients in eudaimonia. This may be the most concise, pregnant lyrical summation of the ethical vision of the classic, pre-tragic Peart:

Leave out the fiction—
The fact is;
This friction,
Will only be worn by persistence

Leave out conditions—
Courageous convictions,
Will drag the dream into existence ("Vital Signs," *Moving Pictures*,
    1981).

The earlier metaphors are rendered clear. We shouldn't tell ourselves stories meant to rationalize our state. Make no excuses in
pursuing your ideals and dreams. And the real source of our internal problems is "the friction," the resistance of reality as manifest
internally through physical and psychological barriers, from self-
limiting beliefs to reduced vitality due to our own lassitude; but
also, externally, the values, judgments, and conduct of other people, many of which themselves are internalized. To surmount this
friction, we ought to be persistent.

This is the character quality, the excellence that must be
learned and put into action. We must stick to our tasks and
goals unfailingly. Constant effort will wear down opposing
forces, if anything can. Endurance is everything in the extended
journey of life. Inspiration must be present, but prolonged per-
spiration brings dreams to fruition. Once again, courage is
invoked so that we might surmount our own fears as well as the
threats of the wider world, not to mention, drag our dreams
into existence.

The message receives its final intensification after a brief musical interlude, as Geddy Lee, somewhere between commanding
and pleading, repeatedly emotes, "Everybody got to deviate—or
"elevate"—from the norm." What a strong, resonating message for
those trying to figure out who they are. I can recall my friend Ron
and I huddled on cold November nights in the Midwest with our
ears pressed against the wall of the local "stoner's" house. We
would furtively listen to the entire *Moving Pictures* album in this
posture while the walls of the shabby frame house rumbled.
Those inside remained oblivious to our eavesdropping. Perhaps
they knew that on a school night, we would never be able to
crank out "Vital Signs" at our homes, where our parents ruled. But
by foregoing our physics homework, were Ron and I really elevating from the norm to a higher plane of human excellence, or

just deviating for the sake of being different, following a classic rebellious tendency of youth?

Filling in the eudaimonic gaps left by Peart, prudent (rather than reactionary) non-conformity is essential because happiness is, to a large extent, finding those activities which give you pleasure, fulfillment, and peace of mind. If you don't pursue your own personal investigation of what suits you, you are less likely to be happy. Some people, such as the fictional Ivan Ilyich, find this out, but way too late. Some never grasp the importance of this truth. But if you discover a pastime or hobby that almost everyone else happens to like, rejecting it out of spite for conformity, like Dostoevsky's "underground man," only detracts from your own happiness. Peart may not tell us exactly what to do, but he stimulates us to do our own reflective thinking about how best to live, whether we're angst-ridden sixteen year olds or adults in the midst of a mid-life crisis.

In any case, as the music builds, Peart unleashes his full powers on the drum kit, punctuating, emphasizing Lee's passionate singing. This synergy explains why Rush's songs resonate so deeply and inspire so many. Because Peart has conceived those words and is intimately familiar with their significance, his fills and accents are always in sublime accord with Lee's vocalizing. For his part, Lee has explained that the songwriting process is a "happy collaboration," and that he cannot sing Peart's words unless he really loves them and can put his "heart and soul" into the performance. Their powers combined create a unique organic impact on the listener that is very different from the unadorned, non-musical, verbal essence of a philosophical treatise.

I Must Help My Mother Stand Up Straight

From fairly early on, Neil Peart has acknowledged the interpersonal realm of human values and virtues—empathy, compassion, and altruism being chief among them. Such Rush songs as "Losing It," "The Pass," "Everyday Glory," and "The Larger Bowl" show that the philosopher-drummer is attuned not just to the achievements of great individuals and the assertive careers of free spirits, but also to the pain and struggles of ordinary human beings. A perfect example is "Distant Early Warning," from *Grace under Pressure* (1984), in which the direct, colloquial diction of the chorus reflects the "new" values and virtues:

The world weighs on my shoulders
But what am I to do?
You sometimes drive me crazy—
But I worry about you

I know it makes no difference
To what you're going through
But I see the tip of the iceberg—
And I worry about you . . .("Distant Early Warning," *Grace
  under Pressure*, 1984)

The second person pronoun "you" predominates. The source of the narrator's angst is the other person, directly addressed! Concern with authenticity, self-determination, and the personal happiness of the isolated free spirit are conspicuously absent, though not necessarily forgotten. But the problem, illustrated throughout *Grace under Pressure*, is how to endure the tough times together. Whether it's the excruciating, focused pain of a death camp ("Red Sector A"), or the nebulous alienation and malaise of a mechanical, post-industrial culture ("Between the Wheels"), we need empathy, compassion, and a sense of our common humanity. We also need action, as the narrator of "Red Sector A" relates, "But I must help my mother stand up straight." Even "Afterimage," which is only about how we ought to live in the most indirect way, celebrates empathy: "I feel the way you would."

Fast-forward about a decade, and we find that Peart's expanded ethical consciousness was not a transitory phenomenon. In "Everyday Glory" (*Counterparts*, 1993), the individual against the mass, as in "2112," has become "we," and our problems do not necessarily originate with a totalitarian regime. We're in this fragile condition together, a condition in which it's all too familiar to observe "a little girl [hiding], shaking, with her hands on her ears / Pushing back the tears, till the pain disappears."

Peart humanely, compassionately portrays the concrete reality of modern family life through the experience of an average little girl, not a literary figure such as Tom Sawyer or a mythological space traveler such as Cygnus. Peart also shows a sensitivity to how mundane "desperation drives the bored to extremes." We are "everyday people" with everyday "shame" and "promise," but there's still hope. In one of the most poignant, gentle, yet rousing choruses for which Peart has ever penned lyrics, Geddy Lee's voice exults to hope, or perhaps predict, that we will "rise from the ashes [in] a blaze of everyday glory."

Despite this expanded consciousness, this re-calibration of his own moral compass such that it's pulled to everyday suffering and unfulfilled promise, Peart integrates his "new" concern for real, obscure individuals with his classic virtues.

> If the future's looking dark
> We're the ones who have to shine
> If there's no one in control
> We're the ones who draw the line
> Though we live in trying times—
> We're the ones, who have to try
> Though we know that time has wings—
> We're the ones who have to fly. ("Everyday Glory,"
>   *Counterparts*, 1993)

To fix what's broken in the modern families and cities that we have created, we must choose free will to control not only ourselves but others in society. We must call upon our courage and persistence to recapture everyday glory, and because time flies, we must change things now. The compass is re-calibrated, but its grounding in autonomy, responsibility, and courage remains constant.

Experience Slips Away

Along with his compassionate, altruistic turn in which real individuals are the focus, the pre-tragic Peart also had a sense of the finite, radically contingent, even absurd character of human reality. This existential consciousness is directly expressed in "Time Stand Still," "Roll the Bones," and "Ghost of a Chance." The post-tragic permutations include "Vapor Trail," and "The Stars Look Down," which are about as dark and resigned as any songs in Rush's repertoire. "Existential consciousness" could be a highfalutin, potentially vague term; but in our context it simply means that Peart has noticed and described some very basic features of human existence, and that these are the very features that make human life problematic and challenging. At the same time, these features render human life exciting and meaningful. In any case, these features are unavoidable if you live as a conscious human being. They are not culturally determined or socially constructed.

One of these features is finitude. Finitude refers to the state or quality of human existence being limited, in time, energy, ability, and so forth. Our existence is not infinite in duration, knowledge, or power. Gods may be timeless, but we're not. We live in time and space, and because we're finite we always live at a specific time and in a specific place. The most profound manifestation of finitude is our mortality, the fact that we are born, live a certain span of hours, days, or years, and then—inevitably—die. But besides the awareness of the ultimate temporal limits of lives, finitude shows itself in life while we are alive in various ways that cut to the heart of our sense of meaning and value.

In "Time Stand Still" (*Hold Your Fire*, 1987), Peart made finitude and our desire to overcome it the central motif. Once again Peart's humanism radiates as Geddy Lee petitions whatever powers that be, "Freeze the moment / A little bit longer / Make each sensation a little bit stronger." However, "experience slips away," and there's nothing anyone can do about it, or is there?

Is there a more or less virtuous response to this basic feature of human existence? Since it's impossible to freeze the moment, the only possibility left open to us is "like some pilgrim—who learns to transcend," to "learn to live as if each step was the end." We are aware of our finitude, which presents a double effect. We're burdened by living with knowledge that our stream of experiences will eventually evaporate, but we're blessed in that we can use this knowledge as motivation to live with maximal effort and sharpened focus. It's not merely a platitude to say that any moment could be your last. This is the human situation. So, if you value living at all, if human life is worthwhile, then any particular moment in your finite stream of moments should be seized and its fullest potential maximized.

But this is easier said than done. You have to embark on an existential pilgrimage—a kind of quest for transcendence of the ordinary—in order to live with the virtues of intensity and engagement. Moreover, the fleeting nature of our experiences can sometimes be so overwhelming that we're incapable of any productive reflection that would lead to more virtuous living.

Consider "Vapor Trail" (from *Vapor Trails*, 2002), a seminal post-tragic composition in which Peart's first-hand encounters with finitude apparently have not led to ethical reflection culminating in a greater impetus for living in the moment. Here, the fleeting nature of experience cuts so deep, even deeper than in a much earlier song such as "Afterimage" (*Grace under Pressure*, 1984) that the only appropriate response is a resigned lament.

> Horizon to horizon,
> Memory written on the wind
> Fading away, like an hourglass, grain by grain
> Swept away like voices in a hurricane.
> In a vapor trail. ("Vapor Trail," *Vapor Trails*, 2002)

Anyone who has ever seen the long, arcing trajectory of condensation trailed from a jet plane thousands of feet overhead can comprehend the central metaphor of this song. The vapor trail is distinct at first, almost stunning. But just as soon as we notice it, it's changing, decreasing, gradually growing fainter, until it's imperceptible—until it's nothing. Peart clarifies that he's symbolizing the tendency for memory to fade, however brilliant or profound the object of the memory, and this is ultra-significant for conscious creatures whose experience is inherently fleeting.

Memory is one way to attempt to "freeze the fading past," but if even memory is subject to gradual disintegration, then freezing either the actual moments of experience or their mental representation is doomed to failure. The oceans, stars, the songbirds, all will fade away. "Vapor Trail" states this simple fact and proposes no solution, ethical or otherwise. A free spirit following Peart's ethical vision can't help but ask, "Is this the final word? Is there nothing to be done? Should I still attempt to live as if each step was the end?"

Fate Is Just the Weight of Circumstances

Another feature of human reality prominent in Peart's existential consciousness is contingency, which is also a building block of the final salient feature that we will consider: absurdity.

Contingency is the opposite of necessity. Something necessary has to be, but something contingent could be or it could not be. (Think of our common expression, "contingency plan.") So, to say that human existence is contingent is to indicate that any fact of our situation is dependent on a prior fact or cause which itself was contingent. Human reality is circumstantial. One seemingly small decision or event contributes to further choices, decisions, or happenings which are actualized in an intersecting web of events, but none of these decisions or facts is utterly pre-determined.

Consider a working man who normally takes the 7:15 inter-urban to his job in the city. The man misses his train and thereby avoids his last train ride ever, as the "normal" train crashes into another head-on, killing all the passengers. An observer, perhaps the man himself, might say, "I wasn't meant to be on that train. I wasn't meant to die today." But through the lens of contingency, a completely different analysis would be given. What is the immediate reason that the man missed his train? He overslept. Why did he oversleep? Because his alarm clock failed to wake him. Why did it fail? Because there was a power failure during the night. Why was there a power failure? Because the overnight engineer at the sub-station, recovering from a hangover, spilled his coffee on the control board. Why did . . .? "Why does it happen? Because it happens."

Now we're in the thematic realm of "Roll the Bones" and "Ghost of a Chance" (*Roll the Bones*, 1991). Contingency implies a rejection of fatalism and the trite, vague saying, "Everything happens for a reason." Since all events are contingent, it would follow that everything that has occurred has at least one prior cause or reason. But if "for a reason" implies an ultimate, pre-determined purpose, then contingency is completely at odds with the cliché. Because of contingency, which rules out predetermined fate, our lives are filled with risk, and certainly, there are no guarantees of success—even if we "get busy."

What Is the Meaning of This?

The theme of absurdity also looms large in Peart's post-tragic ethics. As employed by classic existentialists such as Sartre and Camus, "absurd" refers to the lack of an ultimate explanation for existence itself or to a lack of rational justification for particularly profound events. Indeed, why does anything exist at all? Why is there something rather than nothing? One initially plausible answer is God. But then one can ask why God should exist. What is the explanation for God? This type of thinking can make your head spin. And this vertigo, brought on by confrontation with the limits of rational explanation, is called the absurd.

The classic significance of the absurd can be apprehended through concrete human situations in which we would prefer that rational human values such as justice would prevail, but they don't. For example, it would be absurd if a brilliant, humanitarian, research biologist on the brink of a great discovery were killed by a falling icicle dagger in midtown Manhattan simply because she happened to be in the wrong place at the wrong time. Once again, like the prior example of the man missing his normal train (at least a happy ending for him), through contingency, we can describe but not justify the scenario. The universe appears indifferent, neither aligned with us or against us. Our desire for sense, order, and purpose is not mirrored by the universe itself. Therefore, the universe presents a fundamental value-neutral resistance to our desire for a rational, ethical order. For lack of a better word, the non-rational, non-teleological universe is absurd.

In Peart's most focused post-tragic meditation on absurdity, "The Stars Look Down" (*Vapor Trails*, 2002), there is no imperative to "get busy" and "roll the bones." There is no hint of ethical reflection. The song hammers away at our pretensions of cosmic, overarching meaning by asking, "Are you under the illusion/That you're part of this scheme?" It also presents some deflating, unflattering analogies, as humans are compared to flies and rats, being turned by unknown wheels and trapped in mazes, respectively. The chorus summarizes our utter frustration with a search for answers to our most basic inquiries.

> What is the meaning of this?
> And the stars look down
> What are you trying to do?
> And the stars look down
> Was it something I said?
> And the stars look down. ("The Stars Look Down," *Vapor Trails*, 2002)

Despite all of our questions, the stars communicate no response. The indifferent, absurd universe will be of no help in overcoming our ignorance of the reasons why things happen, nor will it give us any solace as we struggle through life. As many of us have asked, semi-seriously, in moments of distress, "What did I do to deserve this?" Peart's post-tragic answer, in congruity with "Roll the Bones," composed a decade earlier, is that there is no answer. And the stars look down.

Peart's existential consciousness is perfectly summarized in "Ghost of a Chance" (*Roll the Bones*, 1991), with a surprising twist. After ruling out destiny, fate forever, or "angels watching from above," what remains possible is to "find someone to love." Human values are still worth pursuing, but it may be that an actual experience of the other is the final tonic for human happiness in an absurd world. That experience would prove crucial for Peart's post-tragic ethics. It is the final ingredient of eudaimonia.

Sweet Miracles of (Secular) Faith, Hope, and Love

The same fundamental, existential truths of human reality—finitude, contingency, and absurdity—that Peart had already reckoned with from a safe distance are brutally forced upon him through the tragic events of the late 1990s. The post-tragic albums *Vapor Trails* (2002) and *Snakes & Arrows* (2007) are the aesthetic, philosophical result. The general becomes specific. The abstract "human condition" is concretely experienced, and this determines a new quality to the reckoning of well being.

The concrete tragedy almost does Peart in, but his primal urge to live, his inveterate optimism survives the onslaught. Rather than nihilism, the ultimate adaptive response for Peart is, ironically, a kind of secular faith with the cardinal beliefs being hope and love. In the long view, we never see an utter disavowal or heresy in Peart's humanism. But we do see spheres brought completely to the fore, almost completely obscuring prior thought worlds but never negating their gravitational pull. All of these worlds, however, remain within the universe of ethics.

Ethics is careful reflection on how we ought to live in order to bring out human excellence and attain the ultimate goal, happiness. With this in mind, Peart's more recent, post-tragic emphasis on hope, love, and the saving power of the other can be seen for what they really are, as his capstone of implied "oughts" for living a life as a rational animal with a unique awareness of finitude, contingency, and absurdity. The awareness is not merely intellectual, as these existential features cause us the deepest psychic and emotional unrest, which can be felt by anyone, but which cannot be ignored by someone whose only child and wife die in a rapid cataclysm of loss and grief. Assaulted by this ultimate deprivation, Peart's consciousness undergoes its final transformation. The existential consciousness becomes a tragic consciousness. However tragic, it is not void of hope, love, and a peculiar kind of secular faith.

In "Sweet Miracle" (*Vapor Trails*, 2002), the most profound of the post-tragic, autobiographical songs, Peart indicates through the first person narrative perspective that "I was . . . lost without a trace / No hope at all / No hope at all." The despair is immediately juxtaposed with an exuberant but calm profession of an unexpected affirmation of life's ineffable value. Crooning in a smooth, lower register, Geddy Lee emotes, "Oh—sweet miracle / Oh—sweet miracle / of life." In the next refrain, the lyrics are slightly but tellingly changed. Now Lee sings, "Oh—sweet miracle / *Love's* [italics added] sweet miracle/Of life." Then in a bridge which approaches pure aesthetic transcendence, and reports on the narrator's own subjective one, Lee's voice rises in a glorious, hymnal falsetto to relate, "Oh salvation / Oh salvation." The hope of love professed in "Ghost of a Chance" has endured, or perhaps returned.

In Peart's life, prior to the composition of *Vapor Trails*, he had re-integrated as a person, met someone, and fallen in love, not only with another human being, but with life. It sounds too simple a dénouement for the intellectual, philosopher-drummer, but deep joy, even if simple, is after all profound. In *Ghost Rider*, Peart's published personal account of his loss, grief, alienation from others and himself, and long process of healing, he refers to the "joy of knowing Carrie, and the inspiration of being loved by her."[1] He further relates that without Carrie, the world would never have heard *Vapor Trails* because it would not have been created. Just as *2112* would not have existed without the courage, integrity, and self-esteem of Rush, *Vapor Trails* would not have existed without the love experienced by Neil Peart and Carrie Nuttall.

Love is one of the lyrical motifs of *Vapor Trails*. In "Earthshine," one of Rush's finest songs of any decade, ". . . the moon tells a lover's story." In "Secret Touch," love is manifest in concrete, bodily forms such as "a gentle hand" and "a healing hand." We're also warned, however, that "there is never love without pain." Dionysus was never so humanized. Finally, in "Out of The Cradle," the last song of the album, "the breath of love is electricity." Love revitalizes, inspires, and literally saves. Any experience so profound and filled with potential to assuage a tragic consciousness must be considered as an ingredient of the good life. Love's salvation is so deeply permeating that it re-invigorates some of the absurd virtues as well. Whereas "Time Stand Still" (1987) counseled us to live as if each step was the end, "One Little Victory" (2002) instructs us to "celebrate the moment / As it turns into one more." We're still deal-

---

[1] Neil Peart, *Ghost Rider: Travels on the Healing Road* (2002), p. 460. I highly recommend Peart's book for a detailed account of his harrowing, self-alienated post-tragic existence that preceded his relationship with Carrie Nuttall.

ing with finite, fleeting existence, with rapid successions of
moments. But, apparently, love's salvation has caused not only
engagement or intensity, but an affirmation of even the most
minute eddies and waves in the stream of life.

One somewhat critical response to this unrestrained, emotional
outpouring from Peart is to bring his own existential consciousness
to bear on the nature and permanence of "love's sweet miracle of
life." Certainly, no one, at least no Rush fan, would deny Peart his
salvation or denigrate it in any way. But this whole chapter has
been informed by a philosophical approach, and part of that
approach is to ask tough questions about a theory, especially the
coherence of a theory or stance.

Given what Peart has related about finitude, contingency, absurdity—and let's take the practical gist of that to be, "no guarantees"—can a finite, contingent experience such as love really
function as the culminating capstone to his ethics? Just for a start,
look at the divorce rate in America, not to mention the untold millions of individuals who have been hurt by love gone sour. As anyone who has lived with any awareness can tell you, the euphoria
of new love passes quickly. For some, once jilted or otherwise per-
manently separated from the beloved, there will be no new love.
Even you free spirits are weighed down by tragedy and heartbreak.
Can the tragic consciousness always find salvation in the other? Is
this universal enough to be a general ethical principle? Love is put
forth as a virtue in the Christian tradition, but can it be spoken of
by a skeptical, secular philosopher like Peart?

There may, however, be a way out for Peart. In fact, he's
already suggested it. His rejoinder is a secular faith informed by a
tragic consciousness which does not ignore the implications of finitude and contingency. There is a direct expression of it in
"Faithless" (*Snakes & Arrows*, 2007).

> I don't have faith in faith
> I don't believe in belief
> You can call me faithless
> But I still cling to hope
> And I believe in love
> And that's faith enough for me. ("Faithless," Snakes & Arrows, 2007)

First, notice his intentional use of a scriptural pre-text in a song
about faithlessness! St. Paul, in 1 Corinthians 13:13, details the virtues

of faith, hope, and love, but in his context they are only available as gifts from God. In Peart's version, by contrast, the usual hard human labor would be needed to cultivate and integrate them into our lives. Peart also plays on the meaning of "faith," paradoxically using the language of faith to express his commitment to not believing without sufficient rational justification. The plot thickens. Even though Peart accepts the moniker, "faithless," he then asserts that his belief in hope and love are "faith enough for me." What's going on here?!?

Faith is multi-dimensional, with secular and religious manifestations. The essence of the concept is belief against the backdrop of uncertainty, commitment to truth without absolute, total proof. With this understanding of faith as multi-dimensional, one could, for example, have faith that the stairs to your first floor landing will not collapse, or faith that a person you trust will not disappoint you. The object of faith is not only an intangible, supernatural entity. In a finite world riddled with uncertainty, some form of faith is required to actively live. This brand of faith is clearly what Peart has in mind, a kind of necessary, secular faith that's effected by a tragic consciousness. One can exist without hope, but one cannot live well. If hope is a kind of inner, passion-imbued, orientation of the will toward the future and all its favorable possibilities, then perhaps it can never be fully explicated or proven through logical, verbal means. But, we can observe the different kinds of life that are associated with hope and hopelessness. Peart couldn't help but observe these different lives from the inside, and he suggests that the life with hope, especially in the face of radical finitude and absurdity, appears to be the better life.

Though hope seems to be the final word of Peart's ethical vision, his latest insight should be seen as complementary to his prior wisdom. The values and virtues praised in "Anthem," "Freewill," and "Vital Signs" are still important for achieving the ultimate end of human life and happiness. But Peart's ethics, or, for that matter, Aristotle's, may ultimately be insufficient to guarantee a happy life. The threat of contingency and the vertigo of absurdity may not be vincible through any philosophical reflection, and secular faith may not be a mindset that everyone can attain. Regardless, Rush's music itself has contributed to making human life worth living. If you can be happy while listening to your favorite Rush song, perhaps that happiness can sustain you as you work for your dreams within an inherently challenging situation.

PART III

I Want to Look Around Me Now

12
A Heart and Mind United

LIZ STILLWAGGON SWAN

The so-called "hard problem" in contemporary philosophy of mind is to explain why we experience the world qualitatively in colors, sounds, tastes, and feels. In getting stuck on the hard problem of consciousness, some philosophers have forgotten the crucial insight that is so beautifully expressed in the story told in "Cygnus X-1 Book II: Hemispheres" (hereafter "Hemispheres," from the album of the same name)—namely that it is human nature to feel, and not just think, our way through the world.

Heart and Mind Divided

The hard problem is most closely associated with philosopher David Chalmers, who has devoted his academic career to understanding the nature of human consciousness. Chalmers identifies the hard problem as the need to explain why there is a subjective component of experience; for example, why seeing red is accompanied by a particular feeling of "what it's like" to see red, or why listening to your favorite Rush song has a particular feel to it that is unlike that of listening to any other song. The crux of the hard problem is that while science can explain the how of consciousness—for instance, how we recognize faces and how we learn a new language—it cannot explain why recognizing and learning different things feel a certain way to us.

The hard problem is contrasted with the so-called "easy problems" of consciousness, which require scientific explanations for our cognitive abilities to: discriminate (these pants are made out of cotton, not polyester); integrate information (the film *Transformers*

159

3 will be even more awesome than *Transformers 2*); report on mental states (I'd rather be listening to Rush), and so forth. The reason these kinds of problems are considered "easy" is because, at least according to Chalmers and those who agree with his view, the natural and cognitive sciences will be able to solve them. In theory, what we know from neuroscience and human biology can be supplemented with insightful models in cognitive science and artificial intelligence, enabling us to figure out in detail how the human brain performs all of these cognitive tasks.

However, proponents of the hard problem contend, even when all of the easy problems of consciousness are solved, we will still be in the dark about why experience has a subjective feel to it—why diving into a swimming pool on a blistering hot day comes with the feelings of extreme pleasure and relief, or why discovering that Rush has no tour dates in your city comes with the feeling of extreme disappointment. But wait a minute, you might say—why wouldn't experience be subjective? Whatever could it mean for me not to experience my world subjectively? To understand how this could even become a question that is taken seriously by contemporary philosophers, we'll revisit a wise tale about the duality of human nature that is recounted by Rush in "Hemispheres."

The Gods of Love and Reason Battle It Out

What's at stake in philosophical debates, broadly speaking, is a genuine understanding of human nature. The philosophical proponents of the hard problem seem to believe that human nature amounts to some sort of "Robot Plus." Let me explain: the hard problem suggests that science can explain almost every bit of us— except for the special, ephemeral icing on the cake of human nature that is consciousness.

In other words, we're no different from robots whose inner workings can be explained by physical and mechanical principles, except for the fact that we have an extra layer of reality, so to speak—one that allows us to experience the characteristic feel that comes along with different experiences. But could our human ability to experience the world qualitatively (as well as simply survive in it physically) really be just the icing on the cake? Just an extra?

To the well-studied Rush fan, this problem may bring to mind the story recounted in "Hemispheres," wherein we learn of the battle between the gods of Love and Reason, Dionysus and Apollo, who, when the world was young, each sought to "rule the fate of Man." The people in the story are divided over which god to follow, struggling with the internal battle over the promise of wisdom and grace from Apollo, and that of a free-spirited and passionate lifestyle promised by Dionysus. The promises that Apollo, Bringer of Wisdom, makes to the people are worth repeating here:

> I bring truth and understanding,
> I bring wit and wisdom fair,
> Precious gifts beyond compare.
> We can build a world of wonder,
> I can make you all aware. ("Hemispheres," Apollo, excerpt
>   1, *Hemispheres*, 1978)

Apollo is promising the gifts of the mind: understanding, wisdom, wonder, wit, and awareness. Knowledge is all the people would need, presumably, to live comfortably in their world:

> I will find you food and shelter,
> Show you fire to keep you warm
> Through the endless winter storm.
> You can live in grace and comfort
> In the world that you transform. ("Hemispheres," Apollo,
>   excerpt 2, *Hemispheres*, 1978)

We learn from the story that at first, the people gratefully embraced Apollo's offers, eager to live the comfortable life of the philosopher. We're told that, "they ran to build their cities, and converse among the wise."

Yet it soon becomes apparent that something is missing from their lives, "yet they knew not what was wrong." Their lack of passion for living is evident when "the streets fell silent" and for some reason "the urge to build these fine things seemed not to be so strong." In order to find out what was missing, "the wise men were consulted. . . . In quest of Dionysus, to find out what they had lost." Dionysus has a very different kind of promise for the lackluster people:

> I bring love to give you solace
> In the darkness of the night,
> In the Heart's eternal light.
> You need only trust your feelings;

Only love can steer you right.
I bring laughter, I bring music,
I bring joy and I bring tears.
I will soothe your primal fears.
Throw off those chains of reason
And your prison disappears. ("Hemispheres," Dionysus,
    Hemispheres, 1978)

The people are seduced by the sensualities promised them by Dionysus, which will free them from the heavy "chains of reason" weighing them down from their reverence to Apollo. They give in to their sensual and feeling side, reawakened by Dionysus, abandoning the cities and taking to the forest where they "danced and lived as brothers":

Food and wine they had aplenty
And they slept beneath the stars.
The people were contented
And the gods watched from afar. ("Hemispheres," *Hemispheres*,
    1978)

The moral of the story begins to unfold as we see how the people, so happy with their free-spirited lifestyle, have forgotten about the practicalities of life, which come back to haunt them.

But the winter fell upon them
And it caught them unprepared,
Bringing wolves and cold starvation,
And the hearts of men despaired. ("Hemispheres," *Hemispheres*,
    1978)

The people have followed both Apollo and Dionysus, each in turn, to see which can fulfill their true human destiny, and we learn that neither alone can fulfill it. Already from Rush we have a profound philosophical insight that is missing from the discussion surrounding the hard problem of consciousness.

Blinded by Apollo

Physicalism is the doctrine that there exists in the world nothing but physical stuff and thus that all phenomena in the world can be explained by physical principles. Thus, all supernatural phenomena such as fairies, devils, spirits, ghosts, reincarnation, virgin births, gryphons, and angels are denied in this worldview.[1] Physicalism has enabled us to understand how both nonliving and living things work. For example, we understand how rock surfaces in the mountains get worn down over time due to the effects of wind and rain, and we know that plants need sunlight and water to grow because we understand the process of photosynthesis. But do the insights provided by physicalism extend to the human realm?

Some might argue that physicalism can explain the purely physical aspects of human nature (such as walking and eliminating) but cannot explain the quintessentially human subtleties such as the feelings we experience when at a Rush concert, drinking in the music and lyrics flowing from the stage out to us in the crowd. To these skeptics, it seems that physicalism can only explain the objective aspects of experience. For example, a psycholinguist who is studying the blood flow in your brain on an fMRI monitor can see that your pleasure centers "light up" when you recall your first Rush concert, but she of course cannot experience the pleasure you are experiencing when you recall that Rush concert. She can observe that you're experiencing pleasure, but only you are experiencing that pleasure. The hard problem challenges us to understand why we experience those feelings at all. In other words, why isn't there just blood flow in your brain without any accompanying aesthetic or emotional experience? If physicalism is true, after all, aren't you just a lump of physical stuff?

The underlying assumption in this line of questioning is that physical stuff cannot have experience, and therefore we need to allow for some sort of nonphysical component of human nature that allows us to feel and have subjective experience. René Descartes articulated this distinction between the physical and the mental in the early 1600s when he concluded that there were two different kinds of substances in the world—*res extensa* (extended stuff) and *res cogitans* (thinking stuff)—which led him to worry about how the two could possibly interact and influence each other (for example, when my desire for ice cream causes me to buy some

---

[1] If that sounds like a bummer to you, you might consider the plausible alternative hypothesis for these kinds of phenomena that *is* consistent with the doctrine of physicalism—they're in your head!

and eat it). His view, which came to be known as Cartesian Dualism, has publicly been abandoned by contemporary philosophers, yet the simple misconception that the brain is physical and the mind is nonphysical shamefully lives on, creating lots of impossible questions concerning how the brain could produce presumably nonphysical phenomena such as thoughts, beliefs, wonders, ideas, and dreams.

Now, granted, our dreams don't weigh anything, our beliefs aren't colored or black and white, and we cannot store our ideas in a closet. Dreams, beliefs, and ideas do seem different in nature from tangible, physical things. But if we're committed to physicalism, then we don't believe that there's anything non-physical, and so we're not going to accept any way of describing our problem which assumes that non-physical entities can exist. So let's put the question this way: How can it be that dreams, beliefs, and ideas are physical happenings in our brains?

Passion and Reason Find a Balance

Proponents of the hard problem seem to believe that if physicalism is right, then as physical beings, we should be able to perceive and respond to any stimulus in the world appropriately, without these processes being accompanied by any qualitative "feel" at all. Although the hard problem is meant to concern human beings, this description in fact applies not to humans, but to robots.

Very clever robots can successfully navigate the space they are in, avoiding obstacles and completing simple tasks to the delight of their creators, all the while being completely devoid of any qualitative or phenomenal experience of what they are doing. Humans, on the other hand, are not like this. Humans process stimuli too but their doing so is always accompanied by the ongoing qualitative "feel" associated with whatever they are doing. We experience the world qualitatively in color and sound, feeling and mood, wherein passing instances make us feel happy, scared, worried, fearful, elated, or bored.

As we saw, some philosophers argue that we need something beyond the mere physical to explain and account for our qualitative experience. This stance, however, opens the door to a whole host of supernatural stuff that we have very good reason to reject or at least be very skeptical of. Why would we allow just one kind of supernatural phenomenon in the world (namely, human consciousness) and deny the rest? That doesn't seem like a sound philosophical position to adopt.

Another option is that we are thinking about physicalism in the wrong way. This is the position I advocate. Why shouldn't physicalism allow for us and other sentient (feeling, perceiving) beings to experience the world qualitatively? Wouldn't it make sense for organisms that have a natural survival instinct to be in constant phenomenal contact with their world? Generally speaking, we'll be safer and survive longer if we avoid dimly lit alleys that make us feel apprehensive, and murky water that smells bad, even if we're thirsty. The contrary assumption—that phenomenal experience is somehow superfluous to the mechanics of being—begs the question of why and how beings would be motivated, at even the most rudimentary level, to do anything at all! Why, for instance, would we know to take a drink of water without feeling thirst, or want to study for a degree in philosophy without a passion for thinking, or undergo procreation without the excitement of romance and sex?

Robots are not in phenomenal contact with their world—they don't feel any particular way about anything they do—but it doesn't matter since they have no interest in their own survival and well-being. Humans are entirely different kinds of beings; we need to be in constant phenomenal contact with our worlds, monitoring how we feel about what is going on at all times in order to secure our survival and well-being. Occasionally we might feel "care-free," but robots don't have a care in the world, literally. We are not simply "Robots Plus"; we are human beings.

A Single, Perfect Sphere

Part III of "Hemispheres", titled "Armageddon: The Battle of Heart and Mind," recounts the story of the dark years when the people were confused and unhappy, unsure of who they really were and which force—Love or Reason—represented their true nature. The world—and, we are to understand, the individual—was split into unhappy hemispheres, divided and in need of ultimate synthesis.

Part IV of the story, titled, "Cygnus: Bringer of Balance" provides that needed synthesis between Love and Reason, feeling and thinking. The narrator of the story passes through a black hole in space, in search of some resolution that will set aright the divided world full of unhappy people in need of finding balance. He approaches the gods, still busy battling each other for dominion

over human nature, and asks them to hear his story—presumably
a plea for an end to the shattered hemispheres of the world. He
tells how

> The warriors felt my silent cry
> And stayed their struggle, mystified.
> Apollo was astonished;
> Dionysus thought me mad. ("Hemispheres," Cygnus, *Hemispheres*,
>   1978)

The choice of words used to describe the respective reactions
of Apollo and Dionysus are worth noting: it is perfectly appropriate that Apollo, god of Reason, would be "astonished", and likewise that Dionysus, god of Love, would think the narrator "mad";
these reactions suit the nature of one ruled by reason and one ruled
by passion, respectively. The gods listen to the narrator's plea for a
resolution that balances reason and passion, and realize he is right:

> They sat a while in silence,
> Then they turned at last to me:
> "We will call you Cygnus,
> The god of Balance you shall be." ("Hemispheres," *Hemispheres*,
>   1978)

The gods of Love and Reason recognize the meritorious contribution of Cygnus, the god of balance, who recognized the truth that
human nature both thinks and feels its way through existence. The
important philosophical insight expressed in the story in
"Hemispheres" is that human nature is a balance of reason and passion, thinking and feeling. The story recounts the pointless and
regrettable struggle that is mounted in an effort to make just one or
the other the reigning nature of humans, when clearly it doesn't
work that way. We're all thinkers and feelers, and have always
been so. Some of us are more cerebral and some of us are more
emotional, but none of us is purely one or the other. And when
philosophers ask why we have phenomenal experience of the
world, they are forgetting this very simple and very true insight.
    As the wisdom of Cygnus X-1 shows, human nature is a com-
posite of reason and passion. We strive for a balance of the two,
but we are all certainly a composite of the two. How we think
about things affects how we feel about things and vice versa. The

solution is not that we need something beyond physicalism to explain phenomenal consciousness. The solution, rather, is to develop, in conjunction with the natural sciences, a deeper kind of physicalism—one that allows for the variety of human experience without taking on supernatural baggage. If we are committed physicalists, then we should strive for a deeper understanding of human nature that recognizes us as fully emerged from and enmeshed in the natural world, not partly separated from, and beyond, it.

I repeat here the same lyrics I chose for my high school senior yearbook quotation since they are just as meaningful and inspiring to me now as they were then:

Let the Truth of Love be lighted,
Let the Love of Truth shine clear.
Sensibility,
Armed with sense and liberty,
With the Heart and Mind united
in a single Perfect Sphere.[2]

---

[2] This chapter has two dedications: First, to my cousin, Melinda, who introduced me to Rush on a family ski trip to upstate New York in 1989. I couldn't wait to get home and buy my own copy of *Exit . . . Stage Left*. And second to Neil Peart, whose heartfelt stories about the darkness and light of human nature have inspired my philosophical thinking for years.

13

More than They Bargained For

DURRELL BOWMAN

Rush often incorporated the technical mastery, virtuosity, formal constructions, and metrical complexities of progressive rock. However, the band then also began to modify and extend its techniques to include synthesizers and related performance devices. It did so fairly gradually from 1976 to 1981, but the band then engaged with music technology at a considerable level of saturation from 1982 to 1987. In *Feminism Confronts Technology* (1991), Judy Wajcman indicates that:

> New technology emerges not from sudden flashes of inspiration but from existing technology, by a process of gradual modification to, and new combinations of, that existing technology. . . . Innovation [involves] extending the scope of techniques successful in one area into new areas.[1]

Rush already consisted of highly-regarded performers on each of drums, bass, and guitar, but how would such musicians necessarily be able to bring hi-tech instruments into such a context? The answer to this quandary may be found in *Technology and Women's Voices: Keeping in Touch* (1988), in which Cheris Kramarae suggests that technical complexities reflect the "male domination of skilled trades that developed under capitalism."[2] Rush's technology-obsessed, late-capitalist approach throughout the 1980s perfectly

---

[1] Judy Wajcman, "Feminist Critiques of Science and Technology," Chapter 1 in *Feminism Confronts Technology* (Polity, 1991), p. 21.

[2] Kramarae, *Technology and Women's Voices*, p. 2.

exemplifies Wajcman's idea of "gradual modification" and Kramarae's concept of "male domination of skilled trades." Bassist-singer Geddy Lee is not a "keyboardist" (by his own admission, in a 1984 *Keyboard* magazine interview), but he nonetheless felt strongly compelled to work with synthesizers and similar tools.

From 1976 to 1978, Rush occasionally used keyboard and foot-pedal synthesizers. However, five of the six songs on *Permanent Waves* (1980) and all seven songs on *Moving Pictures* (1981) each use at least some synthesizer elements. These include elements played by Lee on a Minimoog, Oberheim OBX-a, or Roland Jupiter-8 (see Figures 13.1, 13.2, 13.3).

Figure 13.1. Minimoog

Figure 13.2. Oberheim OBX-a

Figure 13.3. Roland Jupiter-8

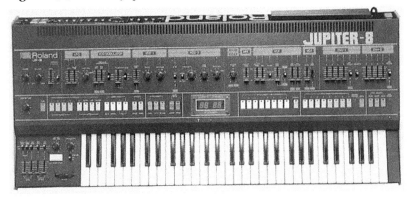

As microcomputers then began to flourish throughout the 1980s, so did digital synthesizers, melodic sequencers, and electronic percussion. In the wake of such developments, Rush made its four most "technological" albums. In this period, a few of Neil Peart's lyrics addressed technology, but Rush's use of certain instruments and related hi-tech techniques (such as music videos, electronic percussion, and sampling) did so to a much greater extent.

"Subdivisions" (*Signals*, 1982)

"Subdivisions," the opening track of *Signals*, begins with the first of several brassy synthesizer patterns that underlie nearly the entire song. No earlier Rush song used a synthesizer to this extent, and it is present for 72 percent of the song's duration, including two "solos." Thus, the song contains nearly as much synthesizer "airtime" as is found in all of Rush's previous work combined.

Not surprisingly, Lee wrote the song on keyboards, and he especially refers to the wide frequency range and "organic punch" of the Roland analog (JP-8 Jupiter) synthesizer he used.[3] This direction resulted in Lee's own historiographical confusion over this album, in 1982 calling it "definitely the direction that we've wanted to go," in 1984 "confusing," and in 1991 "a failure in getting the right balance."[4] The later comments suggest that Lee wished to apologize for

---

[3] Greg Armbruster, "Geddy Lee of Rush," *Keyboard* (September 1984), pp. 56, 60.

[4] Pete Makowski, article-interview with Rush, "Adrenalin Rush," *Sounds* (18th December 1982; <http://yyz.com/NMS/HTML/artindex.html>. Derek Oliver, article-interview with Lee, "Rush Release," *Melody Maker* (5th May 1984), p. 12.

the shortcomings of *Signals*, especially that it often buried Alex Lifeson's guitar. Lee's comment from 1982 suggests that the band thought of its recent music as comparatively accessible and that "big points" (such as 1970s-style individualism) and "weird times" (such as complex metrical constructions) no longer mattered. On the other hand, "Subdivisions" still addresses relatively serious issues, and it certainly does still use complex time signatures.

Despite the song's extensive engagement with synthesizer technology, the lyrics of "Subdivisions" do not address technology. The song describes the desire of restless young persons, especially "dreamers and misfits," to escape from suburbia, which "sprawl[s] on the fringes of the city . . . in between the bright lights and the far unlit unknown." The music video for "Subdivisions" portrays a solitary, male teenager (a "loser") playing video games and wandering around the downtown area of a major city: Rush's hometown of Toronto, Ontario. The young man endures the ridicule of "cooler" students, and, intertextually, watches a video of Rush performing this song. An annoyed parent turns off the TV and rudely flings his homework on top of him (see Figure 13.4).

Figure 13.4. Teenage misfit from "Subdivisions" (*Signals*, 1982)

Schulte, "Rush: Straight from the Heart," *Canadian Musician* 13:5 (October 1991), p. 36.

Rush had earlier experimented with music videos, such as for 1977's "Closer to the Heart" and for concert backdrops, but it was in the "MTV" era of the 1980s that the band sometimes explored relatively mainstream "concept" videos such as this.

"Subdivisions" partly conforms to early Rush's frequent "progressive" 7/8 time signature, as in the beginning of the song's introduction. Also, the middle portion of each half-verse switches from 4/4 to 7/8 (0:58–1:10, 1:20–1:32, 2:51–3:03, and 3:12–3:24). This metrical change underscores lyrics about the suburbs' "geometric order, [functioning as] an insulated border in between [city and country]", with its "Opinions all provided . . . the future pre-decided . . . detached and subdivided." Later, the same metrical shift inscribes the cities' "timeless old attraction," with individuals "cruising for the action" and "lit up like a firefly" at night, but losing "the race to rats," getting "caught in ticking traps," and, ironically, starting to dream of the suburbs.

The musical-lyrical parallel recalls the band's use of the same music to represent both Apollo and Dionysus in 1978's "Hemispheres" and both London and New York in 1981's "The Camera Eye." The song's title references the suburban subdivisions with which the song concerns itself lyrically (and in the video), but it also references the metrical subdivisions that musically underscore Verse 1's dislike of the suburbs and Verse 2's ambivalence about having left them. In beginning to use music technology so extensively, Lee probably recognized an ironic parallel of Peart's urban "ticking traps."

"Countdown"

Like "Subdivisions," "Countdown" (*Signals'* closing song) uses a "brassy" synthesizer sound. Lyrically, it uncharacteristically bridges the band's enthusiasm for general technology (NASA's space shuttle program) with its use of music technology. In 1981, the band had attended the first space shuttle launch (the Columbia), and their enthusiasm in the song parallels Ayn Rand having attended—and then enthused about—1969's launch of Apollo 11.

Grace under Pressure (1984)

In a controversial move, Rush abandoned its long-time associate Terry ("Broon") Brown and engaged former Supertramp producer

Peter Henderson to co-produce *Grace under Pressure*. The band wanted a change in production approach, but its desire for a renewed balance in technology and co-production resulted in a difficult recording period. The band took three months to write the album and five months to record it. The album title, its inner photo of an egg precariously lodged in a C-clamp, and Hugh Syme's cover art (see Figure 13.5) reflect the stylistic difficulties of this period.

Figure 13.5. *Grace under Pressure* (1984), cover art by H. Syme

On the evocative album cover, an android observes a circuit board (?) suspended between ominous storm clouds (pressure, abbreviated "p") and a shimmering oceanic liquid (grace or "g").

Geddy Lee mused in interviews about his mid-1980s approach to synthesizers:

> I look at myself as . . . a melodic composer with the synthesizer. . . . I can't play a lot of complex chord changes or move through a very complex structure, but I can find lots and lots of melodies. I can write

lots of songs on a synthesizer. I can zone in on the sound that I want and make it speak for the mood I want to create.[5]

In addition to his bass guitars, from 1982 to 1988 Lee used as many as five keyboards on stage. Later selections in that period also included a PPG Wave 2.3 (see Figure 13.6) with Waveterm digital sampling, Emulator II, Yamaha DX-7, Roland D-50, Prophet VS, and Yamaha KX-76 controller. In addition, in the 1980s Lee continued to use pedal systems, initially Moog Taurus and Taurus II units (Figure 13.7) and, later, a Korg MIDI unit. He also used melodic and/or rhythmic sequencers, including an Oberheim DSX, Roland TR-808 (Figure 13.8), and/or Yamaha QX-1.

Figure 13.6. PPG Wave 2.3

Figure 13.7. Moog Taurus II pedals

---

[5] Armbruster, "Geddy Lee of Rush," pp. 63–65.

Figure 13.8. Roland TR-808 Rhythm Composer

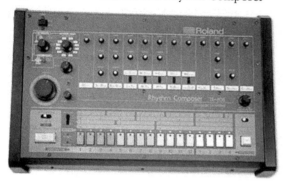

"Distant Early Warning"

A high-concept music video was made for *Grace under Pressure*'s opening song, "Distant Early Warning." Directed by David Mallet and filmed in front of a stylized map of the world, it borrows from Stanley Kubrick's film *Dr. Strangelove or: How I Learned to Stop Worrying and Love the Bomb* (1964). The song and video update the context from the earlier days of the Cold War to the height of the conservative era (Thatcher and Reagan) of exactly twenty years later. The imagery includes flight control instrument panels, a bomber jet, a melting wax mock-up of Geddy Lee's face ("destroyed by acid rain"), and a young boy riding the bomb over nature and cities (similar to *Dr. Strangelove*). The set aesthetic presents a hi-tech vision. In addition, Lee plays a compact Steinberger bass (and wrote the song on a keyboard) and Peart's Simmons electronic drums appear prominently (see Figures 13.9-13.10).

Figure 13.9. Lee, with Steinberger bass
Figure 13.10. Peart, with Simmons drums (1984)

Peart had earlier rejected electronic drums as insufficiently visceral but by 1984 had changed his mind. Also, the song's instrumental introduction includes the sounds of static, suggesting radiation or perhaps a Geiger counter measuring it. In part of Lifeson's solo (3:15–3:28), he uses a Delta Lab Harmonicomputer to play in octaves. The song's main instrumental hook (initially at 0:28–0:39) is in 7/8 with some 5/8. Lee uses keyboards and bass pedals for that section.

Paul Théberge points to H. Stith Bennett's discussion of the disparity between recorded music and its live performance.[6] By introducing bass pedal units, synthesizers, sequencers, arpeggiators, triggers, effects boxes, and samplers within its live performances between 1977 and 1988, Rush acknowledged this potential disparity. Indeed, the band chose to recreate its studio creations through a meticulous application of such technology. Later, the band concerned itself less with this disparity. In 2002, Lee included only two keyboards on stage, and he rarely played them. When the band performed its keyboard-heavy songs from 1982–87, it allowed off-stage computers and samplers to play most of those sounds, although these elements were always subtly triggered by the three band members on-stage.

"Red Sector A"

The music video for *Grace under Pressure*'s song "Red Sector A" shows four synthesizers and Moog Taurus pedals on Lee's part of the stage. Notably, he does not play bass at all during the song. By 1987–88, Lee's off-stage equipment also included as many as four synthesizers (including two Roland modules), seven samplers (Akai 900 modules), and two Yamaha QX-1 sequencers.[7] The video shows that Lifeson also sometimes used Moog Taurus pedals (see Figure 13.11).

By 1985, Lifeson also used a pair of bass pedal units, two off-stage Emulator II keyboards, and a digital sequencer. In addition to his early-1980s guitar pedal effects (including MXR, Delta Lab,

---

[6] See Théberge, *Any Sound You Can Imagine*, p. 109 and Bennett, "Notation and Identity in Contemporary Popular Music," *Popular Music* 3 (1983), p. 231.

[7] See Robert L. Doerschuk, "Geddy Lee: Rush to Perfection on 'A Show of Hands,'" *Keyboard* (March 1989), pp. 16–17 and Stern, "Rush," *Canadian Musician* 10:1 (1988).

Figure 13.11. Lifeson, with Moog Taurus I pedals

Roland, Yamaha), he added numerous ones in 1985 (including Loft, Ibanez, Boss, Scholz-Rockman).[8] For his part, Peart wore head-phones in concert for certain songs around 1984–88, so that his drumming could match the tempos of electronically-generated sequences and arpeggios. Also, Peart's drumming continued to involve Simmons electronic drums, as well as samplers and other electronic equipment (see Figure 13.12).

On tour, Peart combined his 1982 Tama Artstar prototype drums (plus Avedis Zildjian cymbals, and so forth) with a satellite set largely involving electronics. In 1987–88, he replaced his glocken-spiel with a KAT electronic MIDI mallet unit. He also used Akai sampling modules and various additional electronic triggers.[9]

"The Body Electric"

"I Sing the Body Electric" (*Leaves of Grass*, 1855) by Walt Whitman (1819–92) involves a wide-eyed enthusiasm for the physiology of the human body. Neil Peart used this inspiration as his lyrical start-ing point for *Grace under Pressure*'s "The Body Electric." However, the song more closely recalls *Star Wars* creator George Lucas's

---

[8] Anonymous article-interview with Lifeson, "Alex Lifeson: *Grace under Pressure*," *Guitar Player* (August 1984), pp. 44–51. Also see Jas Obrecht, article-interview, "Alex Lifeson of Rush: The Evolving Art of Rock Guitar," *Guitar Player* (April 1986), <http://yyz.com/NMS/HTML/artindex.html>.

[9] Banasiewicz, *Rush Visions*, pp. 65, 86. See also the *Rush Backstage Club newsletter* (March 1990).

Figure 13.12. Peart, with headphones and Simmons drums

early film *THX-1138* (1971), with lyrics referring to a "humanoid escapee," an "android on the run . . . trying to change its program." The song later expands the computer imagery with references to "data overload," "memory banks unloading . . . bytes break[ing] into bits," and, especially, to the binary code sung during the chorus (though already implied in the song's main drum pattern): "1-0-0-1-0-0-1" (which also represents the decimal number 73 and, more importantly, the letter—or word—"I"). The paranoid and panicky situation of the song's lyrics recall the film through words such as: "S.O.S.," "in distress," "trouble," "break down," "struggle," "resist," "a pulse of dying power," "a hundred years of routines," and "pray[ing] to the mother of all machines." The song's music video also uses *THX-1138* imagery, combined with Plato's less-technological cave.

After the song's initial drums/bass/guitar groove, Lee uses synthesizers in 72 percent of the song, although he often provides them simultaneously with bass guitar. These synthesizers provide voice-like or "crystalline" timbres, via a recently acquired PPG digital synthesizer. Lee sometimes played the PPG via a melodic

sequencer or foot-pedals. The keyboard parts support the central
rhythms up into the higher frequencies. This approach also corrects
one of the most common complaints about *Signals* (1982): that the
keyboard-oriented songs on that album often diminished, or at
least substantially veiled, the band's traditional instrumental interplay of guitar, bass, and drums. Further to this point, the song's guitar solo features only guitar, bass, and drums, in a highly
contrapuntal ("traditional Rush") texture. Overcoming these sorts of
"balance challenges" resulted in the album's title: *Grace under
Pressure*, which derives from the definition of "guts" that Ernest
Hemingway (one of Peart's favourite authors) provided to Dorothy
Parker in an interview in 1929.

Interlude: Influences, 1984–86

In a 1984 interview in *Keyboard*, Geddy Lee referred to inspiration
from current pop-rock, such as Peter Gabriel (including synthesist
Larry Fast and various drummers), Simple Minds, Ultravox,
Eurythmics, Howard Jones, and King Crimson (its recent album
Three of a Perfect Pair). Around the same time, Alex Lifeson mentioned his appreciation for the album *Win This Record* (1982), by
the extremely eclectic California musician David Lindley (bluegrass,
world beat, blues, rock'n'roll, among others). In a 1986 interview,
Neil Peart mentioned his enthusiasm for big-band music and its
drummers (such as Gene Krupa), jazz-rock fusion (Weather Report
and various drummers), other progressive-influenced rock drummers, and world music. He also discussed how Rush's music had
progressed from being "progressive:"

> We think that the face of our music is changing from having been pro-
> gressive to not being progressive. For us, we're progressing. That's all
> that progressive music can be, and it's just as difficult for us to think
> of and to play. To us, it's totally satisfying and progressive. Perhaps
> from the view of an outsider who judges only on the superficiality of
> technique, it might seem simpler. Believe me, it's not.[10]

Peart's childhood piano lessons probably explain his predilection
for melodic percussion (such as chimes, glockenspiels, marimbas,

---

[10] See Scott K. Fish, article-interview with Peart, "Neil Peart," *Modern
Drummer* (January 1986), <http://yyz.com/NMS/HTML/artindex.html>.

and, later, MIDI- or sample-based instruments) as well as his ongoing interest in jazz drumming.

Power Windows (1985)

Starting with *Power Windows*, Rush achieved a renewed level of comfort in producing its music along with an outside co-producer: Peter Collins. Collins's background included writing and producing jingles as well as producing techno-pop recordings. However, his production associates would hardly have dissuaded Rush's use of hi-tech equipment in 1985 and 1987. These included programmer/keyboardist Andy Richards, who had recently contributed to the UK dance pop sensation Frankie Goes to Hollywood. For its two 1985–87 albums with Collins, the band also recorded mainly in the UK (plus Montserrat and partly in Toronto), after five years recording at Le Studio near Montreal, Quebec, Canada.

Hugh Syme's cover art for *Power Windows* (see Figure 13.13) shows a teenaged boy apparently using a remote control to open his bedroom window. Behind him, three televisions that do not quite look like televisions—presumably one for each member of Rush—stand askew in the middle of the room.

Figure 13.13. *Power Windows* (1985), cover art by H. Syme

The boy stares at us, as if to solicit our blessing for him to explore the brave new world (adulthood?) outside. A lightning flash shows through the window, recalling the storm imagery of part of Syme's album cover for *Grace under Pressure* (1984). On one of the television screens, a faint doppelganger of the same boy stares at us through binoculars. The remote-controlled bedroom window, the televisions, the binoculars, the lightning flash, and the electrical outlet below the window all provide visual puns for the album title.

"The Big Money"

Power Windows's opening song, "The Big Money," picks up on the band's ongoing ambivalence about media and industry contexts, and, appropriately, the band performs the song's music video mainly on a large "Monopoly"-like set. The "TV boy" from the album cover appears in a number of sequences and the band members themselves also seem to get sucked into TV screens, but otherwise in the video the band somewhat downplays its use of technology. For the song's main synthesizer line, Lee simultaneously plays a keyboard and the Moog Taurus I pedals at the base of the keyboard stand (Figure 13.14).

Figure 13.14: Geddy Lee, still shot from the video for "The Big Money" (1985)

Parts of the song feature Peart's electronic drums or voice-derived samples, including some played by drums, which decidedly blurs the categories of electronic drums, samples, and background vocals and makes them quite difficult to differentiate aurally. The song's second introduction uses real drums (which the song's video shows Peart playing), but it also includes keyboard parts and sample-based orchestral hits. This approach contrasts the prominent display of Peart's Simmons electronic drums in certain 1984 videos. The chorus (in 4/4) features Lifeson's raw guitar sound, Peart's aggressive drumming (on a traditional, if large, rock kit), and Lee's active/"popping" bass guitar. By comparison, parts of the verses (in 6/4) include voice-like synthesizer sounds, duplications of Lee's voice, and also samples of Lifeson's guitar played on keyboards. The verses of Peart's lyrics refer to "Sometimes pushing all the buttons; sometimes pulling out the plug," but the song also inscribes this musically.

"Manhattan Project"

The activities of rock musicians and fans in the post-counterculture resemble the tendency among twentieth-century males to produce technically compelling inventions first and ask questions later. Brian Easlea quotes the US nuclear weapons coordinator J. Robert Oppenheimer as saying that "when you seen something that is technically sweet you go ahead and do it and you argue about what to do about it only after you have had your technical success."[11] The *Power Windows* song "Manhattan Project" concerns the drive for Oppenheimer and others to display this kind of technical prowess in the context of nuclear weaponry. Feminist Simone de Beauvoir, as paraphrased by Judy Wajcman, suggests that "male accomplishments in the field of science and technology serve to bestow a virile status on the respective male achievers and thereby underwrite a claim to masculinity" (p. 139). Related to this, but also largely contradicting it, male and female hardcore Rush musician-fans valorized Lee, Lifeson, and Peart's technical abilities, powerful playing, and songwriting in order to underwrite their virility as musicians, not as men or women.

"Manhattan Project" inscribes Peart's ambivalence about the inevitable "big bang" (nuclear weaponry) having produced "more

---

[11] J. Robert Oppenheimer, quoted in Judy Wajcman, "Technology as Masculine Culture," *Feminism Confronts Technology*, p. 138.

than they bargained for." The song thus reflects a critically ambiva-lent worldview, not an apocalyptic one. The verses consistently include synthesized and sampled sounds and thus convey a sense of technological irony. In a related matter, Lee points out that key-board associate Andy Richards contributed a "fretless bass" part on a synthesizer which Lee then had to replicate with an inferior sam-ple-based method in order to play it live.[12] On the other hand, the chorus features a more traditional Rush sound: a complex rhythm featuring guitar. A later instrumental section (3:20–3:45) incorpo-rates a string section (along with extensive wordless vocals) play-ing a vaguely Russian-sounding string arrangement by Anne Dudley of the UK, postmodern techno band Art of Noise. (Like Richards, Dudley had contributed to recordings by Frankie Goes to Hollywood. She later wrote scores for the 1992 UK film *The Crying Game* and the 1997 UK film *The Full Monty*, winning an Oscar for the latter.) "Manhattan Project" ends with a fade-out featuring a reflective distillation of Lifeson's main earlier guitar part and a sim-ilar reprise of Peart's opening "military" (cautionary?) snare roll.

"Mystic Rhythms"

The eighth and final song of *Power Windows*, "Mystic Rhythms," also fits the album's themes of power and of the blurring of tech-nology. As Geddy Lee explains:

> Everything in it is going through a synthesized something. We spent a day sampling African drums, tablas, roto-toms, and all kinds of bizarre sounds. We found four appropriate ones, locked into four dif-ferent AMS's [delay units with sampling capabilities] that were trig-gered by Neil playing his Simmons kit. There's a very unique guitar sound, too. It's an Ovation acoustic guitar going through amplification and it comes off with a very synth-like sound.[13]

The song's video also participates in these types of ambiguities: unlike the modern TV screens in the video for "The Big Money," the video for "Mystic Rhythms" incorporates old-fashioned variants

---

[12] Tom Mulhern, "Geddy Lee," *Guitar Player* (April 1986), p. 86.

[13] Perry Stern, article-interview with Lee and Lifeson, "Rush: Baroque Cosmologies in Their Past, the Boys Focus on 'the Perfect Song'," *Canadian Musician* 7:6 (1985).

of projection technology, thus somewhat reminiscent of the trio of odd-looking TVs on the album cover. Images of water, reflection, and light (and nature generally) contrast with an elaborate mechanical toy, glowing spheres, a Claymation-like Godzilla, nautical-like portholes looking in on Rush, and a skeleton containing other beings. The skeleton and toy reflect the "embedded" nature of the song's sampled/synthesized soundscape, which comprises, for example, electronic drums consistently triggering sampled percussion, twice as much synthesizer "airtime" as bass guitar (83 percent versus 41 percent), and a few "seagull" noises reminiscent of the electronic bird sounds (a.k.a., the "music score") of Alfred Hitchcock's film *The Birds* (1963). The melodies and chords favor pentatonic elements (thus referencing "nonwestern" constructions), and the lyrics refer to the natural/mystical world outside:

> The more we think we know about, the greater the unknown.
> We suspend our disbelief, and we are not alone. . . .
> We sometimes catch a window: a glimpse of what's beyond.
> Was it just imagination stringing us along? ("Mystic Rhythms" excerpts, *Power Windows*, 1985)

Music technology can embed such "unknown" things, and, paralleling its gradually-building introduction, the song ends with an extended fade-out to a virtually inaudible—and thus technologically deceptive—synthesizer "real ending" to conclude the album. As Neil Peart put it (more succinctly), the song provides a "good marriage of lyrics and music."[14]

"Force Ten" (*Hold Your Fire*, 1987)

Hold Your Fire continued Rush's experiment in bridging music technology and hard rock. The opening song, "Force Ten," uses the maximum level of the Beaufort wind velocity scale as an analogy for the storms of life. Neil Peart based his lyrics on something provided by Pye Dubois, thus paralleling the origins of Rush's best-known song ("Tom Sawyer," *Moving Pictures*, 1981). The Hemingway-like lyrics encourage listeners to transcend not only their inability to predict things but also the powerful forces that

---

[14] Neil Peart, *Guitar for the Practicing Musician* (1986).

they cannot control. Sampled choir, crowd, and guitar sounds begin the song, followed by jackhammer samples (later reprised to end the song) and a woman's laugh—powerful forces comparable to the force ten wind storm of the song's title.

Lee's open fifth-centred main riff (C/G and D/A above an A pedal) and Lifeson's related guitar derivations join Peart's aggressive rock drumming. This underscores the vocal introduction: "Tough times demand tough talk, demand tough hearts, demand tough songs . . . ." The verses (in 4/4) feature a call-and-response pattern between Lee's vocals and Lifeson's guitar gestures (recalling "Afterimage," 1984), as the lyrics oscillate between extremes: "We can rise and fall like empires, flow in and out like the tide . . . ." (recalling the lyrical ambiguity of "The Big Money," 1985). A middle section returns to open fifths (but now in 6/4), and it features ethereal-sounding synthesizers for a kind of mellow chorus: "Look in to the eye of the storm. Look out to the force without form. . . ." The instrumental "solo" section (2:51-3:26, in 4/4) at first features Lifeson's atmospheric guitar gestures over Lee's open fifths, but this gives way to a rhythmically eccentric section (derived from cross-rhythms) featuring keyboards, bass, guitar, and drums. The song ends with additional 6/4 choruses and then material reprising the song's introduction (back in 4/4).

"Time Stand Still"

Hold Your Fire's "Time Stand Still" features guest backup vocals by Aimee Mann (recently of the band 'Til Tuesday). This produces an emotional resonance for some of the song's lyrics:

> Time stand still: I'm not looking back, but I want to look around me now.
> Time stand still: see more of the people and the places that surround me now.
> . . . Experience slips away. . . . The innocence slips away. ("Time Stand Still" excerpts, *Hold Your Fire*, 1987)

It also suggests Rush's "progressive" desire to look outside itself and to a wide variety of colleagues and influences, including a female singer-songwriter who also appears in the song's video as a movie camera operator and backup singer (see Figure 13.15).

Figure 13.15. Lee, Peart, and Aimee Mann, "Time Stand Still" (1987)

The video makes pervasive use of "blue-screen" effects, where separate video elements can be spliced and moved around separately, so that the individual band members (with their instruments) and Mann (with the camera) often float around on a set or outside in nature. As a supporting singer on the song itself (sometimes contributing short passage of "lead" vocals), Mann's presence in the video also provides realistic supporting images. When the "innocence slips away" at the end of the song, Mann pleasantly waves goodbye and she and her movie camera magically disappear off into the background. Her pleasant departure and the band's apparent lack of concern about this suggest fleeting influence rather than a lasting collaboration.

Peart reports that he sampled Asian temple blocks in order to use them at pitches other than their native ones.[15] The song uses non-subtle keyboards mainly in the comparatively gentle chorus that also features Peart's sampled temple blocks (47 percent) and Mann's vocals. The instrumental middle section features semi-virtuosic guitar, bass, and drums, a certain degree of sampled sound effects, and the 7/4 time signature that comprises over one-quarter of the song. Lifeson's guitar (98 percent) and Peart's drums (99 percent) participate almost constantly throughout, but the song forgoes

---

[15] See William F. Miller, article-interview with Peart, "Neil Peart/Rush," *Modern Drummer* (December 1989).

a guitar solo in favour of short, virtuosic bass flourishes in between various sections.

"I Want to Look Around Me Now"

In its music and concert tours from 1980 to 1988, Rush expanded its ongoing strategy of "permanent change" by including influences from post-punk/new-wave rock, post-progressive hard rock, and jazz/rock fusion. Lyrically, the band addressed a wide spectrum of the human condition, including: pride, freedom, fame, self-doubt, war, ambition, conflict, originality, burning out, vulnerability, outside forces, and loneliness. Rush's music exemplifies Pierre Bourdieu's concept of the habitus: a "system of structured, structuring dispositions."[16] For Rush and its fans, this system involves the virtuosic interaction of guitar, bass, drums, and voice. In the 1980s, Rush's habitus provided the band, to use Bourdieu's terms, with "relative autonomy" from the "external determinations" of the "immediate present" of music technology. Rush snatched music technology away "from the contingency of the accidental and constitute[d] it as a problem by applying it to the very principles of its solution" (p. 55).

Instead of abandoning synthesizers, samplers, and sequencers as a problem, the band worked through certain timbral and textural possibilities and added these to its "embodied history." However, in its new music from 1989 to 1996, the band then gradually decreased the sounds of music technology. It did so while applying related techniques (i.e., computers and recording software) within its songwriting and arranging. By the time of its studio recordings of the 2000s, Rush had reinvented itself, according to a new version of a "minimal technology" power-trio aesthetic.

---

[16] Pierre Bourdieu, *The Logic of Practice* (Polity, 1990), p. 52.

14

Contre Nous

NICOLE BIAMONTE

"Entre Nous" (French for "between us") is a Rush song from *Permanent Waves* (1980). The lyrics are about recognizing that we can transcend individual differences between ourselves and others.

The music uses a technique called text-painting, in which musical gestures imitate the meaning of a word or phrase. The differences described in the lyrics are reflected by the vocal pauses in the chorus after "just between us," "time for us to recognize," "spaces in between" and "leave room," which represent points of separation. The larger message of the song, about overcoming such differences, is expressed by musical elements that create unity: the verse and chorus are in closely related keys (D and G), and the guitar and synthesizer play together in the bridge but there is no individual solo.

A song called "Contre Nous" (French for "against us") would have the opposite meaning, focusing on how differences can act as barriers that create separation and distance from others. This idea could be text-painted using contrasting musical elements like distantly related keys or abrupt changes in instrumentation, texture, or style. In fact, these techniques have been used to symbolize otherness in music for hundreds of years. Throughout history, composers have drawn on little-used keys or scales, exotic instruments or tone colors, or quotations or imitations of a foreign musical style to convey differences in place, culture, or time. In the "raga rock" of the late 1960s, for instance, the Beatles, the Kinks, the Byrds and other bands incorporated sitars, drones (continuously sounding notes), and other elements evoking Indian music and culture into numerous songs. The introduction to Metallica's "Wherever I May Roam" from 1991 is a more recent example of a sitar representing distant places.

How Does Music Mean?

We cannot define the "other" without first defining ourselves. To effectively portray otherness, exotic elements need to be placed in a familiar musical context. This juxtaposition—and meaning and expression in music generally—depends on the listener's knowledge of a musical style and awareness of its conventions, called "listener competence." Think of a sad song you know. Even if you can't explain in technical terms what makes the music sound sad, you recognize that it suggests sadness. Now think of a culture whose music you don't know. You would have no idea whether a song from that culture sounded sad or not, because you are not a competent listener in that musical tradition.

There might or might not be anything inherently sad about the sad song; scientists and scholars who study music perception and cognition are still figuring out exactly how we understand music. The important point is that when you know the conventions of a particular musical style, you can recognize the symbolism of its gestures and relationships. For example, minor chords are often described as sounding sadder than major chords. This is a sweeping generalization, but as with all generalizations, there is some truth to it. Most songs (if they have chords at all—in many musical cultures, they don't) use both major and minor chords, but don't alternate between sounding happy and sad from moment to moment. Yet changing a minor chord into a major one built on the same note can sound like a ray of sun coming out of the clouds. In the chorus of Rush's "Different Strings" from *Permanent Waves*, compare the sound of the A-minor chords at the lyrics "two of us," "along," and "part of us" to the final A-major chord on "song." The last chord sounds warmer and brighter. However, someone unfamiliar with our musical tradition probably would not hear it that way.

Minor keys, as well as chords, are often described as sadder than major keys. It's true that funeral marches, for example, are in minor keys, while "Happy Birthday" is in a major key. But the beginning of Rush's "Something for Nothing" from *2112* is in a minor key (to be precise, it's in the Dorian mode, a type of minor), but is not especially sad. In contrast, "Tears" from *2112* is sad, but begins in a major key (up to the lyric "so long," when it becomes clear that the overall key is actually D minor, not F major). The keys and emotional characters of these two songs deviate from the norm partly because other musical elements contribute to their effects: "Tears" has a slower tempo, simpler texture, and softer tone color than "Something for Nothing." However, this reversal of characters also demonstrates that hearing major keys as happy and a minor key as sad is a learned convention.

In the same way, exotic musical elements could be authentic aspects of a different musical culture, or they could be entirely invented—all that matters is that listeners perceive them as representing otherness. Many conventional exotic gestures are generic folk elements that are very old and are found in numerous different national styles. For example, drones are common in Indian, Arab, Scottish, Australian, and various types of Eastern European folk music. A gapped scale called the pentatonic scale shows up in music just about everywhere in the world, including American and British rock and blues.

Whether a generic exotic element suggests a specific location depends on additional musical, lyrical, or external cues. In the introduction to Metallica's "Wherever I May Roam," a drone is combined with the distinctively Indian timbre of the sitar. AC/DC's "It's a Long Way to the Top (If You Wanna Rock'n'Roll)" has a similar lyrical theme, describing the seemingly endless travel required of a touring band. The solo section of this song features a bagpipe drone and melody characteristic of Highland Scottish music.

Like many progressive bands, Rush is known for using a variety of musical style references, extended song forms, asymmetrical and changing meters, and a wide vocabulary of scales and harmonies. Since the band's normal musical language is so diverse, they range further afield for exotic effects, incorporating unusual timbres (tone colors), chord progressions. and scales. There are two broad categories of otherness in Rush's music: geographic otherness, which evokes foreign or alien locales, and moral otherness, which symbolizes manifestations of evil.

Evoking Other Places

The most obviously exotic Rush song is "Tai Shan" from *Hold Your Fire*, which describes Neil Peart's journey to the top of Mount Tai, a holy pilgrimage site in Shandong Province, China. This setting is evoked by a sampled Shakuhachi flute (actually a Japanese instrument) in the introduction and verses. The flute plays a gapped melody based on a distinctively Asian form of the pentatonic scale, not the universal form mentioned earlier. The plucked guitar sound in the second verse and the ending is reminiscent of a pipa, a Chinese four-stringed lute. In contrast, the chorus of the song features a thick layer of synthesized strings that is not exotic—although the end of the first chorus is punctuated with a gong. The beginning of "Territories" from *Power Windows* is organized in a similar way. The first verse, which concerns China's attitude toward Hong Kong, uses sustained and plucked string sounds, gongs, and a drone bass, while the chorus reverts to a standard rock-band texture. Both of these examples demonstrate the general rule in rock music that choruses are more stylistically conservative than verses.

In Rush's "A Passage to Bangkok" from *2112* (1976), the Eastern setting of the title and chorus are text-painted by a brief musical cliché nicknamed the "Oriental riff" or "Asian riff" (a riff is a short, repeated melody or chord progression). The "Oriental riff" occurs at the end of the introduction (at 0:07), and again at the end of the solo, before the final two choruses. It acts as a structural marker, framing the beginning and ending of the song. This riff stands out because of its distinctive rhythm, characteristically gapped pentatonic melody, and because it's played at a high pitch, segregated from the rest of the musical texture. In contrast, the melodic quotation of Tchaikovsky's 1812 Overture in Rush's "2112: Overture" is somewhat hidden in the texture, because it's played in the same range as the rhythm guitar. The partial disguise of this musical pun adds to its playful effect.

Versions of the "Oriental riff" have been used in music since the late nineteenth century. The one in "A Passage to Bangkok" was made famous by Carl Douglas in "Kung Fu Fighting" (1974), which uses the riff after the first and third lines of the chorus. Rush's version has the same melody and rhythm, but intensifies the riff by harmonizing it in parallel fifths. Parallel fifths and parallel fourths (which can be heard at the beginning of David Bowie's "China Girl") are another faux-Asian musical cliché.

The main instrumental riff used throughout the verses in "A Passage to Bangkok" is a gapped pentatonic melody with the same intervals as the "Oriental riff." The verse riff is generically exotic: if you hold out the first note and repeat the last note, it becomes the "war chant" sung by sports fans of various Native-American-themed teams. A beginning piano book I had as a child included a song titled "Ming Hing, Laundry Man," with the same melody accompanied in parallel fourths. With a more even rhythm, the melody is almost the same as the beginning of the round "Hey, Ho, Nobody Home," from Renaissance England. So while the "Oriental riff" is associated with Asia, and usually China in particular, this generic exotic riff can sound characteristically Asian, Native American, or old English. It represents a nonspecific otherness.

Alex Lifeson has cited Led Zeppelin's "Kashmir" as an indirect influence on "A Passage to Bangkok" because of its "similar sort of odd-tempo arrangement to the verses" (interview in *Guitar World*, June 3rd, 2009). He might have meant the heavily syncopated vocal melodies of both songs, in which almost all of the notes fall between the beats rather than on them, creating a stretched-out effect. Or he might have meant the disjunction between the instrumental riffs and the vocal melodies, which have slower rhythms and irregular phrases that don't quite line up with the riffs. In both songs, the result of this rhythmic layering is that the melody seems to float above the accompaniment, disconnected from it. This floating, disjointed effect is highly appropriate to the lyrics of "A Passage to Bangkok," which describe a global sampling tour of "only . . . the best" pot, hash, and opium. Zeppelin's "Kashmir" is also a travel song with otherworldly lyrics, although it is less obviously drug-related and more musically exotic than "A Passage to Bangkok." The disconnect between voice and instruments in these two songs is more evocative of a state of mind than a physical place.

In Rush's "Rivendell," ethereal timbres depict the elven sanctuary of J.R.R. Tolkien's *The Lord of the Rings*: gentle mid-range vocals, classical guitar (played by Geddy Lee), soft and slow electric guitar, and no bass or percussion. In the electric guitar part, the volume fades in and out on each note, making their attacks and releases inaudible. This dissociates the sounds from the physical act of playing, enhancing their unearthliness. Lifeson uses a related technique to illustrate 'A Lerxst in Wonderland,' one of the dreamscapes of the extended work "La Villa Strangiato."

Another exotic literary landscape is portrayed in Rush's "Xanadu" from *A Farewell to Kings*, a song inspired by Samuel Taylor Coleridge's poem "Kubla Khan." The lost kingdom of Xanadu is suggested by the wide variety of pastoral nature sounds, synthesized timbres, and unpitched percussion in the long (five-minute!) instrumental introduction. Lifeson uses the same volume-fading technique as in "Rivendell," with a comparable otherworldly effect. The varied timbres in different pitch ranges create a sense of space, and the lack of a consistent regular beat creates a sense of timelessness. The interludes after both choruses, following the invocation "Xa-na-du", evoke its remoteness through abrupt changes in key, instrumentation and texture. A standard rock-band texture in E minor gives way to a delicate glockenspiel and synthesized string sound over an arpeggiated guitar in D major, and the pedal point (a short-term drone) and tubular bell from the introduction return.

Evoking Outer Space

While exotic settings around the globe can be depicted with melodies or rhythms from other musical cultures, exotic settings beyond Earth are best illustrated by avoiding any recognizable melodies and rhythms. Space music has been its own genre since the 1970s, although it was influenced by electronic music and psychedelic rock from the 1960s. The vastness and emptiness of space are typically represented by slow tempos, sustained sounds, echo effects, and very high and low pitch ranges, avoiding the middle—human—pitch range. A classical example that uses most of these techniques is *Thus Spoke Zarathustra* by Richard Strauss, better known as the theme from the movie *2001: A Space Odyssey* (1968). The very low sustained note combined with the high trumpet melody and empty middle range convey a sense of immensity. This is what makes the piece such an effective soundtrack for *2001*, although the music was originally composed to represent the dawn. As a side note, Rush used this theme as an introduction on the *Counterparts* tour (and the *Test for Echo* tour), to accompany a video of the album cover's nut and bolt slowly rotating in space and finally screwing onto one another.

Rush's *2112* song cycle is set on a future Earth governed by the Solar Federation and no longer inhabited by "the elder race of man." The 'Overture' begins with two layers of high-pitched electronic sounds: sustained notes and slow oscillating glissandos (long sliding pitches) over an intermittent low bass. Some of these same effects are used in "Hemispheres" to portray the narrator's passage through the black hole Cygnus X-1 and are also used over the

"Hyperspace" riff in "Natural Science" (beginning at 2:19). The beginning of Hawkwind's "Master of the Universe" from *In Search of Space* (1972) is similar to the opening of *2112* and so is the version of Pink Floyd's "Set the Controls for the Heart of the Sun" from *Live at Pompeii* (1972)—although with low-range pitches instead of high ones.

The generalized space sounds that open *2112* represent a planetary view of the future Earth. In contrast, the nature sounds at the beginnings of "Discovery" (at 6:48) and "Soliloquy" (at 15:58) depict the narrator's specific setting, in a cave behind a waterfall. This shift in perspective is the musical equivalent of a camera zooming in from outer space to a human level. The same shift happens in reverse in the first two sections of "Natural Science" from *Permanent Waves*. The bird calls, lapping water, and strummed guitar in the verse of "Tide Pools" text-paint the natural scene described in the lyrics. In "Hyperspace," the metaphor of tide pools as natural microcosms of human society gives way to an opposing metaphor of computers as artificial microcosms of an increasingly mechanized universe. Although these two sections are connected by a transition (beginning at 1:45, "wheels within wheels"), they are musically opposed in almost every possible way, as shown in the chart below.

"Tide Pools"	**"Hyperspace"**
relaxed tempo	fast, driving tempo
soft to medium dynamics	loud dynamics
regular 4/4 meter	uneven 7/8 meter
no bass or drums	heavy bass and drums
natural sounds	synthesized sounds
clean guitar timbre	distorted heavy-metal timbre
strummed chords	single-line melody
added-note chords	Phrygian mode
mid-range vocals	high-range vocals
long, sustained phrases	short, fragmented phrases

The transition section returns (at 4:30) to connect "Hyperspace" to "Permanent Waves." This final section mediates between the contrasts of the first two sections. The standard rock instrumentation of "Permanent Waves" occupies a middle ground of timbre, texture, dynamics, and tempo. The meter is a strongly defined 4/4 with intermittent metric shifts, blending the regular beat organization of "Tide Pools" with the asymmetry of "Hyperspace." The lyrics call for integrity as a means of reconciling science and nature, art and commerce, and the individual and society. "Permanent Waves" acts as a synthesis of both the music and the lyrics of the previous two sections.

In Rush's "Cygnus X-1" from *A Farewell to Kings*, the distorted spoken prologue is set to a space-music texture of sustained electronic sounds and echoing bell tones, depicting the black hole of the song's title. These sounds return after the narrator's spaceship has crossed the event horizon and been swallowed by the black hole (beginning at 7:13). Another alien musical signifier is the unusual scale at 3:30, 6:34 and 7:03. This scale, called the double harmonic major or "Ahava Rabba" scale, is used in the music of various Eastern cultures and has two scale steps that are abnormally wide (augmented seconds). The lyrics at the second statement of the scale (at 6:34) suggest that it represents the black hole's gravitational field sucking in the narrator's spaceship: "the black hole gains control." The scale is reprised in "Cygnus X-1 Book II: Hemispheres" (at 11:49), when the narrator recounts the descent of his ship into the black hole. Yet another symbol of otherness in "Cygnus X-1" is the series of strangely unrelated chords from 3:20 to 4:54. These chords represent the black hole's interior, which becomes clear when they return in Part III (at 8:33) as Geddy Lee's vocals, sung in a truly inhuman pitch range, describe the descent and dissolution of the narrator inside the black hole.

Evoking Evil

The underlying structure of most music depends on the interplay of tension and stability. Dissonant, unstable intervals or chords often portray moral otherness, or evil, in music. One of the most dissonant intervals in music is the tritone. The tritone has been nicknamed "diabolus in musica" (Latin for "the devil in music"). Although the rumor that this nickname dates back to the Middle Ages is probably not true, it has been in use for at least three hundred years. In any case, for a very long time unresolved tritones, especially when used melodically, have represented evil or ominous things. Two examples of melodic tritones are the first two notes of *The Simpsons* TV theme, and the first two notes of "Maria" from *West Side Story*. These examples do not have negative connotations, because their tritones are resolved by the third melody note (which is the same in both songs).

In Rush's "The Necromancer" from *Caress of Steel* (1975), about an evil wizard who resembles Sauron in *The Lord of the Rings*, the very first two notes form a tritone. A clearer example is the band Black Sabbath's song "Black Sabbath," from the album (surprise!) *Black Sabbath* (1970), about an encounter with Satan. The verse motive is built entirely out of a tritone: the first two notes of the riff are an octave apart (they have the same letter name), and the third note is a tritone away from both of them. In Rush's "Witch Hunt" from *Moving Pictures*, which is about mob hatred and is part of their "Fear Trilogy,"[1] the first two notes of the repeating bass pattern from a tritone. Rush expands on this gesture by using two adjacent chords—not just individual notes—that are a tritone apart: in the first verse, they are the chords at "moon" and "air is thick," repeated at "on" and "lonely torchlit." The first of these chords (on "moon") is unsettling because it is far removed from the overall key (the chords are B minor and F major, in the key of G Dorian). The 'Monsters!' sections in "La Villa Strangiato" feature a prominent tritone between the first and third notes of the riff (from 5:49–6:09 and 7:52–8:16). This melody is actually a quotation from a tune called "Powerhouse" by Raymond Scott, which was used by Carl Stalling in the soundtracks for various Warner Brothers cartoons.

The most famous tritone in Rush's music is at the beginning of "YYZ" from *Moving Pictures*. The song title is the aviation code for Toronto's Pearson International Airport. In the introduction, the two notes of the guitar riff form a descending tritone, and the slow-moving synthesizer line above it spans an ascending tritone. (The synthesizer melody is an unusual example of the Locrian mode, which Metallica established in the 1990s as normative in heavy metal. For centuries before that, it was regarded as unusable because of its tritone above the final, or keynote.) The guitar riff returns briefly at the end to frame the song. In "YYZ" the tritones do not represent evil, just the constant agitated motion of an airport. Neil Peart has explained that the song is "loosely based on airport-associated images. Exotic destinations, painful partings, happy landings, that sort of thing" (*Rush Backstage Club Newsletter*, March

---

[1] Although it now includes four songs, what is still called the "Fear Trilogy" consists of "The Enemy Within" from *Grace under Pressure,* "The Weapon" from *Signals,* "Witch Hunt" from *Moving Pictures,* and "Freeze" from *Vapor Trails.*

1990). A tritone is an especially appropriate symbol for a cross-roads, because it is a symmetrical interval that divides the octave exactly in half: for example, the interval from the note B up to the note F is the same distance as the interval from F up to B. The tri-tone is the only interval that has this bidirectional quality. The sense of instability in "YYZ" is enhanced by the asymmetrical meter of 10/8, a result of the irregular (although catchy) rhythm, which is a musical translation of the Morse code for the letters Y-Y-Z.

Listen to My Music, and Hear What It Can Do

Several of Rush's songs are built around a contrast between acoustic and electric timbres, including "A Farewell to Kings," "Cinderella Man," "The Trees," and "2112." The acoustic-electric contrast in "The Trees" is emblematic of the parable's conflict between the powerful oaks and the oppressed maples, although the different timbres are not specifically associated with either species. In the introduction to "A Farewell to Kings," acoustic gui-tar, flute-like synthesizer, glockenspiel, and birdsong suggest a pas-toral innocence, while the standard rock instrumentation in the body of the song depicts the "cities full of hatred, fear, and lies." The song ends with a cleverly intertextual reference to another song on the album, "Closer to the Heart," which espouses the same themes of idealism and individualism. Neil Peart has described "A Farewell to Kings" and "Closer to the Heart" as identifying societal problems and solutions respectively (Neil Peart, "A Condensed Rush Primer," *A Farewell to Kings Tourbook*, 1977).

In "Cinderella Man," which is loosely based on the movie *Mr. Deeds Goes to Town*, the acoustic-electric distinction more clearly reflects the conflicts between idealism versus authoritarianism, and between the individual versus the state. The lyrics describing Cinderella Man are accompanied by acoustic guitar, punctuated with short bursts of drums and bass, while society's condemnation of him is set to a conventional electric rock texture. There's a sim-ilar musical distinction in "2112" between the idealistic protagonist and the authoritarian priests. In both "Cinderella Man" and "2112," the contrast of acoustic and electric timbres is intensified by a con-trast between Geddy Lee's low and high vocal ranges.

The earlier examples of musical otherness in this chapter—exotic elements, space-music textures, and unresolved dissonant intervals—are easily linked with specific associations. The contrast between acoustic and electric timbres, on the other hand, is a very general one, and need not mean anything at all. Lots of bands use a variety of timbres to maintain interest over the course of an album or concert (Led Zeppelin comes to mind). But electric timbres are normative in rock music, and acoustic ones are more typical of folk music. If one of these two categories represents the "other" in rock, it is the acoustic one. Yet this seems aesthetically inappropriate to represent moral otherness: evil is more convincingly portrayed by electric guitar and bass than, for example, flute and harp. This is partly because of the sonic qualities of these instruments, having to do with range, the way notes are articulated, and the shape of their sound waves, but partly because of the original status of rock music as a genre of rebellion. Its electrified sounds were immediately perceived as transgressive, which is why so many people felt betrayed when Bob Dylan went electric at the 1965 Newport Folk Festival. In the decades since, these sounds have become established as a familiar and even comforting norm. Nevertheless, if Rush are a force of good in the world, as I believe they are, it's ironic that they use their most characteristic musical sounds to represent the bad guys. Perhaps the overall lesson to be learned here, which brings us back to "Entre Nous," is that otherness and difference are not inherently negative qualities. Opposing entities or ideas can be synthesized into a greater whole.[2]

---

[2] Thanks to Justin Biamonte, Jerry Cain, Linda Meyer, Tom Owens, and Glen Vilches for helpful comments on this chapter.

15

The Inner and Outer Worlds of Minds and Selves

TODD SUOMELA

Imagine a close friend invites you to a party and your friend is the only person you know at the party. At the party you meet a young man, probably a college student, and you start talking about the different kinds of music you enjoy. "I love Rush," the young man says to you. How do you respond? If you're a not a philosopher or a skeptic you may agree and then proceed to talk about favorite albums or songs. But to a philosopher the question of belief is a perennial problem. How can you trust what another person says? What are beliefs or opinions? Are they actual mental events or just the firing of certain neurons in the brain? Is there a difference between the contents of the mind and the physical behavior of the body?

The skeptic is ready to doubt anything. Modern philosophy began with René Descartes's famous encounter with skepticism. According to Descartes the only thing he could be sure of was the fact that he was thinking—thus, "Cogito ergo sum" or "I think, therefore I am." Everything else Descartes experienced—other people, physical events such as the melting of a candle—could be doubted. His senses could always deceive him. But when he looked inside himself—looked at the process of thought itself—he believed he had found a ground upon which philosophy could stand. The fact of thought proved existence.

At first it seems natural to agree with Descartes that I have direct access to my own thoughts. It seems as if I can sit in a chair and just think without any other prerequisites. The Cartesian picture is remarkably seductive and easy to grasp because I don't feel any doubt about the process of my own thoughts. There's little room for confusion when I think about my favorite Rush song or remember what it was like to see them in concert, as long as I'm not crazy. But ignoring the possibility that I'm delusional it seems that everyone has the same experiences of being alone with their personal thoughts. Moreover our thoughts seem profoundly private and sometimes difficult to convey to other people through words, but we still know that they're inside our minds. Our personal experience reaffirms the sensation of our own internal thought world every day.

Philosophers are never content to let a basic idea go to waste so they push it as far as possible. René Descartes started with doubt about everything he saw until he felt he came to the certainty of his own thought. Solipsism is the belief that the only things that exist are the ideas in one's own mind. A solipsist would believe that the world is his dream. Physical objects, including other people, are figments of his imagination. No philosophers have actually been solipsists, of course, but many philosophers have been troubled by the fact that it is difficult to come up with a way to prove solipsism wrong. Contemporary philosophers have referred to this as the brain-in-a-vat problem. In popular culture it's like *The Matrix*.

René Descartes acknowledges the radical problem of skepticism, that once you start to doubt everything it becomes impossible to stop. You go on doubting until you reach a foundation and from that foundation you begin to build up your beliefs; philosophy becomes the search for certainty and assurance, for a base that will justify all beliefs, thoughts, feelings, and sensations, everything that we consider to be part of human experience. For Descartes, the final foundation of human experience and thought was God; only God could provide the final ground of our existence and our minds.

Today God is still a powerful motivator and foundation for many people but it isn't the only one. Many scientists and philosophers don't believe in God. The question is: how do they respond to the radical skeptical challenge posed by Descartes and other philosophers since the seventeenth century?

Inner and Outer Worlds

The problem of internal and external worlds is a question posed by Rush in their songs and is a persistent theme across many of their albums, especially those produced during the 1980s—when Rush was internationally more popular than ever before.

Starting with *Moving Pictures*, the lyrics of Rush songs dealt with the problems of reconciling the internal and external worlds again and again. In the song "Limelight" Neil Peart writes about the bizarre experience of fame. "Living on a lighted stage / Approaches the unreal," according to Peart, "I can't pretend a stranger / Is a long-awaited friend." But the problem of fame is just an extreme example of the skeptical thought problem we started with. How can someone in a world-famous rock band tell if the person talking to them is a real fan or just someone who wants to flatter them for some other purpose?

In "The Camera Eye," Peart laments the obliviousness of the people he sees in the city. They seem to move through the rain without recognizing the "sense of possibilities" that he feels. The people around him just continue walking onwards without pausing to see the wonder of the world around them.

The theme of awareness or its lack continues through all five of Rush's subsequent studio albums of the 1980s: *Signals*, *Grace under Pressure*, *Power Windows*, *Hold Your Fire*, and *Presto*. In some songs, the problem is framed as one of escape, whether from the "Subdivisions" on the edge of the city or through "Middletown Dreams." Sometimes it's set as a thin veneer that covers our hidden emotions from other people, or a thin veneer that covers our civilized facade from deeper feelings of anger or resentment. In order to discover these internal depths we need an "Emotion Detector" or a "Lock and Key" that will reveal our actual feelings.

"Show Don't Tell," the first song from *Presto*, is a perfect example of the theme of awareness, trust, and facades.

> Who can you believe?
> It's hard to play it safe.
> But apart from a few good friends,
> We don't take anything on faith. ("Show Don't Tell," *Presto*, 1989)

Apart from close friends we ask for evidence of other people's beliefs and convictions. When someone at a party tells us that they enjoy Rush, we should follow up with further questions. A person who has seen Rush in concert seems likely to be a better fan than someone who hasn't, because he or she has actually acted on their enjoyment of Rush by attending a concert. If we are able to see that person's home, we may observe more evidence of their musical taste by counting the number of Rush CDs or MP3s they own, or observing a concert poster on their wall. Over time, we may get to know a person better and extend trust to them more easily without demanding confirmation, by then they have become a friend just like Neil Peart described in his lyric.

"War Paint," another song from *Presto*, continues the same lyrical theme of dreams, illusions, mirrors, appearances, and vanity. "The mirror always lies," sings Geddy Lee. What we think we see in the mirror, our self-image, is flawed. It shows us what we want to see and hides our feelings from ourselves as much as it hides them from other people. The problem of internal and external confusion has reached its ultimate end point where we don't know whether we are "all puffed up with vanity" or something else more authentic. Peart suggest that our failure to escape from these delusions is part of the reason why we fight wars and get into arguments with other people.

In addition to the lyrics of the songs there is a change in the form of the music during the 1980s that parallels the skeptical problem. Throughout the 1980s synthesizers became an important part of the Rush instrumental toolkit. A synthesizer is an instrumental analog of the problem of skepticism. Synthesizers are able to reproduce sounds from other instruments, and they essentially act as a fake for another instrument. There may be no way for the listener to tell whether a sound came from a synthesizer or some other source. Without actually being at the recording sessions we can only take the words of the artist about where the sounds came from. We must be just as trusting of Rush as of anyone else we might meet.

Pain and Internal Experience

Let's return to the party where we began. In the middle of trying to decide whether the person you just met is really a Rush fan or someone who's lying, there is a sudden sound of breaking glass from the kitchen. You and the potential Rush fan walk into the kitchen to see what has happened. Apparently the host, your friend, dropped a wine glass on the floor and he is now bending over to pick up the pieces. He cries out, utters a curse, and starts clutching his hand. "Damn, I cut myself on the glass," he says to the two of you and you can see the blood on his fingertip. Your friend tells you to get a band-aid from the medicine cabinet. When you return he's washing his hand under the tap. He puts on the band-aid and says "That hurt like hell." So far so normal, but the philosopher keeps pushing us forward. What is this thing called pain? Is it anything like the opinions we have about the music of Rush?

Pain is another mental phenomenon that has challenged philosophers. How can we explain what it is like to be in pain? We all seem to remember what it's like to be in pain, whether it be from a paper cut, a broken wine glass, a headache, or stubbing a toe. These events don't occur every day but they do happen often enough to seem like they have something in common. Philosophers call the common subjective sensations "qualia." They are the properties of our experience that determine "what it is like" to have a particular mental state. Each person has their own unique experience of pain because there doesn't seem to be any way that we can participate in their experience.

Beliefs and opinions, such as whether you like the music of Rush, are, at first glance, similar examples of mental phenomenon. But there is a question whether beliefs are just dispositions to behave in a particular way or if they are internal states. Behaviorists assert that the only real part of a belief is the behavior we observe. So in the case of the Rush fan you met at the party the only way to know if they really do like Rush is to observe their behavior for confirmatory evidence. This is the motto "Show Don't Tell" turned into a complete philosophy.

But saying that the only way to tell if someone likes Rush is to observe their behavior feels as if it misses the experience of having opinions. You, the reader of this book on Rush and philosophy, must surely feel something about Rush that is different from a worker at the printing press who picks up a copy and looks at it to see if the binding is correct. The reader is actually reading and thinking about the words on the page, deciding whether he or she agrees or disagrees with them. To the reader or fan, Rush really is an important band—a band he or she cares about enough to read a book about their music and philosophy.

It is this internal, subjective feeling of possessing opinions, feeling pains, and experiencing other mental states that makes the behaviorist position so difficult to accept. We don't want to accept that we are nothing more than the sum of our actions in the world. We want to believe that there is something unique inside of us that makes our perspective on the world important and valuable to ourselves and others.

The radical skeptic followed doubt until it turned into solipsism. Now the behaviorist has taken us in the opposite direction. Instead of believing in only the internal world of the solipsist the behaviorist only believes in the external actions of other people. For the pure behaviorist there is no internal world of feelings, opinions, or beliefs, just the evidence of the actions that we take. "Show Don't Tell" is a powerful philosophical stance that can be taken too far, to a point where we lose as much as we gain.

Ludwig Wittgenstein Tries to Understand Pain

At the beginning of the twentieth century, a group of philosophers in England and America started a new form of philosophy which came to be called analytic philosophy. For these philosophers the solution to many of the common problems of philosophy could be found by closely examining language. The very words we used to describe the problems of philosophy often caused as much confusion as clarity. By closely examining the underlying logic of language they hoped a solution to problems like the ones we have been discussing could be found.

One of these analytic philosophers was Ludwig Wittgenstein (1889–1951). He was originally from Austria but he spent most of his academic life working at Cambridge University in England. There he met Bertrand Russell, the most famous living philosopher in the first half of the twentieth century. With Russell's support and encouragement, Wittgenstein wrote the *Tractatus Logico-Philosophicus*, the only work he would publish during his lifetime.

Reading the works of Ludwig Wittgenstein is unlike reading any other philosopher. He wrote in a very terse style using numbered paragraphs and sections. In the *Tractatus* these sections were hierarchically ordered (1.0, 1.1, 1.234) and together formed an argument for language as a logical picture of the world. We know language is correct when the picture we have matches up with the rest of the world.

It wasn't until after his death that a new set of manuscripts were published that seemed to contradict the picture of language presented in the *Tractatus*. The most famous of these posthumous works is *Philosophical Investigations*. Like the *Tractatus*, *Philosophical Investigations* is composed of numbered paragraphs and sections, but this time they are merely ordered consecutively from 1 through 693 (for Part I) instead of being arranged in a hierarchy. But reading them is still just as difficult, if not more so. Some sections seem to connect into a single theme, while others comment on the whole by speaking through the voice of the skeptic or the behaviorist. None of the sections seem to present actual arguments; instead they take the form of questions. For Wittgenstein, philosophy does not reach conclusions through argument. Instead, philosophy works more like therapy.

> 133. It is not our aim to refine or complete the system of rules for the use of our words in unheard-of-ways.
>
> For the clarity we are aiming at is indeed complete clarity. But this simply means that philosophical problems should completely disappear.
>
> The real discovery is the one that makes me capable of stopping doing philosophy when I want to. . . .
>
> There is not a philosophical method, though there are indeed methods, like different therapies."[1]

One of the major ideas that Wittgenstein proposes in *Philosophical Investigations* is the view that the meaning of words comes from their use. To a non-philosopher this may seem obvious, but there had been many philosophers before Wittgenstein and more since that words mean by virtue of some connection between the words and the world. When we say that a book is about "Rush" we are referring to a particular trio of Canadian men, who recorded rock music in the late twentieth and early twenty-first centuries.

For Wittgenstein this view of meaning as reference was insufficient. Through a series of examples and questions he attempts to show that names cannot be reduced to their descriptions or any other simple referent. Words could just as easily be perceived as a set of rules that we learn from each other. If a word is present in our language then its meaning comes from its use among the people who share that language. Language was like a game played between people. Through experience and time these people adopted a common set of signs that they used in consistent ways.

From this view of language as a communal activity Ludwig Wittgenstein moved onto one of the most famous portions of *Philosophical Investigations*, the private language argument.

---

[1] Ludwig Wittgenstein, *Philosophical Investigations* (Prentice Hall, 1958), p. 51.

Labeling this an argument is something that later philosophers have added to his work. It is probably more accurate to call private languages a problem than a full-blown argument.

Let's recall the pain we saw our host express after he cut himself on the broken wine glass. Our friend performed a number of actions that we associate with pain, he grabbed his hand, cursed, and told us that he had cut himself. In a move akin to the behaviorist, Wittgenstein asks us to look closely at what we have seen. Does the behavior of our friend really provide evidence for his pain? Could we imagine the same thing happening without the grimace, the grabbing, or the cursing? And if he did respond without those actions wouldn't we question whether he was actually in pain or not?

How do we learn to use a word like "pain?" Doesn't it seem likely that people learn to say pain when they see other people behaving in a certain way? When their parent yells out after stubbing his or her toe, or when a friend at the playground falls to the ground and starts crying, the child learns to call that behavior "pain."

But what happens inside a person's head when they say they are in pain? Here Wittgenstein makes his radical move. There is no way for anyone to know what happens inside another person's head when they experience pain. All we can know is how they react: what words they use to tell us about the experience or the expressions that cross their face. So far this seems like the standard behaviorist explanation. But there is an even further level of questions raised by Wittgenstein. He asks whether it makes any sense to speak of a private sensation or expression of pain or any other mental state.

What would a private expression of pain be like? Suppose someone marks down the letter "S" on a calendar whenever they experience a particular sensation. The problem is indicating what internal sensation is identified by this repeated use of the symbol "S." How can a person know that their memory is accurate or that they are recording the same sensation as before? According to Wittgenstein there is no way to be certain about the repetition of this sensation. "The essential thing about private experience is really not that each person possesses his own exemplar, but that nobody knows whether other people also have this or something else."[2]

---

[2] Wittgenstein, Section 272 of *Philosophical Investigations*.

To further solidify his point Wittgenstein proposes a thought experiment:

> Now suppose someone tells me that he knows what pain is only from his own case! –Suppose everyone had a box with something in it: we call it a "beetle." No one can look into anyone else's box, and everyone says he knows what a beetle is only by looking at his beetle. — Here it would be quite possible for everyone to have something different in his box. One might even imagine such a thing constantly changing. —But suppose the word "beetle" had a use in these people's language? —If so it would not be used as the name of a thing. The thing in the box has no place in the language-game at all; not even as a something: for the box might be empty. —No, one can 'divide through' by the thing in the box; it cancels out, whatever it is.
>
> That is to say if we construe the grammar of the expression of sensation on the model of 'object and designation' the object drops out of consideration as irrelevant."[3]

The true problem is in our language. The grammar of our expressions forces a certain mode of thought upon us when we are doing philosophy. We talk about "having pains" or "having an opinion" and are already committed to a model where an opinion is an object and the word "opinion" designates that object in the mind. When we go searching for the object in the mind we run into a wall of confusion. Instead of finding a pain or opinion that we can point to or remember we are left with a vague insistence that we know what our own thoughts and pains are because we just do. For a philosopher this is not good enough.

Ludwig Wittgenstein realizes that our mental states are not objects like those we see around us every day. Like Descartes, he is willing to question our assumptions about what we think we know for sure, and conclude that internal thoughts are not sufficient because they can be ignored, like the beetle, without doing any damage to language or our actions. We don't need to be certain of what an opinion actually is in order to go on living in a language community with other people. We can continue to be like Rush and wait for other people to show us what they mean instead of telling us what they think.

---

[3] Wittgenstein, Section 293 of *Philosophical Investigations*.

Does Rush Offer a Way Out?

Is there any way to escape from the skeptical confusion we seem to have gotten ourselves into? Neither the solipsist solution of doubting the external world or the behaviorist solution of doubting the internal world seem satisfactory.

Ludwig Wittgenstein pushed the problem even further by examining the role of language with regard to the problem of internal and external states. If the meaning of words is determined by their use in a community of speakers, it seems impossible to have any purely internal solution to the problem. Pain and other mental entities are too diffuse to have a solid referent that we can consistently identify.

Rush offers us a challenge with regard to internal and external feelings and experiences. The only way we can make contact with other people is to open ourselves up to them and be vulnerable. In "Turn the Page" from *Hold Your Fire* (1987), Peart writes:

> Nothing can survive in a vacuum
> No one can exist all alone . . .
>
> It's enough to learn to share our pleasures
> We can't sooth pain with sympathy
> All that we can do is be reminded. ("Turn the Page," *Hold Your Fire*,
>   1987)

Ludwig Wittgenstein wanted to show us that the confusion we feel between the internal and external, between the mental and everything else, is a confusion of our language. We are stuck with a system of words that assume a mental object when none may actually be present. Once we see that the confusion is part of language we're free to continue with our lives, we have been shown the way out of the fly-bottle. Rush finishes the thought by showing us the outside of the fly-bottle where the only thing we have left is other people.

16
Cruising in Prime Time

NICHOLAS P. GRECO

What to say about Geddy Lee's singing voice? Critics seem to think a certain thing about Lee's singing voice, while fans often think the opposite. Critics similarly think a certain way about Neil Peart, whether they're referring to his meticulous and detailed percussion patterns, or his otherworldly, philosophical lyrics. *The New Rolling Stone Album Guide* puts it this way: "Lyricist Peart's mystifying cosmic bent and lead singer Lee's Donald Duck-on-acid howl inspire similar love-it-or-loath-it debates."[1]

Reviewers for *Rolling Stone* magazine have often been most outspoken regarding the nature of Lee's singing voice: "Rupert Hine's deft production [for *Presto*] . . . camouflages Geddy Lee's typically shrill vocals to great advantage."[2] One reviewer calls Lee's voice a "shrill screech" while another comments that "his extremely high voice—either a triumphant cry or a grating yowl—is still a bone of contention. Though Lee can control his singing, he's often unnecessarily strident."[3] Another calls Lee's voice a "dog-calling falsetto shriek."[4] In a more recent review,

---

[1] Mark Coleman and Ernesto Lechner, "Rush," *The New Rolling Stone Album Guide*, fourth edition, edited by Nathan Brackett (Fireside, 2004), p. 710.

[2] Bob Mack, "Recordings: *Presto*," *Rolling Stone* 570 (25th January 1990), p. 51.

[3] David Fricke, "Records: *Power Windows*," *Rolling Stone* 466 (30th January 1986), p. 46; Michael Bloom, "Records: *Hemispheres*," *Rolling Stone* 287 (22nd March 1979), p. 64.

[4] Kurt Loder, "Records: *Grace under Pressure*," *Rolling Stone* 424 (21st June 1984), p. 57.

one critic has the gall to suggest that Lee "sends his voice to the rafters through his nose."[5]

In a discussion regarding the "best rock drummer" on the Internet discussion forum, "HiFi WigWam," user Leonard Smalls writes:

> I tend to have the feeling that Rush don't quite have it . . .
> I mean Geddy's a great bass player, Peart's a great drummer and the Other Guy is a great geetar [sic] player, but somehow it doesn't completely gel for me. There's some bollocks missing (probably Geddy's wot with the state of his voice).[6]

About Rush's earlier work, one critic writes that "Rush's music . . . was typified by Lee's oddly high-pitched voice."[7]

Peart's drumming, on the other hand, is considered "awe-inspiring," and he is praised for being "fluent at a large double kit, also adding colorations on various bells and blocks."[8] In the entry for Geddy Lee in the allmusic Internet database, Peart gets a special mention:

> When Neal [sic] Peart replaced [John] Rutsey [the band's original drummer] one year later, the band's sound and musical direction immediately changed. Gone were the long Zep-jams and in came technically demanding and challenging hard rock, complete with thought-provoking lyrics (courtesy of Peart).[9]

Peart is credited for the complete—and positive—artistic change exhibited by the band. Peart continues his band preservation and improvement, as suggested by J.D. Constantine in a review for

---

[5] Richard Abowitz, "Album Reviews: Rush: *Vapor Trails*," *Rolling Stone* (24th April 2002); available from <www.rollingstone.com/artists/rush/albums/album/302822/review/5944055/vapor_trails>.

[6] Leonard Smalls, "Forum Post: #121—Best Rock Drummer," *HiFi Wigwam*, available from <http://hifiwigwam.com/view_topic.php?id=4478&forum_id=4&jump_to=126205>.

[7] Author Not Cited, "Rush," *The Encyclopedia of Popular Music*, fifth concise edition, edited by Colin Larkin (Omnibus Press, 2007), p. 1211.

[8] Azerrad, "Albums: *A Show of Hands*," p. 100; Bloom, "Records: *Hemispheres*," p. 64.

[9] Greg Prato, "Geddy Lee," *allmusic*, <www.allmusic.com/cg/amg.dll?p=amg&sql=11:h74zeflkhgf4~T1>.

Signals: "Geddy Lee's congested vocals float through the songs like swamp gas. Ultimately, it's up to drummer Neil Peart's hyperkinetic thrashing to hold the performances together."[10] In the music of Rush, though, you can't often listen to Peart's drumming without listening to Lee's singing voice (unless you're listening to one of the instrumentals).

Many fans think differently from the critics, and this contrary view to the critics is particularly strong. Durrell Bowman suggests that "Rush—by making musicianly, instructive music out of combinations involving progressive rock, hard rock, and heavy metal—responded to those rock fans who found rock critics to be a wearied and self-indulgent lot."[11] Bowman goes on to suggest that *Rolling Stone* was suspect as a legitimate countercultural publication, harbouring commercial interests. Why, though, would the critics react toward Rush negatively, citing Lee's voice as the catalyst for hatred? Bowman suggests that such a reaction is a result of the disconnect between critics and Rush:

> Rush fans—working-class and middle-class—pointed to the band's professionalism, strong work ethic, good role model, unique music, and its ability to succeed outsider of popular trends—in other words, many of the things about industrial/capitalist individualism that mystified the community of Marxian-leaning rock critics. (pp. 77–78)

Furthermore,

> Marxian rock critics found Rush's music annoyingly inconsistent according to class and subcultural criteria—rock was supposed to respond, not evolve; to react, not adapt; to hit your gut first and ask questions later. On the other hand, many post-countercultural rock fans felt that Rush's music did all of these things. (p. 80)

Getting Help from Roland Barthes

Fans of Rush like most aspects of the band. Many fans love Geddy Lee's voice (bah humbug to the critics) just as fans are enraptured

---

[10] J.D. Constantine, "Records: *Signals*," *Rolling Stone* 381 (28th October 1982), p. 74.

[11] Durrell Bowman, "Permanent Change: Rush, Musicians' Rock, and the Progressive Post-Counterculture" (UCLA, PhD dissertation in Musicology, 2003), p. 71. <http://durrellbowman.com/PDFS/DBowman_dissertation.pdf>.

by Peart's lyrics. Often as is the case, though, when a fan picks up a new Rush album—or any album for that matter—she might not like it right away. It might not click. It might take a few listens.

What's going on here, then? What keeps the fan listening for those first few listens, before the music clicks? How is that pleasure teased from the fan in these first listens? Well, for one thing, the fan knows from past experience what to expect. Secondly, there are elements, of distraction, say, that keep the fan enthralled. A friend once told me that he needs to work at listening to "Tom Sawyer" because of Lee's voice, but finds an infinite amount of pleasure from hearing Peart's drumming in that song. For my friend, Peart's drumming is a welcome distraction from the incessant singing by Lee. How different might this be from those times when we listen to a new album and need to "work" through it—listen to it multiple times—just because it fails to click with the first listen?

Roland Barthes (1915–1980) often writes about desire and how we gain pleasure when we read a novel or some type of literature. His ideas have been applied to the study of various other "texts," like music and even television interviews (I've done this), to try to get to the bottom of why and how we, as "readers" of these "texts," gain pleasure from them. The point is, why do we enjoy these kinds of things?

Barthes tries to get at this by introducing the term "cruising." He attempts to define what he means by stating, "Cruising is the voyage of desire. The body is in a state of alert, on the lookout for its own desire."[12] Like much of Barthes's writing, this definition can be befuddling. Barthes is making an analogy: the idea of "cruising" a text for pleasure is like looking for sexual liaison or, as he calls it, the "erotic quest"—the idea of "cruising" for a lover. Here, Barthes is writing about the consumer of a "text," and, in our case, the listener of Rush. He suggests that cruising is "an act that repeats itself, but its catch is absolutely fresh." We return to listening to Rush's music, continually listening for those pleasurable moments; we expect them, but somehow they continue to be fresh with each listening. My friend will go back to listen to "Tom Sawyer" and repeatedly struggle through the "howls" and "shrieks" of Lee's singing voice to experience the "awe-inspiring" moments of percussion from Peart.

---

[12] Roland Barthes, "Twenty Key Words for Roland Barthes," *The Grain of the Voice: Interviews 1962–1980* (Hill and Wang, 1985), pp. 230–31.

For Barthes, "cruising" is "related to the catch of sentences, citations, turns of phrase, fragments." In other words, part of what goes on while "cruising" a text is a kind of relishing in something Barthes calls "the catch of sentences." The idea of a "catch" in music will be discussed in more detail later. For now, it seems that this pleasure is also found in what Barthes considers "fragments." Perhaps it's in this way that one might approach the music of Rush and, in particular, the drumming of Neil Peart.

Catch the Spit

The music of Rush is full of "catches," or "hooks." The music of Rush is divided, fragmented into phrases. The listener takes in these naturally repeating fragments, but which it can be argued; continue to be "absolutely fresh." Examples of such repeating fragments are the choruses and verses that make up a Rush song. The listener "cruises" these sung sentences, these turns of phrase, these moments, for a kind of "happiness of chance, but chance that is wished-for, quite thought-out," as Barthes would characterize it.

The listener might expect pleasure in turning on a song in the first place. After all, if the song is by Rush, it happens to be a showcase for a particular band and a particular style of music. The music can make up a promotional or advertisement for the album. Back to Barthes, he also writes about the author of a text—or, in this case, the songwriters and performers of a song or album— which might inform thinking about the role of the song as a text to be "cruised." He suggests that the text is created in order to be "spied upon," to be the object of a gaze, in a way. In terms of listening to a single, the voice and music are subject to an aural gaze, a "cruising" gaze that is looking for pleasure, for chance happiness found in the fragments, a pleasure that is repeated in the "catch" of sentences. If thought of in this way, then, the single asks to be listened to, to become a source of pleasure for the listener. This is especially the case when the song is by Rush and listened to by their fans.

Barthes's term seems to fit well with how others have thought about pleasure being gained from listening to all sorts of popular music. One of the well established tropes of pleasure in popular music is the "hook," the musical or lyrical fragment that acts as a base from which—and to which—the listener is "hooked." For Barthes, "cruising is an act that repeats itself, but its catch is absolutely fresh." It is "the search for novelistic features. What offers itself in the surprise of the 'first time.'" In other words, there is knowledge of what is found at that site of desire, but there is a novelty to it as well, as if there is a first meeting, "freshness" to the particular "catch." As Rush fans, we continue to listen to the band because we just know that good things are going to come to us from every new album.

In an article exploring the nature of musical "hooks" in popular music, Gary Burns suggests "the word 'hook' connotes being caught or trapped, as when a fish is hooked, and also addiction, as when one is hooked on a drug."[13] He goes on to explain, "a radio listener, passing by, so to speak, is caught or trapped by 'a "catch" phrase or melody line' and may become hooked in the addictive sense as a result of how memorable and recurrent the phrase is." Devin McKinney suggests that hooks fall into the category of "jagged musical tool," and that they are "hard sharp implements designed to hold a thing in place."[14] There is the idea, then, that a "hook" is both pleasurable as well as repetitive (the fact that Burns uses terms like "trapped" and "addiction" might work rather strongly against the idea of pleasure, though). They are also, according to McKinney, constrictive and perhaps violent or dangerous; the sharpness of a hook holds not only the listener (McKinney's "thing") but also the piece of music. These hook moments are both the ground (stability) and the air (freedom and pleasure)—the sites of pleasure for which one searches.

McKinney suggests that the critic's role of analyzing what he calls the "mechanics and mystery of the pop moment" is "cruising a road to nowhere: 'cruising' with its pleasurable associations of ease, adventure, and incidental delight, 'nowhere' with its darker implications of displacement, disarticulation, confusion of identity and idea" (p. 312).

As the Wheels of Time Just Pass You By

Barthes not only writes about "cruising" as a voyage of desire, but also explores "cruising" as a kind of power of distraction:

---

[13] Gary Burns, "A Typology of 'Hooks' in Popular Records," *Popular Music* 6:1 (January 1987), p. 1.

[14] Devin McKinney, "Cruising a Road to Nowhere: Mechanics and Mysteries of the Pop Moment," *Popular Music* 24:3 (October 2005), p. 319.

here is the list of distractions I incur every five minutes: spray a mosquito, cut my nails, eat a plum . . . check the faucet to see if the water is still muddy (there was a breakdown in the plumbing today), go to the drugstore, walk down to the garden to see how many nectarines have ripened on the tree, look at the radio-program listings, rig up a stand to hold up my papers, etc: I am cruising.[15]

The apparently mundane tasks that Barthes describes are embarked upon with a kind of passion by the early socialist visionary Charles Fourier, "the passion of papillonnage [flitting like a butterfly], the craving for periodic variety in the phases of life, and for frequent variety in our occupations."[16] In other words, the mundane adds variety and excitement. These activities make other activities possible; through these distractions, Barthes finds pleasure. Thus, cruising is a kind of distraction, a break from the mundane through the mundane.

Barthes further hints at what he means by "cruising" in the preface of Renaud Camus's novel *Tricks*:

Repetition is an ambiguous form; sometimes it denotes failure, impotence; sometimes it can be read as an aspiration, the stubborn movement of a quest which is not to be discouraged; we might very well take the cruising narrative as the metaphor of a mystical experience.[17]

Nicholas de Villiers calls this mystical experience "the desire for the new, the unexpected, for difference—thus not 'picking' or 'choosing' but 'cruising.'"[18]

As mentioned, then, a "hook" can be thought of as a "catch" and or, as Barthes calls it, a "stubborn movement of a quest," but also a distraction from the everyday. It removes the listener from the task at hand, whatever that might be. It may remove the listener from his immediate context and transports the listener to the site of

---

[15] Roland Barthes, *Roland Barthes* (Berkeley: University of California Press, 1994), 71-72.

[16] Charles Fourier, "Of the Role of the Passions," *Selections from the Works of Fourier* (Swan Sonnenschein,1901), p. 60; available from <www.questia.com/PM.qst?a=o&d=1294467>.

[17] Roland Barthes, "Preface to Renaud Camus' *Tricks*," *The Rustle of Language* (Hill and Wang, 1986), p. 294.

[18] Nicholas de Villiers, "A Great Pedagogy of Nuance: Roland Barthes's *The Neutral*," *Theory and Event* 8:4 (2005), paragraph 11.

pleasure, of experiencing pleasure. The "hook" can also be a kind of distraction from the mundanity of the song itself. The moments of pleasure occur within a musical context that is not necessarily completely pleasurable; the "hook" catches the listener and allows her to continue to listen to a song. When we listen to Rush's song "Tom Sawyer," for instance, for Neil Peart's drum parts only, those parts act as "distractions." My friend, who needs to work at listening to "Tom Sawyer" because of Lee's voice, "cruises" the song for the drumming parts that allows him to patiently listen to the other parts of the song. Such a point can be made also when a listener "works through" a new song by a group that she likes, before she "likes" that song (when, perhaps, "it takes a few listens" to like it).[19]

The mundanity of the moment itself might also be a source of pleasure. McKinney states:

> One thing we enjoy about the moment is that it's only a moment, it has no future, it obviates the idea of a future. Suddenly we're free to not care what a thing does, where it leads, what good or bad it will do to us, what it will teach anyone about life and how to live it—i.e. free not to care what the thing means.[20]

If Barthes's notion of "cruising" suggests the promise of pleasure, the expectation and repetition of pleasure in time, McKinney's notion suggests the pleasure that occurs out of time. Barthes writes about looking for chance encounters as sites of pleasure, while McKinney explores what it means at these sites of pleasure. McKinney's notion might be more akin to Barthes's distraction, where one is "free not to care what the thing means," but simply that it would break up the day, and allow one to escape from the mundanity of regular time.

The analog that both Barthes and McKinney use, that of "cruising the text," allows us to begin to understand the process behind the desire for pleasure that comes from the text, which, in this case, are songs by Rush. The intricate drumming of Neil Peart acts as a kind of distraction, an example of "cruising" which allows the listener to work through the song, to listen to the mundane parts of the song in order to reach Peart's drum flourishes, which "hook" the listener.

---

[19] I am indebted to Michael J. Gilmour for this point.
[20] McKinney, "Cruising a Road to Nowhere," p. 320.

Cruising in Prime Time

In "Between the Wheels," from Rush's 1984 album *Grace under Pressure*, the listener is carried through the song by the rhythm section, and a prime mover in this is Neil Peart. Geddy Lee's vocal delivery is somewhat lackluster and straightforward. Unlike some of his other vocal performances ("Closer to the Heart" comes immediately to mind), this one is devoid of explicit emotion. While some of his lyrical delivery seems to have some power behind it (for instance, when he sings, "Cruising in prime time," a lyric which hearkens back to Barthes's theoretical notion), the emotion seems to be quelled by the smooth production made evident by the keyboard bed laid down beneath the vocals. Alex Lifeson's guitar seems to serve simply as accompaniment (and standard accompaniment, at that), until his particularly potent guitar solo toward the end of the song. The constant in the song, and the element which injects the song with its innate energy, is Peart's drumming. The sheer drive of the rhythm that Peart produces might be somewhat overwhelming to the listener, and thus might constitute a kind of "mundane," something that the listener uses to "pass the time," so to speak.

Another example of this kind of drumming might be heard at the very beginning of "Animate" from *Counterparts* (1993). This does not mean that Peart's drumming is worthless in the musical context of the song, but rather that the drumming serves as a distraction from the other elements of the song. Peart's drumming can be thought of as the impetus for the listener to continue to listen, and, like Barthes's daily routines, allows her to find pleasure in the fragments.

Peart's drum rolls, as well as the various moments of rhythmic stress, seem to act as a kind of distraction from the mundanity of the vocal performance and the guitar accompaniment (for now, Lee's bass lines are simply ornamentation—the keyboards seem to be more prominent in this recording than even Lee's bass lines). In a way, the listener might seek those rhythmic moments—rolls, the syncopations that Peart performs on the cymbals just prior to and during the chorus—as a break, a distraction, from the rest of the song. One might need these things to get them through the task of slogging through the song. And, in fact, these moments (and, it might be argued, Peart's performance as a whole) serve to bring pleasure to the listener. The listener "cruises" the text of the song by riding Peart's cymbals in that syncopated section, by waiting for one roll and being propelled toward the next. Pleasure comes in these breaks and fragments, where the "richness" of Lee's voice is broken, paused, and the precision of Peart's rhythm is allowed room to shine.

"Tom Sawyer"—The Distracted Audience

Walter Benjamin writes of distraction in the context of film. He suggests that the film, unlike more traditional forms of art, works against the idea of a spectator being absorbed by a work of art. Film moves quickly, without time for the viewer to contemplate what is going on in the sequence of images. Instead of being absorbed by or immersed in the work of art (being enveloped by a painting, for instance), "the distracted mass . . . absorbs the work of art into itself."[21] Benjamin calls this reception of art as "reception in a state of distraction that to an increasing extent is becoming apparent in all fields of art." Benjamin seems to make a critical remark regarding these new kinds of art suggesting that, now, "the audience is an examiner, but a distracted one."

A distracted audience, one that absorbs a work of art, might find pleasure in the distractions which it encounters in a song like "Tom Sawyer," from *Moving Pictures*, released in 1981. Not only is this one of Rush's most popular—or certainly, one of the most recognizable—songs, but it has gained a kind of esteemed position in popular music culture. In some ways, it has become a bit of a caricature of Prog Rock, in that it is just too much. It has been the song of choice for many air guitarists (and a cadre of air drummers, of which I am a part). The complex rhythm, which Peart supplies as a basis for the song, propels the song forward, and, in turn, propels the listener forward.

One notable portion of the song is the guitar solo. Here, even while Lifeson begins to play the solo, the bass and percussion are more easily heard against the frantic single melody of the guitar. There are other moments in the song when there is very little musical accompaniment to Lee's vocal line; the accompaniment is made up of Peart's steady drum beat and Lee's own static synthesized

---

[21] Walter Benjamin, *The Work of Art in the Age of Mechanical Reproduction* (Penguin, 2008), 1–50.

sustain (a sound which might also include Lifeson's guitar, but also as a sustained sound, rather than as an active melody or rhythmic figure). In these moments (the fragmented moments, to return to Barthes's ideas), the listener is drawn, I would argue, to the drums which propel the song forward. These moments are kinds of mundane moments, moments in which Peart's rhythm has room to move. As McKinney suggests, it's only a moment, it has no future and we as listeners are free to not care what the moment does, or how the moment functions. We find pleasure.

The keyboard parts in "Tom Sawyer" are almost like Lee's vocals in this recording; that is, they sound dated. Arguably, the listener treats these keyboard parts like the vocals: they need to work through these parts, to slog through the lesser parts to those portions that bring particular (and short-lived) pleasure. It is the drumming that is most evident during Lifeson's guitar solo, and the drummer's ability to propel the song forward, landing finally on a percussive flourish of monumental proportions. Once these distraction moments—these moments of pleasure—pass, the listener must continue to work, to again find pleasure when it comes. The listener works, absorbs the song into herself, examining the work for those moments of pleasure, looking for those distractions to get through the mundanity of the song, cruising the song for pleasure.

Counterparts: Lee's Voice and Peart's Drums

What to say, then, of Geddy Lee's singing voice? It acts as a counterpart to Neil Peart's drumming. Because of the singing voice, the listener turns to the drumming as distraction from it. In that distraction, the listener finds pleasure. Because of the interaction of these counterparts, the voice and the drums, the distracted listener "cruises" the text. In that "cruising," the listener finds pleasure, a pleasure that a listener, as a fan of Rush, expects to find, but one which is novel as well. With all of the disparaging remarks concerning Lee's voice, it is an integral counterpart in the quest for pleasure in the music of Rush.

The Blacksmith
and the Artist

17

What Can This Strange Device Be?

TIMOTHY SMOLKO

Do we realize how much we resemble machines in our daily activities? Did citizens in pre-industrial societies live more "authentic" lives? Do we use technology or does it use us?

Each of us confronts technology in both frightening and enlightening ways on a daily basis, even if we are not fully conscious of it. The struggle with technology is pervasive in our culture, our technocracy, from the high-school kid learning to use his new iPhone to the unclear scientist (ahem, nuclear scientist) studying quarks and leptons.

Neil Peart is one such citizen technocrat who has spent much time pondering the dilemmas that confront us and articulating them in Rush's lyrics. Throughout their careers the three members of Rush have written numerous cautionary tales about technology, and used a vast amount of technology to broadcast them! Peart's lyrics show an ambivalent attitude towards technology, while Rush's music and stage shows demonstrate an affirmative stance towards it.

What does Aristotle have to teach us about technology? Are the ancient Greeks even relevant in this discussion? According to Martin Heidegger in his 1954 essay, *The Question Concerning Technology*, the answer is clearly "yes." Understanding the Greek notion of technē, and how Heidegger contrasts it with our modern view of technology, will give us insight into what Neil Peart has written about it.

Our word "technology" comes from the Greek word technē. Yet to the Greeks technē meant much more than our conception of technology. In Book VI of his *Nicomachean Ethics*, Aristotle wrote that technē contains within it the concept of alētheuein, which means "revealing," or "getting things true." Heidegger fleshes out this connection between technē and alētheuein in Greek thought by saying that technē seeks to reveal the essence of the materials that are used to create things. Richard Rojcewicz puts it this way: "technology is seeing, rather than doing; and its proper realm is truth rather than instrumentality, knowledge of Being rather than manufacture of artifacts."[1]

So, is our view of modern technology equivalent to the Greek view of technē? Do we reveal the essence of the materials we use to make things? What do we make? What do you make? Look around your world, your workplace, your house, your town or city. What artifacts of human invention surround you? What we create reveals much about ourselves and our view of the planet. If we create objects that are meaningful and enduring to others and ourselves, then that reveals meaning, care and purpose in ourselves. Conversely, if we create objects that are vacuous and ephemeral, then that reveals emptiness and purposelessness in ourselves.

Lamentably, much of what we create today is disposable. We value creating things that make our lives more convenient in the short term, rather than things that make our lives truer in the long run. What does that say about our attitude towards the Earth? The Earth is disposable and we view it and value it in terms of raw materials. We use it for our convenience. Much of modern technology has gone beyond working with nature to utilize its bounty, to using nature's resources to create products of convenience. Heidegger writes in his essay that we are challenging nature, ravishing it, and stripping it of its essence.

Neil Peart has addressed this state of affairs in several Rush songs. When Peart writes about the effects of technology on our culture, he takes a cautionary tone more often than an affirmative one. "Beneath, Between, and Behind" recounts the growth of America with lines such as: "Tame the trackless waste. No virgin land left chaste." "Grand Designs" is an observation on mass production: "So much style without substance. So much stuff without style. Shapes and forms against the norms."

"Closer to the Heart" speaks to this issue most pointedly. Peart and co-lyricist Peter Talbot address several human vocations such

---

[1] Richard Rojcewicz, *The Gods and Technology: A Reading of Heidegger* (State University of New York Press, 2006), p. 62.

as politicians ("the men who hold high places"), blacksmiths, artists, philosophers and ploughmen and entreat them all to pursue alētheuein in their technē. They should all strive to create something meaningful, something that has long-term value, something from the heart. The unspoken critique implicit in the lyrics is that too much of what we make is "away from the heart," away from the essence of the materials we use. Another line from "Grand Designs" is relevant here: "so much mind on the matter / the spirit [meaning the essence] gets forgotten about."

I'm Working All the Time

Any discussion about the effects of technology on our culture leads us to that great bearded wonder, Karl Marx. Both Marx and Rush have had something to say about the predicament of the worker under capitalism.

Two of the more important problems that Marx exposed within unregulated capitalism and the Industrial Revolution were that they created a new conception of time which governed the lives of laborers, and that they alienated laborers from what they made, and from themselves. In Chapter 10 of his great work, *Das Kapital*, Volume I, Marx considers the typical working day of a laborer in mid-nineteenth-century England. The working day was frequently twelve hours, and work usurped the laborer's time for education and intellectual activity, social intercourse, rest and sleep, fresh air and sunlight, and the healthy maintenance of the body.

In the sparse lyrics of "Working Man" (from *Rush*, 1974), we see a day in the life of a typical modern worker, who appears to be in a similar predicament. The protagonist gets up at seven, goes to work by nine and gets home at five. The song is primarily about how much time he spends working and how little time he has for actually "living": "I got no time for living, yeah, I'm working all the time."

In his book, *Technics and Civilization*, Lewis Mumford wrote that to make time "arbitrarily rule over human functions is to reduce existence itself to mere time-serving and to spread the shades of the prison-house over too large an area of human conduct."[2] Echoing Mumford, Neil Postman writes "beginning in the

---

[2] Lewis Mumford, *Technics and Civilization* (Harcourt, Brace, 1963), p. 271.

fourteenth century, the clock made us into time-keepers, and then time-savers, and now time-servers. In the process, we have learned irreverence toward the sun and the seasons, for in a world made up of seconds and minutes, the authority of nature is superseded."[3]

Although Geddy Lee wrote the lyrics of "Working Man," Peart expresses similar sentiments about our continued subservience to time in our post-industrial age. In "The Camera Eye," Peart describes the denizens of New York City as "pacing in rhythm, race the oncoming night, they chase through the streets of Manhattan." Life is reduced to pace, race, and chase. Peart also likes to speak of time as a machine, and in "Between the Wheels" Peart refers to time as a wheel, a metonym for a machine. The song has such lines as "Wheels can take you around. Wheels can cut you down." He also describes, in dystopian terms, the condition of humanity as a victim of time, a casualty of time: "To live between a rock and hard place in between time," "a dizzying lifetime," "the wheels of time just pass you by," and "struck between the eyes by the big-time world." Time, as dictated by modern industry, is a machine that humanity cannot control.

Artisanship versus Mass Production in "2112"

To consider the second Marxian dilemma, that modern industry alienates workers from what they make, and from themselves, let's look at "2112" (from 1976). This tale is about an idealistic young man in a future oppressive culture (The Solar Federation) ruled by "priests." In the lyrics and narrative sections of "2112", the priests are portrayed using allusions to machines.   They have "grey, expressionless faces," and their "great computers fill the hallowed halls."

They use technology to control their subjects, as evidenced by the daily activities of the young man (in the liner notes that accompany the album): "I used to think I had a pretty good life here, just plugging into my machine for the day, then watching Templevision or reading a Temple Paper in the evening." The iconography on the gatefold record sleeve (showing computer circuits and the "man against star" logo, a symbol of the individual against the masses) also reinforces the impression that the protagonist is up against a society that finds its identity through modern technology, a "tech-

---

[3] Neil Postman, *Amusing Ourselves to Death* (Penguin, 1985), p. 11.

nocracy." Peart describes Megadon, the city where the protagonist lives, as if it were a factory with the citizens as worker drones, cogs in the machine of the Federation.

The protagonist doesn't realize the full extent of his oppression until he finds a guitar, a relic from the twentieth century. He teaches himself how to tune and play it and presents it to the priests, hoping they will see the value in it. The priests regard it as a threat to their culture, ridicule him and destroy the instrument. He then has a dream about how life was before the Federation took over. Humans valued personal expression and used their individual gifts and skills to create things that benefited themselves and others directly: "I see . . . the pure spirit of man revealed in the lives and works of this world" and "I see the works of gifted hands that grace this strange and wondrous land." These lyrics from "2112" closely echo the sentiments in "Closer to the Heart," discussed earlier. The protagonist sees people banding together and coming to overthrow the rule of the priests, but then realizes it is only a dream. He dies in despair.

In this tale Peart is expressing a dichotomy between artisanship and mass production. Playing the guitar (the active pursuit of self-expression) is set against "plugging into my machine for the day" (the passive pursuit of mindless work). In the former, the protagonist works with the machine to create something of value to him and others. In the latter, the protagonist is "plugged into" the machine and his identity is circumscribed by it. The culture fashioned by these priests has no alētheuein in its technē. It alienates the protagonist from his own essence. He is viewed simply as raw material, like the Earth, in the eyes of the priests. Moving on from technē and modern technology, in the next section I will explore other ways in which Peart reflects on the impact of technology on our culture.

Handle with Kid Gloves

Technology philosopher Andrew Feenberg defines technocracy as "a wide-ranging administrative system that is legitimated by reference to scientific expertise rather than tradition, law, or the will of the people."[4] In other words, a society that makes its decisions based primarily on scientific reasoning and rhetoric is a technocracy.

---

[4] Andrew Feenberg, *Questioning Technology* (Routledge, 1999), p. 4.

A major problem in a technocracy like America is that many times the impact and ramifications of a new technology cannot be ascertained until the technology has been embedded into the culture. "Our causes can't see their effects," as Peart writes in "Natural Science." A scientist or engineer may speculate on how a new technology will impact the lives of humans in the future, but history has proven that technology takes us into social, political and ethical areas we could not have foreseen.

In "Manhattan Project" (1985), Peart addresses this issue in connection with the bombing of Hiroshima at the end of World War II. Although President Truman alone had the authority to bomb Hiroshima and Nagasaki, to what extent were J. Robert Oppenheimer and the other scientists accountable for the decision? Did the sheer fact that the construction of such an atomic bomb was possible make the use of it inevitable? In this case, Peart seems to think so: "whoever found it first / would be sure to do their worst / They always had before . . ."

Although most historians agree that the bombing was necessary to end the war with Japan, some think that it was a heinous war crime, a psychological attack mostly on the civilian population rather than a military maneuver, and the opening of a Pandora's box full of weapons of mass destruction making the doomsday paranoia of the Cold War a certainty. As stated in "Manhattan Project": "All the powers that be / and the course of history / would be changed for evermore . . ." by the bomb.

Technology progresses so quickly and influences human activity so pervasively, that we have little opportunity to ponder the possible implications or repercussions of it. Philosophers of technology call this view "technological determinism." As Jeff Goldblum's character Dr. Ian Malcolm says in *Jurassic Park* (1993): "Your scientists were so preoccupied with whether or not they could, they didn't stop to think if they should."

Some philosophers, such as Jacques Ellul and Jean Baudrillard, have gone so far as to espouse the view of "Autonomous Technology," which asserts that we have already lost control of our technology (as the scientist Frankenstein lost control of his monster in Mary Shelley's novel). They believe that we have passed the era when we had an opportunity to choose whether or not to use a new technology; now it inexorably thrusts itself upon us and we must accept it. Peart doesn't go this far and believes that technology is still within our control (for now!). He sees the dangers of technology not simply in technology itself, but in the human employment of it. As he says in "New World Man," a personification of America: "He's got a problem with his power / with weapons on patrol / he's got to walk a fine line / and keep his self-control."

Video Vertigo

The working conditions of the Industrial Revolution and the nuclear annihilation scare of the Cold War era are long ago and far away now (phew!) and we have finally learned to control our technology, right? Unfortunately, this is not the case. The forests are still turned to factories (to borrow a phrase from "Scars") and the Doomsday Clock is never more than a few minutes from midnight. And we now have a vast new array of machines to plug ourselves into!

Along with such media theorists as Marshall McLuhan and Neil Postman, Peart has voiced his concerns about how media technology has changed news reporting. In theory, television news is supposed to be the "medium" between the viewer and important events that occur in our world. Following McLuhan's line of thinking ("the medium is the message"), Postman has pointed out that the news event is no longer the focus of reporting. The manner in which news is reported is now the "event."

In "Test for Echo" (1996), Peart refers to this as "video vertigo." An automobile accident is treated as if was an action film: "Camera curves over caved-in cops cars." A legal case is turned into a soap opera: "don't touch that dial—we're in denial until the showcase trial on TV" (a reference to the O.J. Simpson trial). The reporting itself becomes the event, the news is transformed into entertainment, and the six o'clock news becomes the "sense o'clock news" ("sense" as in sensation, not as in wisdom!). So where does all this leave us? Surely Rush has some positive things to say about technology? Indeed they do, which makes this topic in their lyrics so intriguing and paradoxical, and reflects how many of us feel about technology.

Technology . . . High

While Peart has written about how machines oppress us, he also has written on how they empower us. The protagonist in "2112" presents to the Priests a guitar, itself a machine. The difference between the machines of the Priests and the machine of the protagonist is that his is "closer to the heart," it is a technē with alētheuein. Peart is an overt proponent of space exploration and has written many songs about it such as "Countdown" (about the first space shuttle launch in 1981, which Rush witnessed). Peart has also written much about how modern transportation has made the whole world more accessible to all people, and how encountering other cultures teaches you about yourself and your preconceived notions of others ("Fly by Night," "Dreamline," "Ghost Rider"). He has written four books on his world travels by bicycle, motorcycle, and automobile. Yet Rush's embracing attitude towards technology comes out most unequivocally in their music. But before we turn to their music, let's take one last look at technology in Neil Peart's lyrics.

Emotion Detector

Neil Peart writes with focus and conciseness, identifying the nucleus of an idea then forming an electron cloud of viewpoints to surround and balance it. His craft lies in sequencing well-balanced phrases, using a variety of modes of expression, borrowing and subtly altering quotes from other writers, analyzing a topic from many different angles, and paring down his thoughts to their barest essentials to give them the most impact. Peart has a distinctive way of using the language of technology and science to give new perspectives on emotions, memory, and relationships.

Peart's lyrics resemble a poetic device called the "metaphysical conceit," commonly associated with seventeenth-century English poets such as George Herbert and John Donne. A metaphysical conceit employs an extended metaphor to describe something in unconventional terms. Can emotions be expressed in rock lyrics not only with the conventional clichés that we're familiar with, but with scientific terminology? In "Vital Signs" (1981), Peart describes how emotions, misunderstandings and memories constitute the unpredictable nature of human relationships. Yet a quick perusal of some of the phrases in the song might lead one to believe that Peart was reading the "troubleshooting" section in the technical manual for his newest electronic drum kit: "circuits get shorted," "signals get crossed," "reverse polarity," "random sample," "process information at half speed." At first glance, the disjuncture between what Peart is describing and how he is describing it can be unsettling. Peart writes of the song:

> Lyrically, it derives from my response to the terminology of "Technospeak," the language of electronics and computers, which often seems to parallel the human machine, in the functions and inter-relationships they employ. It is interesting, if irrelevant, to speculate as to whether we impose our nature on the machines that we build, or whether they are merely governed by the inscrutable laws of Nature as we. (Perhaps Murphy's Laws?) Never mind![5]

In "Chemistry" (lyrics by Lee, Lifeson and Peart), more "Technospeak" is used to explore the ways in which humans communicate without using language. With words such as "signals," "energy," "reaction," "telepathy," and "synergy," the lyrics describe body language, eye contact, the symbiotic connection between musicians and the connection between musicians and their audience. In "Virtuality," Peart describes how relationships and human communication have reached new dimensions through the technology of the Internet. He applies the "message in a bottle" trope to cyberspace: "put your message in a modem and throw it in the Cyber Sea." "Net boy, net girl, send your heartbeat 'round the world."

If insight into human emotions and communication can be gained by using technological verbiage, what does that say, philosophically, about us? Is the human body really a "soft machine"? Can our emotions be mapped through cyberspace, or along the neural network in our heads? When have we crossed the line from human to machine? In "The Body Electric," Peart crosses that line in telling the story of an android who can exercise his own will, feels human emotions, and has religious sensibilities.

Carol Selby Price, in her book *Mystic Rhythms: The Philosophical Vision of Rush*, maintains that the robot is just a metaphor for a human, "a compliant consumer and conformer"[6] who is seeking freedom from an oppressive society. An equally legitimate reading would be that Peart is describing an actual robot

---

[5] Neil Peart, Tour book from Rush's *Moving Pictures* tour, 1981, available at <www.2112.net/powerwindows/MPtourbook.htm>.

[6] Carol Selby Price and Robert M. Price, *Mystic Rhythms: The Philosophical Vision of Rush* (Borgo Press, 1998), p. 29.

here and is exploring the boundaries between human and robot. These boundaries have continually confounded philosophers because each time new technology influences human beings, the definition of "human beings" must be tweaked, if not completely overhauled. For instance, many people would say one thing that separates humans from machines is that machines cannot express emotions. Yet in the past decades, scientists in the fields of Artificial Intelligence and Robotics have created robots that clearly "express" emotions (but "feeling" them is another matter). As cognitive neuroscience progresses, the gap between science and science fiction narrows.

All This Machinery Making Modern Music

In today's music industry, musicians not content to play on a street corner have to acquaint themselves with a vast array of electronic gadgets and scientific principles in order to propagate their music successfully. The journey from writing a song, to recording it, to playing it live, and to hearing it played on the radio takes a musician through such harrowing terrain as acoustic science, wireless electronic instruments, digital recording consoles, and sound compression. Yet in album after album, tour after tour, Rush has succeeded in mastering the technology they use. One reason why they are regarded as a "progressive" band is that they employ technology in ever-new ways to reinvent their music.

Ever since 1976, when the success of *2112* allowed Rush to invest in some new musical equipment, their use of music technology has grown by leaps and bounds. All three members of the group have learned to play new instruments and have learned to utilize the technology necessary for them to play these multiple instruments on stage. They have also been able to duplicate the complexity of their studio recordings on stage. During an interview with Martin Sargent for the TechTV show *The Screen Savers*, Geddy Lee and Alex Lifeson were quite candid about the effect that technology has had on their stage shows. Lee stated:

> Technological advances are important. Being a three-piece band [technology has] enabled us to explore other areas of sound by using sequenced strings and choral sounds and keyboards. We have a complex array of foot pedals that trigger a whole bank of samplers,

sequencers and various sounds that are programmed offstage and changed for each song.[7]

The only detriment to these advances is that the average concert-goers' ability to actually see the musicians has become increasingly difficult! Neil Peart is surrounded on all sides by his acoustic and electronic drum kits and Geddy Lee is often ensconced behind a fortification of keyboards and foot petals. Alex Lifeson is the only member who is free to frolic on the stage, with Geddy occasionally breaking free from his "control panel" to frolic with him. Anyone who has been to a Rush concert has marveled at Peart's ability to utilize so many drums, cymbals, and percussion instruments, and Lee's ability to simultaneously sing, play intricate lines on his bass guitar or keyboard, play a foot pedal keyboard, and trigger "sound events" and effects using other foot pedals.

Not only have Rush's stage shows and musicianship benefited from technology, their songwriting has developed in unforeseen ways because of it. In the tour book for the *Signals* tour from 1982, Peart recounts the origin of "The Weapon" as if it were some highly controversial science experiment:

> With a Roland drum machine and assorted synthesizers, Geddy and friend Oscar secret themselves in Ged's music room to create some music of a highly confidential and experimental nature. Among the Top Secret projects that they produce is the basic foundation for this song, including a highly mysterious and bizarre drum pattern which Oscar coaxes out of the drum machine. (I'm supposed to learn how to play that?) Well, I do love a challenge, and once we start to tackle this at one of the rehearsals, I discover that if I play totally backwards, and bend my hands a few ways they don't normally go, I can do it. The shame of being reduced to learning from a machine! However, I must admit, I would never have come up with something like that on my own![8]

This is not the only song whose composition was directly influenced by technology. In the *Moving Pictures* tour book Neil writes

---

[7] Interview available on YouTube: <www.youtube.com/watch?v=YRe1jO87Fdo&feature=PlayList&p=EA6C6351843CBBB8&playnext=1&playnext_from=PL&index=37>.

[8] Neil Peart, Tour book from Rush's *Signals* tour, 1982, available at <www.2112.net/powerwindows/SIGtourbook.htm>.

that "the instrumental section of 'Tom Sawyer' grew from a little melody that Geddy had been using to set up his synthesizers at sound checks . . ." and ". . .'YYZ' is the identity code used by Toronto's Pearson International Airport, and the intro is taken from the Morse code which is sent out by the beacon there."[9] Peart recounts the process of writing the album *Vapor Trails* in 2001: "all the writing, arranging, and recording was done on computer, a lot of time was spent staring at monitors, but most of the time technology was our friend, and helped us to combine spontaneity and craftwork."[10] Despite "staring at monitors," during the writing process, this album has an impulsive, spontaneous feel to it. While the members of Rush have been critical of technology, they have always been open to how technology can make them better songwriters and better musicians. They use technology, and are not used by it.

At the beginning of this chapter, I wrote that Rush is a band that uses technology to critique technology. Not coincidentally, this direction in Peart's lyrics became more overt just as they began to employ an increasing amount of keyboards, digital sampling and digital sequencing in their music. While some Rush albums have a large amount of keyboards, digital sampling and digital sequencing— *Power Windows* (1985) through *Roll the Bones* (1991)—it has never obscured the message of their music nor overwhelmed their trusted template of guitar, bass and drums. As Peart writes in "The Spirit of Radio," "All this machinery making modern music can still be open-hearted. Not so coldly charted it's really just a question of your honesty." Rush has always striven to find alētheuein in their technē.

Straining the Limits of Machine and Man

Starting in August 1997, Neil Peart experienced a horrible double tragedy. His daughter, Selena, died in a car accident at age nineteen on her way to start her first year of college. Less than a year later his wife Jackie died, presumably of cancer (although Peart attributed it to a broken heart over Selena's death).

Peart dealt with the pain and depression of losing his family by clinging to his friends and parents, and by getting on his motorcy-

---

[9] Neil Peart, Tour book from Rush's *Moving Pictures* tour.

[10] Neil Peart, Tour book from Rush's *Vapor Trails* tour, 2002, available at <www.2112.net/powerwindows/VTtourbook.htm>.

cle and riding for fourteen months through Canada, the United States and Mexico, describing himself as "the ghost rider." Although he didn't know where he would end up, by losing himself in the hum of the motor, the blur of the landscape, and the perspective from his rear-view mirror, he found himself and the will to carry on. For him at this juncture in his life, a machine became an instrument of his recovery. In his book *Ghost Rider: Travels on the Healing Road*, he wrote:

> Whatever torments the night had brought; whatever weather the new day threw at me, when I loaded up the bike and swung my leg over the saddle, my whole perspective changed. Focus tightened into the mechanics and mentality of operating the machine, and awareness contracted to that demanding paradigm. As I let in the clutch and turned the throttle, my world-view expanded as I moved into a whole new paradigm of landscapes, highways, and wildlife. Infinite possibilities.[11]

Technology is taking all of us on a ride, one that is both frightening and enlightening.

---

[11] Neil Peart, *Ghost Rider: Travels on the Healing Road* (ECW Press, 2002), pp. 41–42.

18

Enlightened Thoughts, Mystic Words

CHRIS McDONALD

Rush's *Snakes & Arrows*, released in 2007, is a highly topical recording. It's a secular response to what Neil Peart sees as the rising tide of religiosity and fundamentalism that has changed the geopolitics of the Middle East as well as the post–Cold War US. Six of the ten songs with lyrics on *Snakes & Arrows* address the conflict between the once-ascendant humanism of the modern West and the resurgent popularity of religious faith.

This topic inspired Peart, an avid motorcycle traveler, partly because of observations he made during his rides through various parts of the United States. Religious billboard signs were prevalent along highways, making the presence of evangelical Christianity ever palpable, and Peart noted, "Just seeing the power of evangelical Christianity and contrasting that with the power of fundamentalist religion all over the world in its different forms had a big effect on me."[1]

This led Peart to a renewed awareness that secular modernity's conflict with religious belief systems never reached a decisive conclusion in the West or East. He elaborated, "I see the world in what I think to be a perfectly obvious and rational way, but when you go out into it and see the way other people think and behave, and express themselves on church signs, you realize, 'Well, I'm not really part of this club'."

Yet, the religious "club" of which Peart speaks has been in retreat for some time, with mainstream religious institutions reluc-

---

[1] Jonathan Cohen, "Rush Wrestles with Faith on New Album," *Billboard* (September 11th, 2006); <http://www.billboard.com>.

tantly adapting or ceding ground to the philosophical, humanistic, scientific and ideological innovations that accompanied the European Renaissance, the Enlightenment and the Industrial Revolution. For a secularist like Peart to find religion seemingly emboldened, revitalized, and empowered is unsettling, and its blatant influence on recent American politics and military conflicts in various parts of the world seems downright regressive. Thus, one aspect that stands out in *Snakes & Arrows* is a defensiveness, a feeling of being stung or wounded by an unexpected attack.

The album's opening track, "Far Cry," establishes this feeling quite plainly. The narrator describes himself amidst preachers, madmen, and young people all caught up in religious babble, conflict, and irrational behavior. Such circumstances are "a far cry from the world we thought we'd inherit," the narrator states. "We"—presumably like-minded humanists—thought our modern culture had moved beyond such religious belief systems, and certainly beyond fighting over them. In the song's chorus, the humanist-narrator says, "One day I feel I'm ahead of the wheel," part of the vanguard of Western civilization, only to be overrun by un-humanistic ideas, pushing ahead like a juggernaut. The humanist in "Far Cry" feels astonished at being decentered, yet is determined to "get back on."

Other tracks build on this feeling of humanism under attack. "Armor and Sword" puts aggressive military imagery to the forefront, characterizing religious faith as something that starts as a means to provide comfort and protection, but is all-too-often manipulated and perverted into a pretext to for hatred, the dehumanization of others, and violence. Faith is described using ominous metaphors, as something that "leaves a thousand cuts," or that transforms from protective armor into "a sharp and bloody sword."

Whatever benefits religious faith could offer, Peart argues through the song, it's too irrational and unpredictable to be trusted. This ominous depiction is supported in affect by one of the song's main riffs, a heavily distorted, rising Phrygian-mode sequence (E to G, then F to A), creeping upward like an advancing disease. Another song, "The Way the Wind Blows," describes the current state of war between Western powers and Middle-Eastern countries and terrorist groups as a profoundly regressive development, a harkening back to the "Dark Ages," a renewal of Medieval conflicts which murkily combine religious confrontation with territorial disputes. No side is taken by the song's narrator in the military conflict between East and West; the real enemy is humanism's antithesis in religious literalism, no matter where it comes from. Humanism's rationality is pitted against religion's superstition using metaphors of health and sickness, as religion gets described as a "plague that resists all science."

In addition to these reactions to religiosity, Peart offers a renewed statement of his humanistic viewpoint in "Faithless," a secular manifesto. Against those who claim that human values and endeavors are divinely planned, he asserts the humanist's central belief: that flesh-and-blood people are the originators of all human values, and that there is nothing discernable beyond this world, no supernatural being or over-parent choosing our values or destinies for us. But the way Peart sets up this argument at the beginning of the song provides an interesting twist, one which leads directly into the central theme of this chapter.

"I've got my own moral compass to steer by," Geddy Lee sings during the first verse, "A guiding star beats a spirit in the sky." Though the song's theme is a rejection of religious belief and an affirmation of humanism, the symbol of the "guiding star," that which orients the narrator, still casts the eyes of the humanist, metaphorically, toward the heavens for direction. In "The Pass" from Rush's *Presto* (1989), there is a similar metaphor ("Dreamers learn to steer by the stars"). Even as the message is secular, the very language which gives it life and expression is celestial. The image harkens back to the very beginning of the Western Renaissance, when sailors pragmatically used the stars to steer their ships, but placed a kind of a faith in the fixity of a phenomenon whose nature they could scarcely then have understood.

Snakes & Arrows, while timely in its theme, is also typical of the kind of secular humanism that Rush has promoted and defended throughout its decades-long career. In fact, surveying the band's repertoire, I think you'd be hard pressed to find popular music artists more directly and self-consciously dedicated to humanism's cause. Yet some critics and reporters associate Rush with a kind of metaphysical air because of the mysterious and mythical overtones that appear in a number of songs and in its visual material (album covers, stage presentations, iconography).[2]

---

[2] Carol Selby Price's 1998 book on Rush's lyrics was entitled *Mystic Rhythms: The Philosophical Vision of Rush*, placing a surprising emphasis on mysticism for a book focusing mostly on Rush's unreligious philosophies.

Do the themes of trajectories between humanism and mysticism in Rush's music conflict with each other, or do they complement each other, achieving a balance or synthesis? Moreover, does Rush's merging of the humanist and the mystical fit revealingly into a broader history of such tensions in Western literature, art and philosophy? What purpose does this pairing of the humanistic and mystical serve?

Rush's Love Affair with Eighteenth-Century Revolutions

At a very basic level, humanism builds on the supposition that all knowledge, values, and ethics have their source in human experience and human motivations. To the humanist, the universe is self-sufficient, not created, and human beings are manifestations of nature. Following from this, knowledge of the natural world and knowledge of human history, culture, thought, and expression are not really separate pursuits (however much they get separated in practice), but are all part of a single project aiming to understand human nature and the human condition.

Such notions followed from philosophical developments in ancient Greece, especially Plato's transcendent forms, Aristotle's theory of physics, and Protagoras's relativism, establishing universally applicable principles, and a picture of the individual as intellectually critical, discerning, even skeptical. These philosophers looked to the mind and human experience for explanations of phenomena, rather than to myth and superstition. Many of these developments were applied pragmatically by the Romans to the notion of a "liberal education" (moral philosophy, grammar, poetry, history, and so on), essential in the molding of the rational, productive, liberal citizen.[3] The term humanism was later applied to the "new learning" of the Italian Renaissance, particularly in its creation of the Humanities, the study of human thought through works of literature, art, and history.

But most important for the development of what is today called secular humanism are the philosophies of the Enlightenment thinkers. Taking their cue from Isaac Newton, who employed a rigorous and critical sort of reason in the study of nature, Enlightenment intellectuals like Voltaire, David Hume, and Auguste

---

[3] James Battersby, "The Inescapability of Humanism," *College English* 58:5 (1996), p. 556.

Comte applied a similar method to the study of people and human society. Thus did disciplines such as sociology, linguistics, psychology, and history develop, and these, as James Battersby puts it, "established the principles of our common nature on new bases and gave defining immediacy to such inseparably human and inalienable values and regulative ideals as equality, justice, freedom, liberty, and individual rights."

The rational study of human societies led to the conclusion that the sources of authority which rested on religious or traditional dogma—the divine right of kings, feudal hierarchies, the justification of laws and ethics on Biblical scripture alone—were arbitrary, irrational or fraudulent. In place of these, Enlightenment philosophers insisted that traditional ways be challenged, and used reason and a secular, humanist spirit to propose new kinds of social arrangements, states, and bases for laws and ethics. Such thinking inspired the American and French Revolutions, where egalitarian and democratic rhetoric chipped at the bases of aristocratic rule, and where constitutions were drafted to establish permanent rights, freedoms, and protections which would apply equally to all citizens.

Early in Rush's career, Neil Peart drafted three sets of lyrics that explicitly cited these Enlightenment humanist revolutions, making Rush perhaps the only band in rock history to have a trilogy of songs devoted to eighteenth-century political movements. The first of these, "Beneath, Between and Behind" (from *Fly by Night*, 1975), recounts the American Revolution, in which "the kingly foe," the colonial master in Great Britain, was vanquished and a "wondrous dream" is given birth in the form of the new American republic. The song paints a picture of the early US as building, growing, and innovating uninhibitedly, once the old feudal ties are severed.

Triumphant Enlightenment values bring into being a country whose ideals of rights, liberty, and freedom of enterprise attract immigrants from around the world. But the song turns from a rosy, admittedly naive, imagining of a fledgling US to a more critical view of contemporary America, where "the guns replace the plow," where fear motivates people more than moral conviction, and where "the principles have been betrayed." The song describes cracks appearing beneath the nation's noble symbols, between the words of its constitution, and behind the beauty of its national mythologies and self-portrayals. To Peart, a Canadian contrasting what he saw in America in the mid-1970s with what the founders intended, the country seemed to be turning away from its humanistic promise.

Another cautionary tale is told in "Bastille Day" from *Caress of Steel* (1975). Describing the catalytic event of the French Revolution, the song begins with an effete French aristocracy who "flaunt the fruits of noble birth," and sow resentment among the hungry masses of Paris. Righteously, the people in the streets rise up against arbitrary and unearned privilege, puffed up with the idea that all individuals should be equal under the law regardless of social status. The Bastille prison is stormed, the monarchy is humbled, and the ascendency of the common French citizenry is expressed in the chorus's key line, "The king must kneel / To let his kingdom rise." But as the song progresses, righteous anger and violence turns on itself. The monarchy is guillotined, but so are other individuals, and soon the population at large becomes terrorized by the storm of violence that builds unchecked.

The lesson of the French Revolution, the song points out during the last verse, is relevant today, even if it is ignored: the desire for power, backed by violence, can hijack and overwhelm the most noble of political intentions. The humanist ideals of the French Revolution became a pretext for the same kind of violence and power-grabbing that had sustained feudalism and the monarchy's absolutism—a sobering realization.

The third song, the title track from *A Farewell to Kings* (1977), continues on a similar line as "Bastille Day" and "Beneath, Between, and Behind." A more general foray into social commentary, Peart compares the tenor of contemporary, modern society with the feudal society which we supposedly left behind. The song begins with a wistful, archaic-sounding opening using classical guitar, orchestra bells and a muted synthesizer (sounding like a distant woodwind), an instrumental introduction that recalls Renaissance music. This is swept aside by the entry of Rush's electrified hard rock, with the band playing a triumphant, major-key passage which sounds a bit like a joyful procession.

The band thus dramatizes their farewell to kings: the old feudal ways represented by the song's introduction are challenged and defeated by the rise of Enlightenment ideas, advancing in procession, heralding the collapse of old traditions and hierarchies. But the entry of the song's lyrics moves us forward anxiously to the present time. The song asks what future generations will think of us: will they see us as having abandoned the ideals of reason, progress, and humanism which had characterized the Enlightenment? Have we turned away from these "castles in the distance," and returned to our old, pre-Enlightened ways? Peart compares today's "hypocrites" who criticize the humanist-inspired quest for truth and progress with "ancient nobles" who preferred that their subjects lived under their shadow in ignorance. The chorus's image of cities seething with unrest, those in power lying and scheming, average people feeling disempowered and desperate, and "the wise" being mocked and silenced, is meant to resonate as an image of contemporary discontent, but also as an image of how things used to be before humanism and Enlightenment ideas took hold.

All three songs, then, seem to look back at the hopeful beginnings of secular humanism and the Enlightenment project as a lost Golden Age, an idealistic vision to which the present scarcely lives up. Intriguingly, these songs show that Rush was concerned about a decline of humanism's vitality and authority quite early in its career, some thirty years before the release of *Snakes & Arrows*, even if fundamentalist religion was not then singled out as the most significant threat. But if these songs show Rush as devotees as well as concerned defenders of humanism, they do not tell us a great deal about what kind of humanism, or what facets of humanism, they emphasize and defend. One aspect that is justifiably stressed in the literature on Rush is individualism, a concept that draws together a number of important humanistic ideas. It helps us to locate Rush's humanism within a definable geographical and political context. It also allows us to contrast Rush's humanism with other aspects of humanism which they have generally not aligned themselves with, at least publicly.

Living (Mostly) for Yourself

Many of Rush's individualistic songs and stories are humanistic in the sense that they portray anything beyond a self-sufficient, individual consciousness (such as mass consciousness, religiosity, determinism, ideology) as mistaken, threatening, or wrong. The individualism that emerges from Rush's repertoire is consonant with what is written about the individual in the American Humanist Association's document, *A Humanist Manifesto II* (1973), whose fifth principle states:

> The preciousness and dignity of the individual person is a central humanist value. Individuals should be encouraged to realize their own

creative talents and desires. We reject all religious, ideological, or moral codes that denigrate the individual, suppress freedom, dull intellect, dehumanize personality. We believe in maximum individual autonomy consonant with social responsibility. Although science can account for the causes of behavior, the possibilities of individual freedom of choice exist in human life and should be increased.[4]

This view of the individual resonates with a number of Rush songs. The notion that the individual should be free to create himself or herself, independent of social, historical, or ideological constraints, is exemplified in songs like "Anthem" (1975) or "Something for Nothing" (1976).

In "Anthem," Rush delivers injunctions to "live for yourself," "hold your head above the crowd" and to find your unique, individual niche, "your place in life." The song also soundly rejects moral or ideological beliefs that one should guide one's behavior based on the conventions of what others do, and it rejects altruism as a moral imperative, insisting that the individual does not, a priori, owe any duty, responsibility or debt to anyone else, other than refraining from interfering with the freedom and well-being of others.

In "Something for Nothing," Rush urges critical self-reflection, and implores the listener to be a self-made individual, and not to "wait for someone [else] to call" and take the lead. The song's bridge offers an almost prayer-like invocation of individualist virtues: your possessions are called your "kingdom," you derive "power" from doing what you love, and your work is your path to "glory." The allusion to the kingdom/power/glory motif from the Lord's Prayer in a secular, individualistic setting is a poetic device that calls out for some explanation.

The kind of individualism Rush invokes here is strongly embedded in the North American context. The emphasis, drawn from classical liberal and libertarian strands of thought, on the individual's freedom from obligations to others is included in the category of "negative rights." Negative rights guarantee a kind of individual freedom that protects one from having to do anything for anyone else, promoting a social environment where entrepreneurial social relations are most valued. In contrast, "positive rights" describes an

---

[4] Paul Kurtz and Edwin H. Wilson, *A Humanist Manifesto II* (1973); <http://www.americanhumanist.org>.

individual's right to something (food, education, medical care) that obliges others to take some kind of action to fulfil that right.[5] Few fully-modernized societies in the West eschew one category of rights entirely in favor of the other, since some balance is generally considered desirable, but an emphasis on negative rights corresponds to a more forthrightly capitalist economy (like that of the US), and positive rights towards a more socialist or social democratic arrangement (common in some European states). Both notions of rights derive from different strands of humanistic thought, though they do appear to conflict. Idealized American capitalism found favor in Peart's early lyrics, while any system emphasizing positive rights was viewed with suspicion.

There were a number of narrative pieces in Rush's repertoire between 1976 and 1981 that tried to illustrate the superiority of a negative rights-based system to one based on positive rights. For example, "2112" (1976) dramatizes an individual's struggle against an oppressive futuristic regime which ruled society through collectivist ideology, a theocratic or priestly mystique and a command of powerful technologies. The society's entire culture was created by the priestly caste and disseminated through computer interfaces. The story's protagonist rediscovers a kind of freedom when he starts making his own music without interference from the priests, instead of consuming the common, synthesized culture the regime provided.

In another example, a cartoon-like fable called "The Trees" (1978), a quarrel erupts between tall oak trees and smaller maples over the unequal distribution of sunlight. The maples win a suit obliging the oaks to be cut down to size, but the unintended result is that the whole forest is made equal "by hatchet, axe, and saw." Meanwhile, "Witch Hunt" (1981) takes aim at the practices of censorship, painting the desire to protect the public from subversive influences as paranoid and ignorant. The song contrasts an implied, benevolent laissez-faire approach to rights, in which all minorities, artists, and individuals are left alone by authorities and the public at large, with a malevolent attempt to censor, regulate or intimidate anyone who affronts traditional standards or the status quo. In all cases, freedom is equated with the right to be left alone to do what

---

[5] Jack Donnelly, *Universal Human Rights in Theory and Practice* (Cornell University Press, 2003), p. 30.

one chooses, to be free from governmental or social interference of various kinds.

Spirits and Visions

One other important way in which Rush's repertoire demonstrates sympathy with humanism is its uplifting aestheticization of the human drive to create and achieve. This theme appeared with growing frequency in the group's repertoire during the late 1980s and 1990s. Songs like "Marathon" (1985), "Mission" (1987), "Available Light" (1989), "Cut to the Chase" (1993) and "Driven" (1996) expressed fascination and admiration for feats of endurance and risk-taking (physical, mental, artistic) as well as for those with visionary ambitions and the capability of realizing them.

During these years, Rush married music of great bombast to these kinds of themes, producing a version of progressive hard rock well-suited to large arena concerts, with emotionally-stirring choruses, sweeping, almost orchestral synthesizers, dramatic tempo and dynamic changes, as well as guitar solos that reached achingly for transcendence. This approach formed the musical context in which Rush delivered paeans to the wonder of human achieve-ment, acting in many ways as secular rock hymns to the greatness to which humans could aspire, and occasionally reach. But what is most centrally celebrated in these songs is the hunger or desire that lies behind ambition, perseverance or achievement.

Each of these songs talks about a desire for something more, a desire that is hard to describe or account for, yet is the key to the subjects the songs broach. In "Marathon," for example, the long-distance runner's desire to push the limits of physical endurance is described as "more than blind ambition" and "more than simple greed." But what is it, then? Why must it be more than these things? Similarly, in "Mission," artistic genius manifests itself through an all-consuming obsession with discovery, but more than this, it is described as something ineffable and mysterious: artists, the song says, are "in the grip of a nameless possession," possessions that become "the secrets that set them apart." But what are they pos-sessed by? Why can't it be named? Why is it a secret—something hidden, mysterious, occluded? The language chosen by Peart itself provides a clue: the song's oft-repeated couplet ("A spirit with a vision / Is a dream with a mission") enlivens the essentially human-ist theme with spiritual allusions, adding mystery and a sense of depth to the song's subject. This is an aesthetic choice, and one which is as prevalent in Rush's repertoire as humanist themes.

"Jacob's Ladder," a track from 1980's *Permanent Waves*, provides another striking example of this sense of mystery. The song, which is mostly a dramatized, programmatic instrumental punctuated by short vocal passages, narrates a thunderstorm. The aim is to put a natural phenomenon into an aesthetic frame, showing how its majesty and power can provide an experience of the sublime, and act as a source of inspiration for people. The eerie, quiet and foreboding introduction of the song mimics the approach of the storm; the ensuing riffs and guitar solo, full of dissonant and aggressive gestures, build in intensity to the storm's climax; a softer, synthesized passage symbolizes the return of the sunlight and the calm following the storm. Then the song builds back up to another majestic, heavy rock climax as Geddy Lee's voice delivers the concluding lines: "Follow men's eyes as they look to the skies / The shifting shafts of shining weave the fabric of their dreams."

Peart's poetic use of spiritual or religious overtones here are clear enough: a sense of awe at the natural world, human eyes cast aloft to the skies, looking for inspiration and invigoration, and a title drawn from a Biblical story. "Jacob's Ladder," from the book of Genesis, is the staircase leading to heaven about which the Hebrew patriarch, Jacob, has a dream. Through this potent symbolic reference, the aesthetic experience of the storm is depicted as a vehicle elevating us spiritually, bringing us closer to the heavens. But the song also supports a humanist reading, insofar as it left to a person to make meaning of the storm. The storm is not described as an "act of God," something emanating from a divine or supernatural consciousness. The storm has no intentionality, but the human perceiving it does.

Baruch Spinoza, the seventeenth-century Dutch philosopher whose work anticipated the secular humanist orientation of the Enlightenment, made a similar point in *The Ethics*: against all orthodox religious interpretations, Spinoza believed that nature is not a creation of God based on a conscious plan; it is simply the totality of all substance in the universe, and it lacks the intentionality possessed by living people. Yet Spinoza characterizes nature in an ambiguous way, describing it in a secular, almost atheistic way, but in the end, calling all substance in nature, collectively, "God." Whatever God is, He is immanent in nature, He does not transcend it. "Jacob's Ladder" also takes an ambiguous position, treating human imagination as something interfused with the natural world, and human creativity as immanent in our environment through our very perception of it. There is no "God" acting through nature, but humans, as implied in the song, may act in response to it. Yet, the storm is poetically colored using a Biblical myth.

There are numerous other examples of spiritual, mythical, or mystical references deployed in Rush's repertoire, functioning in a variety of ways. The afore-mentioned use of a motif from the Lord's Prayer in "Something for Nothing" co-opts an aura of importance, or sacredness, for a concept which is not religious in nature by referencing a culturally important, widely-recognized religious text.

The band sometimes used mythical or fantasy-world narratives to illustrate ideas; for example, gods from the Greek pantheon were used in "Hemispheres" (1978) as allegories for the concepts of reason, passion, and balance or equilibrium. The song "Mystic Rhythms" (1985) dealt with the desire for a sense of mystery in life and with the humbling realization that humans still know very little about their universe. "Nature seems to spin a supernatural way," Geddy Lee sings during the chorus, while observing how tempting it is to suspend one's disbelief because of how entertaining, reassuring or intriguing it can be to be open to the possibility of unseen, mystical forces acting from afar.

The album *Presto* (1989) centers on the themes of illusion and transformation, and uses magic as a recurring trope, both on the album cover (featuring a magician's hat) and in the title track. *Roll the Bones* (1991) explores themes of fate, luck, and fortune, and uses tools of divination (dice, bones, the wheel of fortune, cards) as symbols both in cover art and in a variety of songs. This theme was revisited in the album art for *Vapor Trails* (2002) where the Tarot deck is used as a recurring visual motif.

These aesthetic choices did much to cast Rush as a band with as much of a "mystical" side as a "humanist" side in the popular press. Early on, this impression was fostered by the band's use of fantasy literature, science fiction and mythology as resources for illustrating their ideas. These thematic influences were typical for hard rock and progressive rock bands in the 1970s, and these musical genres were filled with mystical and supernatural symbolism, which Rush similarly drew from. In the 1980s, Rush stopped writing narratives steeped in fantasy and sci-fi, yet an openness to mystical language and symbolism remained, even as the songs focused more on real-world observations.

Humanism Needs Its Evangelists, Too

Religious language has a kind of gravitas that plain, everyday language and rational, academicized discourse has rarely been able to match. Humanist ideas may be, in one sense, most accurately represented by the latter, but such language may leave behind a need that they be expressed in a way that gives greater force, weight, and interest to them.

This is a problem that Richard Norman acknowledged in the conclusion of his book, *On Humanism*. His impassioned argument for the continued relevance and soundness of secular humanism as a foundation for modern thought led to a frustrating realization that most of these ideas have become so commonplace, so obvious, so banal, that people find something disenchanting about them. People seem to want a kind of mystery and enchantment that humanism seems to lack on its own.[6]

Edward M. Bruner, an anthropologist pondering the same problem, notes that humanists have struggled for some time to find the right kind of language to elevate human experience, to give it the same sense of solemnity, wonder and spirit-lifting allure that religious myth and ritual has long provided. Secular humanism, Bruner believes, is supposed to empower individuals to "self-create," and it must provide ways to "ritualize the construction of one's self."[7] The problem, Bruner feels, principally centers on language: "under radically secular conditions, the problem facing the humanist is not so much one of replacing the gods but finding a language to replace the Word with new sacred words that will allow us to celebrate the survival of the human spirit." In the case of Rush, we have seen this linguistic or poetic challenge playing itself out: if humanist ideas are to replace religious ones, the same feeling of sacredness, power and mystery must still attend them.

There need be no shame in this rhetorical strategy, says Wayne Booth, who notes that humanists risk being out-evangelized by their opponents if they refuse to aestheticize their ideas in compelling ways. Using mystic-type metaphors in the argument for humanistic ideas may be a necessary strategy for humanists,

---

[6] Richard Norman, *On Humanism* (Routledge, 2004), pp. 132–33.

[7] Edward M. Bruner, "Ordinary and Extraordinary Experience," in Victor Turner and Edward M. Bruner, eds., *The Anthropology of Experience* (University of Illinois Press, 1986), p. 46.

because if they do not show the "wonder" and spiritual efficacy of their ideas, what will inspire anyone to follow them?[8]

At an even deeper level, the interfusing of secular ideas and spiritually-tinged rhetoric may play an important role in defending humanism, and as we have seen throughout this chapter, Peart clearly sees humanism, at this point in history, as being out-manoeuvred on a number of fronts. The ways Rush presents humanist ideas through the media of fantasy and fiction transposes humanism into timeless, imaginary and mythical domains where they appear, not as historically-contingent arguments or sites of intellectual disagreement, but as universal, ever-consistent princi-ples that become almost like tenets of faith. Presented mythically, humanism seems less vulnerable than it might be otherwise. Humanism, historically, has not been a consistent stream of thought, but a site of disagreement, and there have been many humanisms, leading to different and quite conflicting traditions (for example Marxism, Liberalism, Freudianism). Indeed, James Battersby points out that in the US, many a Supreme Court case "involves the conflict of one Enlightenment value with another." Such division and contradiction does not inspire, but casts doubt and confusion. Humanist ideas, however, relayed mythically and with a sense of sacred purpose, are "magically" cleansed of this weakness. Couched in the rhetoric of myth, humanism becomes something more than philosophical argument or theory; moreover, its historical nature, constructedness and contingency is erased and replaced by a sense of immutability, universality and eternal truthfulness.

This context leads to the conclusion that Rush's songs, though frequently and self-consciously broaching philosophical topics related to secular humanism, are mostly rhetorical statements affirming humanist ideas, while presenting few real arguments, hypotheses, or proofs supporting them. That Rush should avail itself of religious or mystical language and texts in the process of this aestheticization is nothing unique to this band, nor problematic to the secular humanist cause. It is an important and useful rhetor-ical strategy. Moreover, spiritual or mystical metaphors, descriptors and myths are inseparable parts of the cultural, literary and imagi-native inheritance that comes down to all of us. Even the most sec-

[8] Wayne C. Booth, ""Systematic Wonder: The Rhetoric of Secular Religions," *Journal of the American Academy of Religion* 53:4 (1985), pp. 697–98.

ular examples of literature bear traces of the Biblical and mytho-logical literary traditions that form the bedrock of Western culture, and it could hardly be otherwise.

Northrop Frye provides an arresting analogy for this: "Just as when we pull a plant up by the roots the surrounding soil will cling to it, so when we examine our experience of the present moment we find it surrounded by the immediate past and future."[9] This image could be related to modernity, which in its secular human-ist form pries itself out of a religious and superstitious past, yet ves-tiges of the culture out of which it grew remain attached. So it is with Rush: so secular, so critical of faith and superstition, yet still open to the mystical language that continues to inspire wonder in us.[10]

---

[9] Northrop Frye, *The Double Vision: Language and Meaning in Religion* (United Church Publishing House, 1991), p. 48.

[10] I thank Dr. Richard Keshen of Cape Breton University's Department of Philosophy for his kind and helpful feedback on earlier drafts of this chapter.

19
Rush's Libertarianism Never Fit the Plan

STEVEN HORWITZ

Can a band labeled as "right-wing fascists" for some of its lyrics be the same band whose lyrics also criticize big government, imperialism, and the religious right? Can the band whose songs include such lines as "What you own is your own kingdom" and "Begging hands and bleeding hearts will always cry out for more" be the same band that has been honored for its charitable work, especially for AIDS-related causes? Does this band even have some sort of coherent philosophical viewpoint behind its lyrics?

Of course, I'm speaking about Rush, and all of these questions can be answered with a definite, though qualified, "Yes"—and I don't mean that other progressive rock band. The problem is that the typical categories of "left and right" or "liberal and conservative" portrayed in the above questions are just as much a false choice as the one between Apollo and Dionysus in Rush's extended suite "Hemispheres." And much as Cygnus brought balance to reason and emotion in that work, the political philosophy of libertarianism takes the best of the right and of the left to provide the set of political ideas that have been reflected in many of Neil Peart's politically-oriented lyrics over the course of Rush's career.

Let Them All Make Their Own Music

To understand libertarianism, it helps to see how libertarians tend to see liberals and conservatives as having much more in common than they might seem to. What liberals and conservatives share is a rejection of the libertarian idea that people should be allowed to live their lives as they please as long as they grant others the same freedom.

Conservatives at least claim to want to give people such freedom in their economic choices, as conservatives tend to support capitalism in some form or other. But they aren't so willing to allow that degree of freedom with respect to what people read, watch, or do with their bodies, as their support for some forms of censorship and laws against prostitution and drug use demonstrates. Their enthusiasm for using military force overseas is another way in which the freedom of the individual, in this case citizens of other countries, is not their primary concern.

Liberals, by contrast, at least claim to be fine with consenting adults reading, watching, or ingesting more or less what they please. However, they are not willing to extend the same freedom to what the philosopher Robert Nozick called "capitalist acts" between those same consenting adults. So liberals and conservatives agree that people can't be trusted to use their freedom wisely. They just disagree on which sorts of freedoms work and which sorts don't. The result is that both liberals and conservatives believe that a large, active government is necessary for the kind of world they'd like to see.

This is evident in much of the debate over health care reform in the US, where the dialogue between conservatives and liberals is stuck with conservatives largely defending a status quo in which government already plays a huge role and liberals asking for even more. Libertarians have argued that real "reform" would involve reducing government's involvement significantly as they believe many of the problems of the current system are a result of the state's already large footprint.

Libertarians think that people should be free to live their lives as they see fit, while respecting the right of others to do the same, no matter whether it's what we read, what we put in our bodies, whom we choose to love, the wage we agree on with an employer or an employee, how we get our medical care, or what we do with our property. Government's only job is to prevent us from harming others, which would deny those others their freedom, equal to the freedom we have. As the old saying goes, my right to swing my fist ends at the beginning of someone else's face.

With Acknowledgment to the Genius of Ayn Rand

Libertarianism comes in a variety of flavors. One of those is inspired by the Russian-born American novelist (and sometimes philosopher) Ayn Rand. (Her first name rhymes with "sign.") In novels such as *Atlas Shrugged* (1957) and works of non-fiction such as the essays collected in *Capitalism: The Unknown Ideal* (1967) and *The Virtue of Selfishness* (1964), Rand developed an entire philosophical system that she named "Objectivism," in which the individual was the center of knowledge, reality, and the social world.

For Rand, humans were endowed with rationality and were therefore the best judges of how to live their lives. The problem Rand saw in modern society was that most moral codes told individuals that the highest good was to sacrifice their own needs to those of others. Which "others" depended on whether the political views of the promoters of that particular ethical code. Rand argued instead that pursuing one's self-interest and living the life that one wanted, again subject to equal respect for others' right to do the same, was the only moral way to live. The implication, of course, was a broadly libertarian belief in small government.[1]

When Peart joined the band in 1974 and took over the lyric writing from Geddy Lee (saving fans from decades of more of the deep insights of "Take a Friend" or "Need Some Love"), he brought his interest in Rand immediately into the writing process. The Randian strain of libertarianism is evident on 1975's *Fly by Night* in several songs, most notably "Anthem." That song's title is taken from a Rand novella that also provided the inspiration for the plot of "2112" two albums later.[2]

The lyrical theme in "Anthem," that selfishness isn't always wrong and that we should live for ourselves because "there's no one else more worth living for," is straight out of Rand's philosophy. For Rand, the demand that we sacrifice our desires to the needs of others was a recipe for social disaster. This was particularly so in the economic realm, where the men and women of ability and creativity who, in her view, are the motors of the world, would find themselves enslaved to their lessers.

This is the dominant theme of *Atlas Shrugged,* in which the capitalist producers, along with the most creative scientists and artists, eventually begin to realize that their acceptance of the moral code

---

[1] Rand never called herself a libertarian, believing that those who did use that term were too often not committed to the non-political parts of her philosophy.

[2] However, see Chapter 20 of this volume for a look at how different *Anthem* and "2112" actually are, despite their surface similarities.

of sacrifice turns them into victims. This realization leads them to go on strike by withdrawing from society. The result is chaos, as without the most productive, the economy collapses and the social order with it. Rand's point was that unless we have a moral code that recognizes that people should be free to pursue profit, including those who profit greatly from their productivity, we will never live truly human lives.

This basic idea is seen in "Anthem" as noted above, but also in other Rush songs as well. "Beneath, Between, and Behind" from *Fly by Night* praises the early Americans who tamed "the trackless waste" along with those who constructed the cities and the inventors, while it bemoans the loss of the principles that guided them and their freedom. The following verse of "Something for Nothing" also captures this Randian individualist libertarianism:

> What you own is your own kingdom
> What you do is your own glory
> What you love is your own power
> What you live is your own story. ("Something for Nothing," from *2112*, 1976)

This is one of Peart's most bluntly libertarian passages, as he strongly defends people's moral right to their property, their pride in achievement, their choice of whom they will love, and how they live their lives. We also see a similar defense of people's "riches" in "Cinderella Man" from *A Farewell to Kings* (1977), whose lyrics were written by Lee. The main character in that song is wealthy, but he's also described as "human," "good," and "moral," and he used his riches "to challenge the hungry" to aspire to his own achievements. Lee has credited the 1936 Frank Capra film *Mr. Deeds Goes to Town* as an inspiration for the lyrics. This moral defense of self-interest is a key piece of the version of libertarianism that is associated with Rand and was a big influence in Rush's early work.

Rand also influenced the band in several other ways not directly associated with libertarianism. In a 2009 interview on CBC radio, Geddy said that her emphasis on artistic integrity and sticking to your principles, particularly as demonstrated in *The Fountainhead* (1943), were also very influential on the band. This can certainly be seen in the lyrics to "The Spirit of Radio" from 1980's *Permanent Waves*, in many ways the quintessential Rush song. Peart's lyrics speak of the struggle for artistic integrity in an increasingly commercialized music world, stating that "glittering prizes and endless compromises shatter the illusion of integrity." In 1987's "Mission" from *Hold Your Fire*, Peart returns to the theme of the power of the creative genius with a clear and principled artistic vision. And the final verse of "Natural Science" (also from *Permanent Waves)* also touches on the importance of integrity and honesty. Finally, Rand's rejection of formal religion and any notion of God is present in Peart's self-described agnosticism in songs such as "Freewill" on *Permanent Waves* and in several songs on 2007's *Snakes & Arrows*, especially "Armor and Sword," "The Way the Wind Blows" and "Faithless."[3]

And the Meek Shall Inherit the Earth

No discussion of Rand's influence on Rush's libertarianism would be complete without a focus on the twenty minute suite "2112" from the 1976 album of the same name. Paralleling the plot of Rand's novella *Anthem* (1938)—but see also Chapter 2 of this book, the song is a powerful statement of many central libertarian ideas, even if it's not always true to Rand's aesthetic.

Anthem is set in a future collectivist society where the concept of the individual, including the word "I," has been obliterated and social life is controlled by various "councils." Members of the society are assigned mates and jobs and are given names that serve the ideological interests of the rulers. As a result, the society has become primitive, lacking electricity and other modern technology and conveniences. The plot revolves around one dissident young man who begins to question the collectivism of the society after finding evidence of a prior society that had advanced technology, including electricity. He tries to do what he thinks is the right thing by bringing these advances to his society through the World Council of Scholars, but they reject his discovery and seek to punish him for daring to think on his own. He ends up running away to the forest to live in the "modern" house he found there, along with his wife-to-be.

---

[3] Editor's note: In addition, "Countdown" from 1982's *Signals* parallels Rand's enthusiasm for the Apollo 11 lunar mission, but updated to the space-shuttle era. See Durrell Bowman, "Permanent Change: Rush, Musicians' Rock, and the Progressive Post-Counterculture" (UCLA, Ph.D. dissertation in Musicology, 2003), pp. 203–05; <http://durrellbowman.com/PDFS/DBowman_dissertation.pdf>.

In "2112," we see a similar plot structure, with a guitar playing the role of the electric light and the action taking place among the planets. The Priests of the Temples of Syrinx similarly control the main character's collectivist society, having "taken care of everything" including all forms of expressions such as books and music. The Priests similarly reject the main character's gift of music that he presents quite sincerely. Though some have argued that, unlike *Anthem*, "2112" ends with the protagonist's despair at the pessimistic-sounding assertion of the Priests, Peart said in an interview on the *Classic Albums: Moving Pictures and 2112* DVD that the end of the song is the good guys returning to defeat the Priests, implying that the protagonist has not died in vain.[4]

"2112" contains several themes central to libertarian political philosophy.[5] The most central is the power of the individual to disrupt the best-laid plans of the collective. The Priests believe they have created an orderly society, and its citizens agree that they are ruled by the Priests' "benevolent wisdom." The Priests, however, cannot stop human curiosity and creativity from finding new and better ways of doing things, whether it's the electric light in *Anthem* or making music in "2112." When the Priests tell our hero that his guitar "doesn't fit the plan," they are expressing one of the essential tensions that libertarianism sees in all forms of collectivism: how to maintain a government-directed pattern of outcomes while still allowing for a significant degree of individual freedom. The Priests have decided to try to stamp out freedom, but they rightly recognize that they cannot have both equality as their "stock in trade" and permit any real freedom.

This point has been raised by many libertarian political philosophers, especially in the twentieth century. Nobel Prize winning economist Friedrich Hayek argued in *The Constitution of Liberty* (1960) that if we want equality of outcomes, we have to treat people unequally, and if we want to treat people equally, we have to accept that outcomes will not be equal. Equality of outcomes will

---

[4] See Durrell Bowman's chapter in *Progressive Rock Reconsidered* (Routledge, 2002) for a detailed discussion of how "2112" works musically.

[5] "2112" also reflects the Randian emphasis on artistic integrity noted earlier, as the song can be read as a metaphor for the band's own struggles against pressure from their label to be more "radio-friendly" after the relative commercial failure of *2112*'s predecessor *Caress of Steel* (1975) and its two songs of ten minutes or more. Whatever the lyrical content, the passion and anger of the music of "2112" have always struck me as the band giving a big middle finger to their critics.

require limiting the freedom of some or many. Permitting freedom will mean that we cannot make everything "fit the plan."

In *Anarchy, State, and Utopia* (1974), Robert Nozick proposes a thought experiment in order to make a similar point. Suppose we desire a society of equal incomes. Suppose we start everyone with equal incomes. Suppose further that we still give people the freedom to spend that income as they please. Suppose even further that many of them really enjoy watching Wilt Chamberlin (or Kobe Bryant, to take a more current Laker) play basketball and voluntarily relinquish some of their incomes to do it. After a while, Wilt will become quite rich and everyone else a little financially poorer and our society will no longer be equal. Freedom disrupts planned patterns. The only way to keep to the plan is to limit the freedom to spend. If you permit that freedom, you won't get your desired pattern of outcomes, whether it's total equality or any other pre-determined distribution of power or resources.

Either you have a plan and a collective purpose, or you have freedom. You can't have both.

Just Think about the Average

Peart plays off this tension between freedom and equality even more powerfully in "The Trees." With themes that strongly parallel Kurt Vonnegut's short story "Harrison Bergeron" where equality among humans is maintained by forcing the strong to wear weights and the smart to hear disruptive buzzers in their ears, the song can be understood to use the allegory of trees to argue that people are not equal and that the only way to make them equal is by brute force. The Oaks presumably have not used force against the smaller Maples, rather they are simply taller and more able to get sunlight. When trees can grow as their own nature or preferences allows, there's no reason to think they will be equal. Again, freedom generates inequality.

The Maples, however, are not content to accept that inequality. With actual trees there are limits to how high different types of trees can grow, but that is not the case if we extend the metaphor to human achievement. Almost any human is capable of reaching heights of accomplishment or wealth. In this case, rather than trying to equal the Oaks by their own effort, the Maples decide that the only way to achieve that goal is by force through the power of government. The result is one of Peart's best lines, finishing the song by noting that after passing a "noble law," "the trees are all kept equal by hatchet, axe, and saw."

Aside from making a point similar to that of "2112" by emphasizing how fitting society into a pre-determined outcome can only come at the price of freedom, "The Trees" makes two other libertarian observations. First, it shows that no matter how much we might hope that the power of government will be used for desirable purposes, once that power is available to be used, it will likely get used for more socially destructive ends. Although many argue that the complexity of modern society is a reason why we need a more powerful government to help control and direct it, libertarianism flips that point on its head. If society is so complex, how can we expect fallible humans like us to control it from the top down via government? In fact, we know from all kinds of natural and social processes, such as the Internet and wikis as well as biological evolution, that complexity is more likely to be produced by undesigned, rule-guided processes than by edict from the top down.

Of course, complexity in and of itself is not automatically good. However we also know that if spontaneous ordering processes such as evolution and market economies have the right filters in place, the complexity they produce is largely good. No such system is perfect but the degree of coordinated complexity that they produce—by making use of a large volume of scattered and often contextual information—cannot be matched by intentional human design. This is one of the central insights of Hayek's work, especially his famous essay "The Use of Knowledge in Society" in his book *Individualism and Economic Order* (1948).

When politicians then fail in their well-intentioned attempts to control the overly complex, the power they've acquired to do so sits there waiting to be grabbed by those whose intentions are perhaps more suspect. Returning to "The Trees," the power of the law is there waiting to be grabbed by the Maples who wish to use it for their own benefit rather than some larger public (or forest) interest. Libertarianism often makes use of what's known as "Public Choice Theory" to explain the way in which politics works. This body of theory argues that people will gladly use the political process to enrich themselves (or harm their competition) if that power is available to them. And politicians will gladly cooperate by doing the bidding of those private citizens as they can provide votes. Like a pile of food to a pack of wild baboons, the coercive power of the state will always attract those who are willing to use force against others. This is why libertarianism argues for strict limits on what governments can do, even if the intentions of those in power are noble.

"The Trees" also illustrates the libertarian argument that trying to enrich one's own narrow special interest through government leads to worse outcomes for everyone. The Maples think they will achieve their goal by passing that "noble law," but the reality is that the trees are *all* kept equal by brute force. Peart's closing line strongly suggests that not only will the hatchet cut the Oaks down, it will cut the Maples down too, possibly because there are yet other trees who see the Maples as a threat. The entire society is made worse off by the excessive use of government coercion, including those who thought they would benefit from it. Libertarians believe that once the door is opened to using the state in this way, there's no stopping how it will be used and by whom. As Peart wrote in "Grand Designs," "So much poison in power, the principles get left out." This is why libertarianism sees the need to limit drastically the scope of government power.

We've Taken Care of Everything, the Words You Read, the Songs You Sing

The view of government held by libertarians could just be written off as pure cynicism if they did not provide arguments for why they are deeply skeptical about what politics can accomplish. That distrust of politics and politicians is evident in a number of Rush's songs, particularly from their later albums.

Lyrical themes in "Bastille Day" from 1975's *Caress of Steel* and "Closer to the Heart" on *A Farewell to Kings* from 1977 reflect Peart's distrust of the "men who hold high places." And nowhere is that clearer in their early music than in the title track from 1977's *A Farewell to Kings*. The title itself is enough to get the point across, as is the album's cover of an apparently dead king still on his throne as all has collapsed around him. The lyrical reference to "scheming demons dressed in kingly guise" and the theme of the current generation's need to break with the past's unwillingness to challenge political authority reflect a very libertarian skepticism about the political process. In "The Weapon" from 1982's *Signals*, Peart picks up this theme again with the opening lyric's cynical reference to Franklin Roosevelt's inaugural address ("we've got nothing to fear but fear itself? Not pain, not failure, not fatal tragedy?") and the suggestion that politicians are employing fear and ignorance as "weapons to be used against us."

The 1985 album *Power Windows* is full of discussions of a variety of notions of power, including political power. "The Big Money" condemns the damage that money can do, but it also refers to the way in which big money can influence the political process with yet another reference to the "kingdoms they would rule." For libertarians, wealth acquired through market exchange isn't dangerous in and of itself, but it becomes dangerous when it is the path to political power. Then the wealthy can rig the rules in their favor. The implication is that the smaller government is, the less likely it is that the wealthy can turn that wealth into political power. In the marketplace, wealth lasts only so long as people wish to continue to buy the seller's product. In the language of political philosophy, markets let us "exit" from the power that wealth brings; politics does not.

The same album has "Territories," with its anti-nationalist and anti-imperialist theme, suggesting a wariness of politicians and their ability to co-opt the citizenry into their military adventures. Just as libertarianism is skeptical of the ability of politics to solve problems at home, it applies the same arguments toward what governments can do in trying to solve problems around the world. "Territories" nicely captures this point.

In *Permanent Waves'* "Natural Science" Peart has a particularly sophisticated statement about the inability of those with power to bend the world to their wishes. More specifically, the song can be read as a critique of what Hayek has called "scientism," or the belief that we can take the methods and results of the natural sciences as a model for how to construct society.[6] Each of the subsections of the song develops one element of the critique.

The opening section's reference to the individual tide pools in which individual creatures are "chasing out their own destinies," ignorant of the broader sea in which they operate, parallels the way in which individuals, families, and firms are seen by Hayek as dif-

---

[6] Hayek's critique of scientism was also a critique of too much faith in the power of reason. His views here were one of the reasons Rand distanced herself from libertarians, as she correctly perceived that the Hayekians did not share her views on important non-political matters.

ferent from the broader social order. In those smaller, more intimate social settings, we can arrange things from the top down. However, when each of these entities comes into contact with other such entities in the broader social "sea," the complexity of their interactions precludes those sort of top-down arrangements. The song's refrain captures this problem of how complexity creates this sort of ignorance and sets up the possibility of unintended and undesirable consequences in the process:

> Wheels within wheels in a spiral array
> A pattern so grand and complex
> Time after time we lose sight of the way
> Our causes can't see their effects. ("Natural Science," *Permanent Waves*, 1980)

Peart is cautioning us against thinking we're smarter than we really are when it comes to knowing how the social world ought to be arranged, paralleling Hayek's definition of economics in his book *The Fatal Conceit* (1988) as demonstrating to people "how little they really know about what they imagine they can design."

The second verse goes right to the role that science can play as a false model for social interaction. It may be obvious that human beings aren't pieces on a chessboard to be directed by some greater human power, as Adam Smith observed in *The Theory of Moral Sentiments*, but our ability to manipulate the natural world has understandably led us to think we can do the same with the social world. This "scientistic" prejudice is at the heart of libertarianism's critique of various forms of social and economic planning. The second verse's tribute to the power of science (even as it also recognizes its "messes" and tragedies) conveys this idea, but it ends with an apt description of the attitude toward society of those who ascribe too much power to science:

> In their own image,
> Their world is fashioned.
> No wonder they don't understand. ("Natural Science," *Permanent Waves*, 1980)

Those who see the power of science, rationality, and planning in their own lives are often too quick to think it's a model for how society as whole (that broader sea) should be structured.

Hayek and other libertarians have argued that it's simply not possible for such planners to acquire the knowledge that they would need to organize the social world that way. The belief that we can dispense with the disorganized, "anarchic" market and other undesigned social institutions and replace them with intentionally designed and rationally planned ones goes back at least as far as Marx. Looking around and seeing what looks like the duplication and waste of competition, many critics have called for just that sort of economic planning by using the methods of science.

Libertarianism, at least in Hayek's hands, claims that the knowledge needed to plan a society from the top is not only too vast, but not even in a form that can be centralized. In addition to being dispersed in this fashion, a good deal of the most important knowledge in the social world is not in a form that we could articulate to such planners even if they could get us all in one place, real or virtual. For example, we know how to ride a bike even if we cannot describe in detail how exactly we keep our balance. These tacit forms of knowledge cannot be communicated through numbers and language, but can be made available to others through our actions in the market, especially in how prices change to reflect our knowledge.

The supposed waste and duplication of competition is not a problem that can be solved by scientific social planning. Instead, it is part of the social learning process that is economic and social competition. Libertarians like Hayek argue that we need competition, and therefore individual freedom in the marketplace, because we are ignorant and it is through competing that we learn by making available to others our inarticulate knowledge by our acts of buying and selling. Consider the analogy to sports: the reason we play the Super Bowl is to figure out which is the better team. We simply can't know who is better without actual competition, as the occasional upset demonstrates. The same holds true for the economy and society more broadly, which is why we have to resist the temptation to create a scientifically planned society.

In the final verse of "Natural Science," Peart recognizes these limits to what we might do with science in much the same way as the libertarian critics of scientism have. The libertarians have not denied the important and vital contributions that science has and must continue to make to human well-being. What they have argued is that science (or science-based technology) works best when it's kept in its place as a way to manipulate the natural world. It creates trouble when its methods are applied to human beings, who have free will and whose knowledge cannot be easily accessed and centralized in order to be organized and ordered from the top. "Science, like nature, must also be tamed" very pithily gets at this libertarian argument.

The libertarian insight that no one knows better how to construct your life than you do is one way to see this rejection of the superior knowledge of political leaders of any political philosophy. In "Witch Hunt" from 1981's *Moving Pictures* Peart's biting sarcasm about "those who know what's best for us" having to save us from ourselves was written in the context of the Moral Majority and other similar conservative movements in the early 1980s, but could also be applied to liberals' unwillingness to tolerate certain economic choices people might make. And its implication that no one knows better than us what's best for us is also a very nice summary of how libertarianism views politics.

Just Think of What My Life Might Be

So it's pretty clear what libertarianism is *against*: government interference with individual freedom. What exactly is libertarianism *for*? The answer is also to be found in a variety of Rush songs, especially in more recent years: libertarianism celebrates markets, cosmopolitanism, and tolerance.

Peart's lyrical output includes very few references to the economic elements of what a libertarian society would look like. I've already mentioned the "what you own is your own kingdom" line from "Something for Nothing," and one could add various lyrics extolling the virtues of hard work and craftsmanship, which are essential to a functioning market economy. And "Red Barchetta" from *Moving Pictures* can be read as a battle between economic regulation ("the Motor Law") and the freedom of the individual. One of Peart's most explicit mentions of the importance of markets is in "Heresy" from 1991's *Roll the Bones*. In the context of the fall of communism, Peart writes:

The counter-revolution
At the counter of a store

People buy the things they want
And borrow for a little more. ("Heresy," *Roll the Bones*, 1991)

Seeing the simple act of buying and selling as "counter-revolution-ary" and as an expression of newfound freedom is consistent with libertarianism.[7]

Markets, however, are essential to the two other libertarian values of cosmopolitanism and tolerance. In a market economy, people with wildly different tastes can still have those preferences met without denying the same opportunity to others. Some people like Hawaiian shirts, others prefer polos. Some people like a good doppelbock beer, others like Budweiser. In a market, we don't have to make one decision for everyone. Compare this point to how politically-granted monopolies work. Either a public school district is going to teach about same-sex marriages or it's not; everyone in the district must accept the decision. Imagine a world in which we had to vote on whether wearing loud Hawaiian shirts was permissible or not. We'd have one decision for everyone and no accounting for differing tastes. Those with unusual tastes would lose out.

Libertarians argue that markets provide a process by which we can tolerate each other's differences by making a variety of options available that meet the diverse preferences of consumers. I might hate Hawaiian shirts, but since we aren't making one decision for everyone, as we would through the political process, I tolerate those who wear the shirts because they are not forcing their preference on me and because they must equally tolerate my choices they don't like. Markets enable us to engage in a level of tolerance of difference that would be much more difficult in a less libertarian world.

Tolerance and cosmopolitanism go beyond markets. "Witch Hunt" is one of many Rush songs that criticize intolerance and make the case for permitting people to engage in what the philosopher John Stuart Mill called "experiments in living." As noted earlier, no one knows better than we what is best for us to read, think, or ingest. A similar theme is present in 1993's "Nobody's Hero,"

---

[7] Peart has also written lyrics critical of materialism in a variety of places as well, from "The Spirit of Radio," to "The Big Money," to "Superconductor" (*Presto*, 1989), to "Faithless." If materialism means believing that material possessions are morally preferable to other values or that money is the only measure of an object's worth, then we can reject materialism but still think a free market is the most desirable economic system.

from *Counterparts*, where the main character's gay friend is perceived not as a threat but as someone introducing the character to a "wider reality" along the lines of Mill's experiments. Several songs on *Snakes & Arrows* deal with problems of intolerance. "Armor and Sword" contrasts the problematic use of faith as a sword to attack others with the more tolerant notion of faith as a way we protect ourselves in times of trouble. The reference to "some by sermon, some by force" in "Faithless" echoes this same theme. And "The Way the Wind Blows" decries fundamentalist intolerance and ignorance of all stripes.

All of these ideas are part of libertarianism's social philosophy. Libertarianism doesn't just limit government's involvement in the boardroom; it treats the bedroom the same way. The state has no business in mandating or prohibiting any behaviors between consenting adults. Just as competition in a free market helps us learn what products people want and how best to produce them, Mill's "experiments in living" and the tolerance it requires exposes us to new ideas and possibilities. Libertarians see this process of social tolerance through social competition as a key feature of the good society.

Nor does this tolerance stop at the water's edge or even at the edge of our own communities, however we define them. The tolerance libertarianism requires of the peaceful, consenting choices of other adults also implies an openness to interaction with those who are different from us. This is clear in a number of Rush songs. "Territories" from *Power Windows* reminds us that our common humanity comes before our nationalistic pride; "Tai Shan" from *Hold Your Fire* celebrates what we can learn from cultures very different from our own; and "Hand over Fist" from *Presto* invites us to treat strangers with openness and warmth rather than fear and anger. The metaphor of the coral reef becomes a way to conceptualize reaching across difference, in this case gender, in "Alien Shore" from *Counterparts*. All of these are part of a cosmopolitan openness to, and tolerance of, difference that are an important part of libertarianism.

For libertarians, economic interaction is the primary way that we cross these lines of difference. Whatever the color of our skin or the nature of our beliefs, we can take advantage of our differences and exchange goods and services to mutual benefit. The lure of profit enables us to overcome our differences by providing a benefit to interacting with those who are different from us. As Jonathan

Sachs, a British rabbi, put it in his book *The Dignity of Difference* (2002): "It is through exchange that difference becomes a blessing, not a curse." For libertarians, there is a seamless thread running from the freedom of the marketplace to the cosmopolitanism and tolerance of the social world.

There's Something Here that's as Strong as Life

In exploring the ways in which Rush's lyrics can teach us about libertarianism as a political philosophy, I have deliberately overlooked a number of songs whose lyrics seem not so consistent with libertarianism. I have also very deliberately side-stepped the question of whether the members of the band are libertarians themselves. The latter question isn't particularly interesting if we're concerned with what the lyrics themselves have to teach us. (The answer, for those who really care, is that Lee and Lifeson are not libertarians and Peart has called himself a "left-libertarian" at times.) The question of those "other" lyrics is not so easily avoided and does force us to consider what might unite all of Peart's work.

Even where Peart seems to reject elements of libertarianism more explicitly, he still holds on to a very clear commitment to the dignity and centrality of the individual and the individual's ability to achieve greatness and overcome tragedy. What we might call Rush's "individualism" (and I do think *this* is a description that applies to all three band members) provides the overarching philosophical theme of their career, from their own choices as a band to their lyrical content. Although libertarianism doesn't require a hardcore sort of individualism, the two certainly are compatible.

Much of Peart's more recent output seems to fall in this category of individualism, from the suburban protagonists of "Subdivisions" and "The Analog Kid" on *Signals* to the quasi-Randianism of "Mission," to "Stick it Out" and "Everyday Glory" from *Counterparts*, to many of semi-autobiographical songs from 2002's *Vapor Trails*. This sort of individualism and its homage to those who stick to their principles, don't blame others for their mistakes, and resist the easy and common is, again, very consistent with libertarianism, but its appeal extends more broadly to those who feel outcast or different along a variety of dimensions. This is also why Rush's fan base, though disproportionately libertarian-oriented compared to the general population, also contains people from every political view imaginable.

Each of the band's fans sees in Rush's emphasis on the individual a reflection of their own struggles to be different and to resist the pressures of conformity they see in their own lives. That desire for individual freedom is broadly shared, even as we all understand differently what such freedom might entail politically. Rush's lyrics generally point in the direction of libertarianism as the set of political beliefs that best fulfills that desire, but like most writers, Peart's work is not easily pigeonholed into one box or another. Even as we recognize the complexity of Peart's own views and the lyrics he has produced, Rush's work still provides numerous opportunities to understand the political philosophy of libertarianism.[8]

---

[8] The author would like to thank Aeon Skoble for helpful suggestions and the smart, funny, crazy, and deeply devoted Rush fans at alt.music.rush for putting up with me posting stuff like this for the last fifteen years.

20

Neil Peart versus Ayn Rand

DEENA WEINSTEIN
and MICHAEL A. WEINSTEIN

"For a start, the extent of my influence by the writings of Ayn Rand should not be overestimated—I am no one's disciple," Neil Peart said. Peart's remark was occasioned by having had to deal with repeated judgments by adverse rock critics, serious commentators and scholars, supporters of Ayn Rand's philosophy, and Rush fans that he was—as he said of himself as a youth—a "Randroid." It was Peart who invited the connection to Rand by writing the lyrics to "Anthem," which borrows its title from a Rand novella; patterning his narrative song cycle "2112" on the plotline of that novella; and publicly expressing admiration for her in the notes to Rush's album *2112*.

Various writers put the Rand brand on Peart. Miles, who interviewed him for *New Musical Express* in 1978, says: "I got the job of interviewing Rush because I was the only one on NME who knew who Ayn Rand was . . . and yes Rush follow her ideas. The epic '2112' is a re-write of her book *Anthem* and they also name their Canadian record label after the same book."[1] Other writers have nuanced Miles's judgment in a variety of sometimes-conflicting ways, but the brand has stuck, at least for Peart's lyrics written in the 1970s.[2] Even those who are not convinced that Peart is a

---

[1] Miles, "Rush: Is Everybody Feelin' all RIGHT? (Geddit . . . ?)" *New Musical Express* (March 4th, 1978).

[2] After the 1970s Peart became more independent of Rand's influence. His influences were broadened to include Ernest Hemingway, William Faulkner, and F. Scott Fitzgerald. Malcolm Dome, "Interview with Neil Peart," *Metal Hammer* (April 25th, 1988), <http://yyz.com/NMS/HTML/articles/mh0488.html>.

Randroid interpret his lyrics by using Rand's writings to determine where the lyrics convey meanings similar to her philosophy and political views.

It is high time to vindicate Peart's repeated claim that he is "no one's disciple" and to re-brand him, even for that period when he seemed to be closest to Rand's thinking and even said that he was.[3]

Dystopias

The literary genre of dystopia emerged in the early nineteenth century as part of the romantic reaction against some of the effects of the industrial revolution and the rise of the mass industrial city— the "metropolis." The Romantic Movement was centered on the deprivations wrought by modern life; in particular, it perceived insensitivity to emotions, destruction of deep social bonds, and hostility to the concrete, particular individual or group that had been effaced by the anonymous atomized mass.

Most generally, a dystopia is an imagined society, in which certain features of the present society are exaggerated to reflect the conflict between the text's values and the reigning social values. Dystopias are "axiological narratives"—dramas of the confrontation between the oppressive and malign system and the contradictory desires of a framing character or protagonist who represents the values affirmed in the text. "Dystopia" was coined by British philosopher John Stuart Mill in a speech in parliament in 1868 against his political adversaries: "they ought to be called dys-topians or caco-topians. What is commonly called Utopian is something too good to be practicable; but what they appear to favour is too bad to be practicable." Dystopias are cautionary tales meant to awaken readers or listeners to dangerous tendencies in the world around them.

Dystopias vary according to what the text finds objectionable in the present society and the values that the text poses against it. For example, among the most famous dystopias, in E.M. Forster's novella "The Machine Stops," a system enforcing extreme isolation through technological means is countered by affirming nature, vitality and human connection; in George Orwell's novel *Nineteen Eighty-Four*, a regime's systematic destruction of truth is opposed

---

[3] Mary Turner and Neil Peart "Rush: Off The Record with Mary Turner," originally broadcast in 1984 <http://yyz.com/NMS/HTML/interviews/otr1984.html>.

by an appeal to honesty; and in Aldous Huxley's novel *Brave New World*, a tightly ordered caste system created and maintained by biological engineering is opposed by the appearance of an individual who is defectively engineered.

There's no single formula for constructing a dystopia. Some texts, like *Brave New World* and H.G. Wells's *The Time Machine*, emphasize tendencies towards hierarchy in modern society—eugenics for Huxley and class inequality for Wells. Others, like *Nineteen Eighty-Four*, identify tendencies towards enforced equality—epitomized, for Orwell, in Soviet Communism. Egalitarian dystopias turn on the feature of an elite—in Orwell's case, the "inner party"—imposing a collectivist order in the name of "brotherhood" or "humanity." The irony is capsulized in Orwell's allegorical fable *Animal Farm* where the dictator—a pig named Napoleon—proclaims: "All animals are equal, but some animals are more equal than others." Most, if not all, dystopian societies are structured hierarchically—in some, they are forthrightly so; and in others the ruling class manipulates an ideology of equality through self-delusion, hypocrisy or cynicism.

"2112" and *Anthem* are egalitarian dystopias, which resemble Orwell's two books in referring to Soviet Communism as the historical model for dystopian tendencies, and generalizing those tendencies to a criticism of modern society. They form a special sub-type in that their dystopian societies are successors to modern society's dynamic of continual change, experimentation and innovation. The ruling classes in the regimes that they depict are reactionary and are devoted to arresting change in a rigid system in which they monopolize a static culture in the name of fraternal equality and, therefore, maintain their grip on power. In that respect, they're different from the dystopia that is most frequently compared to *Anthem*—Yevgeny Zamyatin's *We*, which also uses Soviet Communism as its base in reality—where the ruling class mobilizes the entire society in the enterprise of building a space ship.

Most generally, "2112" and *Anthem* oppose the value of the individual's creative freedom to the deadening leveling of individual difference, indoctrination and conformity of a totalitarian society operating under the myth of equality. The similarities between the two texts allow their differences to stand out in sharp relief when they are subjected to a critical contrast that focuses on their respective axiological narratives.

"2112"—Rush

Philosophical ideas are embedded in many cultural forms, among them rock songs. Some rock lyricists infuse their music with reflections on the meaning of life and the relations of the individual to society—two of the great philosophical themes of the twentieth century. The album *2112* is one of the most frequently cited examples of this turn to "serious rock."[4]

The first half of the album is a cycle of songs, "2112," each component of which is a chapter in a coherent narrative that chronicles the oppression wrought by the ruling class of an egalitarian society. As an egalitarian dystopia, "2112" shares with other works in that genre the confrontation of an individual who separates himself, or is separated from, the egalitarian order and from its ruling class, which smacks down any individuality or distinctiveness. The confrontation reveals the values and sense of life for which the individual stands against the egalitarian order and its ruling class – the philosophy of the work.

"2112" opens with a musical overture, which concludes with a single line, Jesus's famous dictum—"And the meek shall inherit the earth."

The story itself begins with the song "The Temples of Syrinx," in which the nameless protagonist contemplates with awe the temples of Federation city where the ruling class—the Priests—administer "every single facet of life" with their "benevolent Wisdom." There is, at the outset, no separation of the individual from the social order; indeed, there is affirmative conformity—the protagonist has been well indoctrinated.

The stage having been set for them, the Priests then have their triumphal say, proclaiming that they have "taken care of everything," constructed a cradle-to-grave welfare state, including in particular the forms of creative art. Their principle is fraternity—"one for all and all for one," working together as "common sons." The stanza ends with the first hint of dystopia; according to the Priests, there is "Never need to wonder how or why." Questioning—the essence of individual thinking—is out of the question.

The following stanza is the triumphal Priests' chorus, in which they exalt themselves and their "great computers." With all the

---

[4] See, for example, Deena Weinstein, *Serious Rock: The Artistic Vision of Modern Society in Pink Floyd, Rush, and Bruce Springsteen* (New World Perspectives, 1985).

"gifts of life" inside their walls, nobody on the outside has reason to be and do other than they have been told; the Priests have arrogated to themselves a monopoly over culture, and over life. The music, written by Alex Lifeson and Geddy Lee to accompany Peart's lyrics, accentuates the power of the Priests, and, in contrast, the weakness of the protagonist.

There is not a hint of overt repression or coercion in Federation city. At least in the case of the protagonist, identification of the individual with the regime is complete; no need for discipline (threats or punishment); persuasion (brainwashing and indoctrination) has done the work.

After the chorus, the Priests reiterate their ideology—the value of fraternity, adding that "equality" is their "stock in trade." With fraternity and equality, we have a "nice contented world" and can unfurl the red-star banner (a nod to Soviet Communism). Federation city takes from the French Revolution's motto equality and fraternity, leaving out its first term, liberty.

In the next song, "Discovery," the scene shifts abruptly and we find the protagonist alone in a room in the back of a cave under a "beloved" waterfall. How the cave was found and why the protagonist sought it is left unsaid. The break, however, is decisive; at the very least, the protagonist's love for the waterfall introduces the value of unspoiled nature—everything good is not the work of the Priests.

What follows is the first turning point in the plot—the moment at which the protagonist distinguishes himself from the fraternal-egalitarian brotherhood of Federation city. The protagonist discovers an "ancient miracle"—a guitar—from a past civilization and has no idea of what it is, except that it is "beautiful." Soon the protagonist learns to play the instrument and wonders at "my own music" and how "different it could be from the music of the temples!" Immediately, the protagonist is seized with the need to "share this new wonder" with "the people." Through exploring the possibilities of the discovery, the protagonist has created something that is better than the Priests have devised, yet the absolute principle of the Priests is that they have a justified monopoly on culture.

The gift that the protagonist has discovered and created—distinctive music—is a perfection of life through art, a good for its own sake that carries with it individualized expression. The act of perfection is self-sufficient and does not lead anywhere else; it is on another philosophical plane than the Priests' ideology, which is only concerned with caring for the collective good. Here "2112" approaches Friedrich Nietzsche's "joyful wisdom"—a transvalued relation of life and culture, in which they become united in moments of consummation.

The protagonist's attitude toward his "discovery" is not initially to exalt the ego—to feel satisfaction with self and to glorify it—but to delight in his art and to understand that he has found and actualized a higher value.

That the protagonist does not realize that presenting the "gift" to the Priests will necessarily meet with rejection shows how effective the Priests' brainwashing has been; in the protagonist's mind, goodness and power are united in the Priests. The protagonist is possessed of Nietzsche's "gift-giving virtue" that results from the overflowing perfections of life and is performed with perfect affirmation and with no sense of obligation.

The second half of "Discovery" is a repetition of the preceding stanzas, ending with the protagonist's dictum, "Let them all make their own music," and the conceit that "The Priests praise my name on this night"—an expectation that betrays the protagonist's need for validation by the Priests and a desire for recognition, which is contradictory to the ideology of Federation city. There's no acknowledgment that the gift would overturn the established order—its monopoly on life and culture; there is also no hint that the ruling class is unjust, only that it is unenlightened.

The next song, "Presentation," recounts the inevitable rejection by the Priests of the protagonist's gift. Having played the guitar for the Priests, the protagonist is met by their "grim, expressionless faces" and "words of quiet rejection" and "sullen dismissal," rather than the "grateful joy" that the protagonist had expected. Then one of the Priests, Father Brown, smashes the "precious instrument" to bits under his feet as the protagonist looks on in "shock and horror," the second turning point in the plot. With the destruction of the guitar, all is lost. Not knowing how to build another one or having lost the will to do so, the protagonist is left with the knowledge that his table of values has no place in society and that he will never actualize it again.

The rest of the song is a colloquy between the protagonist and the Priests in which the former pleads that in his music there is "something as strong as life," and the latter respond with their justification of their monopoly over life and culture. The music, they say, is "nothing new" and the guitar is "just another toy" that helped destroy "the elder race of man," which has been superseded. The protagonist's "silly whim" does not "fit the plan." The protagonist mounts an appeal once more, adding that the world "could use this beauty," but the Priests dismiss the protagonist, asserting: "Just think about the average / What use they have for you?"

The presentation is an abject failure for the protagonist, who merely pleads and never admonishes the Priests. On their side, the Priests never lose their calm, indifferent, and disapproving composure. There is no punishment to be meted out to the protagonist, who only had to be stopped from disrupting the plan. Their admonishment was a request or demand to see things through the eyes of the average, the others; to feel shame, not guilt, so as to fit in once again.

The next song, "Oracle: The Dream," finds the protagonist alone, having awakened from a visionary dream in which an oracle shows an alternative world with incredibly beautiful "sculptured cities" in which "the pure spirit of man" (not of the individual self) is "revealed in the lives and works / Of this world." The protagonist understands that the beautiful city represents "a complete different way to life" that had been "crushed by the Federation long ago," and sees "how meaningless life had become with the loss / Of all these things. . . ."

The rest of the song recounts how the protagonist wandered home after his gift had been rejected and "fell into a fitful sleep," attempting to "Escape to realms beyond the night." The dream is then retold, extolling the vision of "the hand of man" arising "With hungry mind and open eyes." The protagonist reveals that the dream describes the works of the "elder race," which had "left the planets long ago" and still exists, learns and grows. He will return one day to his rightful home to "tear the temples down" and bring "change."

For the protagonist, only the dream of a utopia is left. There's nothing to be done; there is only hope, if even that, for others to provide a restoration of value. "Oracle: The Dream" marks a moment of what Hegel called "unhappy consciousness" for the protagonist—a complete separation of the ideal and the actual, of fantasy and reality.

The onset of unhappy consciousness becomes full blown in the next song, "Soliloquy," in which the protagonist falls into existential despair. Alone in the cave behind the waterfall, his "last refuge in total despair." Unable to live under the Federation's control, yet with nowhere else to go, the "last hope" is to die and "pass into the world" of his dream and "know peace at last," relief from his perpetually frustrated will. The protagonist desires only that the dream does not fade from their memory.

Then the protagonist takes the existential plunge as he thinks of what his "life might be / In a world like I have seen," and expresses doubt that he "can carry on this cold and empty life / Oh, . . . noo!" The song ends with an expression of the most severe unhappy consciousness: "My spirits are low in the depths of despair/My lifeblood spills over."

As far as the protagonist is concerned, the despair of Hegel's "beautiful soul," the romantic figure of unhappy consciousness who is too good for the world, is the final word. Superiority does not follow, in the protagonist's case, from a false over-estimation of the self—as it does most often—but from knowledge of self-sufficient value that has been annihilated—life is not worth living in a world deprived of joyful wisdom.

"2112" is a romantic tragedy of a protagonist who discovers value, is rejected, and is relegated to despair. The protagonist is not a defiant rebel or a revolutionary; but merely the recipient of a gift and the would-be giver of that gift, never separated by individual will from the others. No future, no exit, perpetual anguish, the despair of living with a dying dream.

The last words in "2112" do not belong to the protagonist and are only heard on the recording, not printed in the lyrics. In the "Grand Finale," a disembodied official voice announces repeatedly: "Attention all planets of the solar federation / We have assumed control." Does this mean that the "elder race" has fulfilled the dream and razed the temples to create the beautiful city? Has the protagonist died and "passed on" to a better world? Is this just another dream? Or has the Federation assumed total control? Have the custodians of the "meek" inherited the planets?[5]

Whatever the final words signify, they have nothing to do with the protagonist's will, which has been irreparably crushed. Like Moses, who was never to enter the land of milk and honey, the protagonist has seen the Promised Land and will never live in it, if indeed anyone ever will. The gift of the instrument was no delu-

---

[5] See Durrell Bowman's chapter in *Progressive Rock Reconsidered* (Routledge, 2002) for a musicological explanation that the powerful, heavy metal music of the end of "2112" could mean that the Priests have re-asserted hegemony over their society and that any further attempts at individualism will also fail. On the other hand, in 2010 Peart described the ending as "the good guys . . . the cavalry coming."

sion; this is the Nietzschian tragedy of a nihilistic world, in which hierarchies of value are destroyed by a will to level distinctions of excellence—egalitarianism as nihilism.

Within the traditions of modern culture, "2112" is an example of the romance of social disillusionment, which arose in the early nineteenth century—most notably in Goethe's novels *The Sorrows of Young Werther* and *Wilhelm Meister*—at the same time as the literary form of dystopia. As a reflection on the embattled individual, the romance of social disillusionment most generally chronicles the fate of an individual who finds that the social order does not honor genuine value and does not even live up to its own code. Most recently, many of the countercultural youth of the 1960s understood themselves to be in this situation, accusing the powers that be of the hypocrisy of failing to live up to the ideals that they had espoused and taught to the young. The gap between the ideal and the actual set up by such an understanding leads the individual to suffer unhappy consciousness, the moments of which structure the romance.

David C. Durst, who draws on the work of Marxist philosopher and critic George Lukacs, has explored the theme of romantic disillusionment historically and conceptually. According to Durst, in the literature of romantic disillusionment, the protagonist "confronts a world of social conventions that remain alien and hostile to his inner aspirations," and, in consequence, "he cannot find the truth of his inner destiny in these alien social conventions."[6]

Following Lukacs, Durst argues that when faced with the conflict between aspiration and convention, the protagonist feels overwhelmed and is forced to acknowledge that his desire for an ideal life is doomed to frustration and that he is consigned to "the certainty of defeat." Inevitable failure leaves the protagonist with the options of either indulging in "the uninhibited activity of abstract idealism" or the "pure contemplation of romantic disillusionment."

Our close reading of "2112" indicates that it is a paradigm case of romantic disillusionment. At the end of the work, the protagonist first dreams of an ideal city in which their aspirations are fulfilled (abstract idealism) and, after awakening, plunges into despair. "2112" is a work of romantic pessimism.

---

[6] David C. Durst, *Weimar Modernism* (Lexington, 2004), pp. 37–38.

Anthem—Rand

At first reading, the parallels between "2112" and *Anthem* are striking. Both the song cycle and the novella are romances of social disillusionment in the context of a fraternal-egalitarian dystopia that has crushed a civilization deemed superior in the texts. Both works feature protagonists who separate themselves from the oppressive order, go outside the boundaries of the city, discover a power from olden times, experiment with that power and perfect it, present their discovery to the ruling class expecting affirmation, are rejected, and experience the aftermath of that rejection.

It is obvious that within the basic plot structures of the romance of social disillusionment and its dystopian variant, many different stories can be told that express different and often clashing sentiments and philosophies of life. The characters of the protagonists need not be the same, the dystopian orders can vary, the discoveries can have different meanings, and the rejection and its aftermath need not lead to the same results for the respective protagonists. In each of those respects, "2112" and *Anthem* are significantly divergent, indeed conflicting, narratives.

Reading *Anthem* through "2112" will not involve close attention to the details of its plot. Instead, the focus will be on its contrasts with "2112," both in the features that the two works share and the elements that are present in *Anthem* and not in "2112." Our aim is to separate "2112" from *Anthem*.

Contrasts appear at the outset in the definitions of the characters of the protagonists. *Anthem*'s protagonist is a young male named Equality 7-2521, whereas the protagonist of "2112" is nameless and ungendered, abstracted from reality and serving as a paradigm for any individual encounter with existence. "2112" has a mythic quality, whereas *Anthem* partakes of the details of a world, even though its world is imagined.

The protagonist of "2112" and Equality are also radically different people. Rather than a complacent and compliant, indeed awestruck, conformist, Equality has always known that he was different from others. He has a burning passion for knowledge and has striven for a place among the Scholars, who monopolize knowledge. Moreover, he has repeatedly committed "transgressions" against the code of conformity administered by the World Council. Indeed, Equality says that he was "born with a curse" and knows that he is "evil," but he cannot help himself, although he has tried "to be like all our brother men, for all men must be alike."[7] (p. 5) Equality is distinguished from the herd by nature; the protagonist of "2112" is one of the many.

When we meet him, Equality has already been rejected as a Scholar, due to his expressions of independence, which have placed him on a trajectory of confrontation. His path will take him from one transgression to the next as the world opens up to him; he will need to overcome guilt for his distinctiveness and superiority, as he fights to affirm his own gifts and the gift that he will offer to the Scholars. The activist character of Equality could not be more different from the passivity of the protagonist of "2112" who never willfully sins against the order of Federation city and is never made to feel guilty, only shamed.

In the chapters of *Anthem* between the stage setting and the discovery, Equality commits the sin of bonding with a particular woman, who will later become his mate. The dystopia specifically excludes romantic relations, and all sex is conducted institutionally for purposes of procreation. Thus, the bond with Liberty gives Equality the basis for a social relation different and apart from the World Council's collectivist order. The protagonist of "2112," however, always remains alone.[8]

Prior to his discovery, Equality, who has been relegated to the job of Street Sweeper, has found a neglected tunnel containing artifacts from the preceding civilization—the Unmentionable Times—and has begun to experiment with them. He's aware of the dangers that loom, because he has witnessed a public execution of a man who had defied the ruling class by uttering the "Unspeakable Word," which we later learn is the first-person pronoun, "I." Rather than the Priests of "2112" who are sublimely indifferent in their doctrinal power, the ruling class of the World Council is punitive, violent, and resorts to torture. As *Anthem* sets up the events to follow, antagonism between Equality and the authorities is inevitable. The Priests in "2112" are beyond antagonism and the protagonist does not have the will and psychological resources to stand against them.

---

7 Ayn Rand, *Anthem* (originally 1938), <http://www.noblesoul.com/orc/texts/anthem/complete.html>.

8 See also Durrell Bowman's chapter in *Progressive Rock Reconsidered* (Routledge, 2002) for further discussions of solitary male protagonists in Rush's "Xanadu" and "Cygnus X-1" (both from *A Farewell to Kings*, 1977).

Through his experiments in the tunnel, Equality discovers electricity and is able to re-invent the electric light, which, despite the fact that he already has been brutally lashed for violating curfew, he is determined to bring before the Scholars, expecting, with a naivety that strains credibility, that they will embrace his gift.

The contrast between the gifts of electricity and of music is telling: technological progress versus personal artistic expression. Indeed, the Priests in Federation city ("2112") possess and glory in the advanced technology of computers, whereas the World Council (*Anthem*) presides over a world lit by candles. *Anthem's* scale of values exalts a world of great humanly constructed works; "2112" ennobles the joyful wisdom of consummatory moments. *Anthem's* motto might be stated as "Individuals and Electrification," a variation on Lenin's dictum, "Soviets and Electrification."

When Equality, still recovering from the lashes that he has suffered as punishment, presents his primitive electric light to the Scholars, their rejection of it is a foregone conclusion. Just as in "2112," the Scholars call the invention "useless" and point out that it does not fit in with their plan, but instead of simply dismissing it, they react with horror and fury, immediately calling for the transgressor's severe punishment, which is to be determined by the World Council. At this decisive moment in the plot, Equality is able to flee, carrying his invention with him into the Uncharted Forest beyond the city, where he will begin a new life with his mate, Liberty, and start to reconstruct the old civilization. All is not lost, as it was when the guitar was smashed in "2112"; rather, there is a new beginning.

For Equality, Liberty is the "Golden One:" for her, he is the "Unconquered." He soon learns to speak the "Unspeakable Word" and glories in his selfhood. He is at the "end of the quest:" "I wished to know the meaning of things. I am the meaning" (p. 41). Far from an existential tragedy, *Anthem* is a modern comedy in which the romance of social disillusionment ends, not in unhappy consciousness, but in affirmative reintegration of the ego in a new world.

Individuals unite; you have nothing to lose but your chains. You have a world to win. That is the lesson of the Unconquered. The protagonist of "2112" remains nameless, with no exit and only a dying dream. The same plotline of social disillusionment has issued in entirely contrasting meanings.

Hardly Rand-y Peart

Our re-branding of "Neil Peart" is done. At least as far as "2112" is concerned, the song cycle does not betray *Anthem*'s sense and philosophy of life, but a radically different one with affinities to romantic pessimism rather than the novella's romantic optimism. If "2112" is a "re-write" of *Anthem*, it is one that merely appropriates a plotline and then overturns its philosophical meaning. The defeated and lonely self caught in anguished despair between a poisoned world and a dying dream is the antithesis and the bad conscience of the unconquered hero setting out to recreate past glories that never were. Textual analysis shows that in "2112" Peart was "no one's disciple," whatever his intentions happened to be when he wrote the lyrics and however much he thought he might be a "Randroid" at that time—the protagonist of "2112" would be anathema to Rand.

None of this is meant to say that the vision of "2112" is more compelling than that of *Anthem*, or that the philosophy expressed in the song cycle is more true to life than the one articulated in the novella. They are radically different, opposed responses to an oppressive fraternal-egalitarian social order presided over by self-deluded, hypocritical, or cynical elites whose plan strips value from life. It's up to readers to decide whether or not the world they live in is dominated by destructive fraternal-egalitarian tendencies and, if so, what response is appropriate to them. The texts of "2112" and *Anthem* are at one in calling for individuals to think for themselves, whatever the consequences.

21
How Is Rush Canadian?

DURRELL BOWMAN

Given Canada's relatively small population (twenty-one million in 1969, thirty-four million in 2009), many—but certainly not all—of the nation's more ambitious musicians have pursued at least some of their career activities in the US and other foreign parts. Rush mainly demonstrates "Canadianness" by combining such British and American influences as progressive rock, hard rock, and individualism. However, the band has also included more specifically Canadian references across its long career.

CanCon

The Canadian government implemented specific content—or "CanCon"—regulations in 1971, and broadcasters were then required to include certain percentages of Canadian material. For music, at least two of a song recording's four main categories of Music, Artist, Production, and Lyrics ("M-A-P-L") must be "Canadian" according to citizenship or location. The interpretation of this changed after 1991, due to a "scandal" involving Bryan Adams failing to qualify as Canadian because of co-writing certain songs, such as "(Everything I Do) I Do it For You" (*Waking up the Neighbours* and *Robin Hood: Prince of Thieves*, both 1991), with such non-Canadians as Mutt Lange and Michael Kamen. (Spelling the word "neighbours" in the Canadian way apparently didn't help.) The outcome is that even though Shania Twain similarly co-wrote the songs on *Come on Over* (1997) with her then-husband Mutt Lange and did not record any of this music in Canada, her album and its songs by that point qualified as Canadian.

To explore the implementation of CanCon on commercial radio, in early 2007 I surveyed a five-hour play-list from Toronto, Ontario's classic rock station Q107. The station played exactly the required daytime hours of 35 percent Canadian songs, and the artists were 33 percent Canadian, 32 percent American, 24 percent British, and 11 percent "other." By comparison, the top artists on Modesto, California's classic rock station The Hawk were 60 percent American, 30 percent British, 5 percent Canadian, and also only 5 percent "other." However, despite this evidence of CanCon as a successful survival tactic against American hegemony, the regulations also ghettoized many Canadians. For example, of the fourteen Canadian artists played during the period of my Q107 survey, probably only the Band, Neil Young, the Guess Who, Rush, and Bryan Adams (36 percent) would be played at all on commercial U.S. radio stations.

Anglo-Americanisms

Based on total album sales, until the ascendancy of Nickelback in 2001 ("How You Remind Me," US #1), Rush was Canada's most internationally successful band. Individual Canadians—especially women—have tended to be more successful than Canadian groups, but only a few of them (including Anne Murray, Celine Dion, and Shania Twain) have sold more albums internationally than Rush. In addition, a certain number of other Canadian bands have been much more successful on the US pop charts than Rush, but most of those groups, including the Guess Who (1970's "American Woman," US #1) and the Barenaked Ladies (1998's "One Week," also US #1, for one week!), have sold far fewer copies of their various albums than Rush has, and even Neil Young has sold fewer albums in the US than Rush.

By 2009, Rush had sold about 45 million albums worldwide: 33 million in the US (including 43 album certifications for 24 different albums), 6 million in Canada, and much of the remaining 6 million split between the UK, Germany, Japan, and Brazil. Rush's success thus cannot be explained primarily as a Canadian phenomenon, and it differs considerably from those artists who became highly successful in Canada while remaining virtually unknown in the US, such as Stompin' Tom Connors, the Tragically Hip, and Jann Arden.

Rush straddled its Canadian-international fusion in a number of ways, including occasional (and usually fairly subtle) lyrics, images, and music-industry activities involving Canada. The band mainly inscribed Canadianness through its combination of tendencies from British progressive rock (such as complex metrical constructions and "philosophical" lyrics) and Anglo-American hard rock and heavy metal (such as distorted guitars, powerful drumming, countertenor vocals, arena venues, and tendencies towards modality and riffs). Such a combination also recalls Canada's own hybrid of things British (such as the Queen as "Head of State" and universal health coverage) and things American (such as individualism, rights and freedoms, and libertarianism). Despite its extensive album sales and tours, other than occasional humorous acknowledgments (such as the *Harvard Lampoon*'s 1993 induction of Rush as "Musicians of the Millennium" and references on TV's *Mystery Science Theater 3000*, 1988–99) and frequent feature articles in US musicians' magazines, for nearly its entire career Rush enjoyed very little mainstream visibility in the United States.

The parents of Rush's bassist-singer-keyboardist Geddy Lee (born 1953) and of its guitarist Alex Lifeson (born 1953) immigrated to Canada from Europe in the 1940s, and by the time the members of Rush dedicated themselves in 1971 to becoming professional musicians, Canada had officially established a policy of multiculturalism, which contrasts the tendency in the US towards a cultural "melting pot." The band's own comments about the greater "flexibility" of Canadians[1] recall Marshall McLuhan's comments about the country's "flexible" and "philosophic or cool" identity.[2] Rush's continuing interest in a wide variety of secondary stylistic elements (such as blues-rock, jazz-rock, new wave, technology, funk, and alternative rock) certainly falls under the rubric "flexible," but the band's particular application of these things is arguably also often "cool and philosophic."

In 1980, Rush performed with fellow progressive-influenced Canadian rock band Max Webster on its song "Battle Scar." Max Webster sometimes opened concerts for Rush but never had a successful career in the US and folded in 1982, with front-man Kim

---

[1] Dan Hedges, article-interview with Lifeson, "Rush Relives 18 Years of Wide-Screen Rock," *Circus*, 30th April 1992. See <http://yyz.com/NMS/HTML/ artindex.html>.

[2] Marshall McLuhan, "Canada: The Borderline Case," in *The Canadian Imagination: Dimensions of a Literary Culture*, edited by David Staines (Harvard University Press, 1977), p. 247.

Mitchell then enjoying a successful solo career in Canada. Geddy Lee also provided the vocals for Bob and Doug McKenzie's (SCTV) "Canadian-themed" 1981 comedy song "Take Off (to the Great White North)." That song charted higher in the US (#16) than Rush's highest-charting US hit, 1982's "New World Man" (#21).[3] Lee also sang the line "Oh, you know that we'll be there" in his high, countertenor vocal style (a minor seventh higher than Neil Young's contribution) on Northern Lights' 1985 charity-rock song "Tears are not Enough." In 2003, Rush played a selection of its 1977–1991 album-oriented rock songs in front of 490,000 music fans at a post-SARS mega-concert in its hometown: "Molson Canadian Rocks for Toronto." The ten-hour event also featured the Rolling Stones and AC/DC (who played last and second-last, respectively, just after Rush) and about a dozen other Canadian and American artists. Tens of thousands of Rush fans probably attended the event, but in such an extremely large context (and even in Canada's largest city, which is also the band's hometown), such fans would have comprised only a very small minority.

In addition to having had only one US Top 40 hit, Rush has never won a Grammy (despite five nominations for Best Rock Instrumental between 1982 and 2009) and has never been inducted into the Rock'n'Roll Hall of Fame (despite having been eligible since 1999). Also, until Rush's appearance on the US late-night "talk show" *The Colbert Report* on 16th July 2008, the band had not appeared "live" on US television since the last of its very early appearances in 1974–75.

In Canada, however, a large number of cultural institutions have compensated for Rush's lack of mainstream exposure in the US. The band had several Top 10 Canadian hits (including "New World Man" reaching #1), and it won eight Juno awards between 1975 and the 1990s, including a special 1990 award (shared with Bryan Adams and k.d. lang) as Artists of the Decade for the 1980s. In 1979, the Government of Canada named Rush its "Ambassadors of Music," and the band later won the Toronto Music Awards Mayor's Award (1990), the Harold Moon songwriting award of the Society of Composers, Authors and Music Publishers of Canada's (SOCAN, 1992), a Toronto's Arts Award (1993), a place in the

---

[3] "Take Off" appears on Rhino Records' seven-CD compilation: *Like Omigod! The '80s Popular Culture Box (Totally)*. It was also used for an episode of *The Simpsons* in which the family visits Toronto (which was also the "home" of *SCTV*).

Canadian Music Juno Hall of Fame (1994), memberships in the Order of Canada (1997), recognition on Canada's Walk of Fame (1999), the designation "Most Important Canadian Musicians of All Time" (JAM! online poll, 2000), and a place in Canada's Music Industry Hall of Fame (2003).

Similar to Geddy Lee's 1982 participation on "Take Off (to the Great White North)," Alex Lifeson memorably guest-starred in a 2003 episode of the popular Canadian cable TV comedy series, *Trailer Park Boys*. In the episode, the guitarist is kidnapped by the show's title-characters (who are Rush fans), and he also ends up teaching the show's character Bubbles how to play the guitar for the 1977 Rush song "Closer to the Heart." The episode also emphasizes the historical truth that Rush had not played in eastern Canada (such as Halifax, Nova Scotia, near where *Trailer Park Boys* was produced) for many years. In 2005, Bubbles then performed along with Rush (and Barenaked Ladies' member Ed Robertson) for that song during a CBC-TV tsunami fundraising concert called Canada for Asia. In 2006, quotations from Rush's 1980 song "The Spirit of Radio" were used in promotional spots for *Trailer Park Boys—The Movie*, the song is heard within the movie itself, and Lifeson appears in a cameo (along with the Tragically Hip's Gordon Downie) as a police officer. Also in 2006, the band's drummer-lyricist Neil Peart (born 1952, pronounced "Peert," not "Pert") appeared on the Canadian current-affairs satirical comedy show *The Rick Mercer Report*, on which he talked about his cycling and motorcycling adventures (which were the basis for several of his published books) then "jammed" with Mercer on adjacent drum kits.

Rush also helped to raise hundreds of thousands of dollars for the United Way, UNICEF, AIDS charities, Artists against Racism, and others, and in 2003 it donated a collection of vintage instruments, stage props, equipment, awards, and memorabilia to the Canadian Museum of Civilization in western Quebec (near Ottawa, Ontario). Rush's success (both internationally and in Canada) enabled it to base its activities in Canada and, in a decidedly libertarian move, to run its own business. Although the group recorded its two 1977–78 studio albums and its pair of 1985–87 studio albums mainly in the UK, from 1973 to 2004 the band otherwise recorded its fourteen additional studio albums mainly at Quebec's Le Studio (north-west of Montreal) or in the GTA (Greater Toronto Area).

Parks and Trees (1975–78)

To apply some terms from Will Straw, Rush explored a "range of musical practices," "varying trajectories of change," and "cross-fertilization."[4] To apply some terms from Keith Negus, Rush functioned as a "synthesist," drawing on emerging cultural elements— thus influencing lyrics and music—and blending them in such a way so as to "create a new distinct musical identity."[5] Rush continued to synthesize its identity over several decades, which reinforced its pedagogical status among its hardcore musician-fans. The band retained certain tendencies, such as individualism, literary lyrics, and instrumental virtuosity. On the other hand, it also engaged with other musical styles (such as post-punk and synth-pop) and other lyrical themes (such as relationships and the environment). Rush's lyrics provide important meanings in most of its songs, and Peart has been influenced by numerous books and authors, with a particular interest in twentieth-century American, British, and Canadian fiction, such as by Saul Bellow, Truman Capote, Samuel R. Delaney, Ernest Hemingway, Jack Kerouac, Jack London, Ayn Rand, and J.R.R. Tolkien. However, Rush's music, which is almost always credited to Lee and Lifeson, reveals at least as much as its lyrics.

In 1974–75, Rush's musical style usually still inscribed blues-influenced, riff-oriented hard rock ("proto heavy metal") or else "pop-rock" of a relatively heavy or psychedelic character, along the lines of such British bands as Cream, Led Zeppelin, and Bad Company. For example, the band's early song "Lakeside Park" (*Caress of Steel*, 1975) uses a relatively straightforward riff and pop-hook inflected style for lyrics about hometown nostalgia and the lost innocence of one's teenaged years, and Peart specifically referenced a park in his childhood hometown of St. Catharines, Ontario. The song also refers to the "24th of May," a Canadian statutory holiday otherwise known as Victoria Day (now generally held on the Monday preceding the 24th and thus creating the summer season's first long weekend). By 1976–77, however, Rush's music more consistently inscribed a sort of "bastardization" that merged elements of heavy metal and progressive rock, such as on *2112* (1976) and *A Farewell to Kings* (1977). Rush thus provided a

---

[4] Will Straw, "Systems of Articulation, Logics of Change: Communities and Scenes in Popular Music," in *Cultural Studies* 5:3 (1991), quoted in Negus, *Popular Music in Theory: An Introduction* (Polity, 1996), p. 22.
[5] Negus, *Popular Music in Theory*, pp. 146–47.

highly-influential exemplar for the international, late-1980s', 1990s', and 2000s' rock sub-genre called "progressive metal." Another "Canadian" element from Rush's early era is inscribed by the fact that the band recorded its first live album (*All the World's a Stage*, 1976) at Toronto's Massey Hall.

Joseph Kerman defines ideology as: "a fairly coherent set of ideas brought together not for strictly intellectual purposes but in the service of some strongly held communal belief."[6] Rush's ideology involves individualism, forging a professional identity, and not allowing outside forces to control one's activities or path. "The Trees," the third song on *Hemispheres* (1978), inscribes a pointed criticism of legislated equality (artificial "balance"). Its lyrics present an allegory depicting one group of trees, the Maples, as being oppressed by another group of trees, the more lofty Oaks. The maple leaf functions as Canada's most important national symbol; thus, one might interpret the Maples in this song as Canada and the Oaks as the United States. Rush does not seem to argue for the Oaks as monologic. Mikhail Bakhtin defines a monologic world view as one that "denies the existence outside itself of another consciousness with equal rights and equal responsibilities . . . finalized and deaf to the other's response."[7]

"The Trees" arguably criticizes the main Canadian initiative intended to correct US media hegemony: the Canadian Content regulations that were introduced in 1971. Rush's aggressive touring and stylistically varied album catalogue ensured its continuing success in the US, the UK, and Canada, despite any such regulations. In the song, the Maples form a union, and at the end of the song an outside force cuts the Oaks down to the height of the Maples. The irony of the song's closing lyrics—"and the trees are all kept equal by hatchet, axe, and saw"—make it quite clear that Rush considers the solution inappropriate. Such lyrics may reflect the band's cynicism about Canadian content regulations (or similar contexts of "affirmative action"), but ironic inscriptions of artificial balance also appear quite extensively within the song's various musical elements.

---

[6] Joseph Kerman, "How We Got into Analysis, and How to Get Out" in *Write All These Down* (University of California Press, 1994), p. 15.

[7] Mikhail Bakhtin, *Problems of Dostoevsky's Poetics*, edited and translated by Caryl Emerson (University of Minnesota Press, 1984), pp. 32, 292–93; quoted in Brackett, *Interpreting Popular Music* (Cambridge University Press, 1995), p. 7.

"The Trees" begins with Lifeson's 6/8 classical guitar introduction (0:00–0:10), after which Lee joins on bass and vocals as the same music underlies Verse 1 (0:10–0:22).[8] Lee sings in his natural baritone register and provides a comparatively simple bass part. The music moves between B minor and its relative major, D, but the G#s within C# and E chords also suggest D Lydian. As Lee sings about the "unrest" of the Maples' discontent, he balances the vocal line by stressing the first and second then fourth and sixth beats of the 6/8 unit (see Example 21.1).

Example 21.1. Verse 1 of Rush, "The Trees" (*Hemispheres*, 1978)

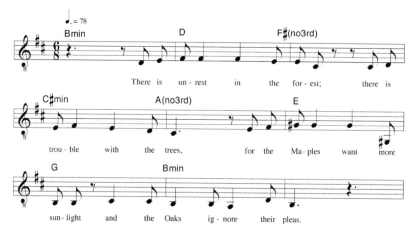

Similar to the use of water sounds in the "Discovery" section of Rush's extended composition "2112" (1976) and the nature sounds found in its mini-epics "Xanadu" (1977) and "Natural Science" (1980),[9] the bird sounds that follow the vocal opening of "The Trees" reinforce the imagery of a "state of nature" in which the Oaks ignore the Maples' pleas. As Lee sings "Oaks ignore their pleas" in the last phrase, he shifts the emphasis to the first and

---

[8] On the band's 1981 live album, *Exit...Stage Left*, Lifeson precedes this song with a brief, classical guitar etude, "Broon's Bane," named after the band's co-producer Terry "Broon" Brown. The piece seems modelled after Cuban composer Leo Brouwer's etude, "Afro-Cuban Lullaby," which Steve Hackett performed as "Horizon's" on *Foxtrot* (1972) by the UK band Genesis. Thanks to Jay Hodgson for this information.

[9] See my article "Let Them All Make Their Own Music—Individualism, Rush, and the Progressive/Hard Rock Alloy, 1976–77," Chapter 9 in *Progressive Rock Reconsidered*, edited by Kevin Holm-Hudson (Routledge, 2002), p. 202.

third beats, which depicts the Oaks taunting, or laughing at, the childish Maples, along the lines of "nya nya nya nya nya nya." Verse 1 tonally and rhythmically inscribes a precarious balance, and Lifeson and Lee reinforce this by repeating this music instrumentally and with Lee compensating for the lack of vocals by contributing a rather more active bass guitar part (0:22–0:34). A brief guitar/bass interlude (0:34–0:40) then summarizes the balance between D and B, but shifting the time signature to 3/4 instead of 6/8 and thereby increasing the rate of the basic pulse by one-third and providing what might have functioned as a subtle bridge into the next section.

Jarringly, though, the following section presents a number of extreme tonal and metrical shifts. For example, the band retains the tempo of the previous 3/4 interlude, but now shifting the time signature to 4/4, introducing a pair of unresolved "secondary dominants" (V/B and V/D), Lifeson shifting to heavy, strummed, rhythmically regular power chords, and Peart entering vigorously on drums (0:40-0:47). As Lee begins singing Verse 2 (about the Oaks being too lofty, 0:47-1:15, see Example 21.2), he switches to his piercing countertenor voice—an octave and a half above the range in which he has just been singing. Agitated, highly syncopated note entries remove all traces of the much more pastoral tone presented in the opening section, thus providing urgency that is not dissipated until the very end of the song.

Example 21.2. Opening of Verse 2 of Rush, "The Trees" (*Hemispheres*, 1978)

Although the song's homophonic texture continues into the new, hard rock instrumentation, this section also sets up contrasting tonal areas. This music outlines A major, but it also contains a series of adjacent major chords, paralleling the ongoing differentiation between the neighbouring Maples and Oaks, but in a heightened, argumentative sense that temporarily displaces their original identities (D major and B minor). After a brief interlude (1:15–1:21), the subsequent Verse 3 (1:21–1:45, D/B, 6/8) continues with the heavy instrumentation and high vocals of Verse 2, but now in 6/8. Thus, it stylistically bridges the two previous vocal sections, and by now the "creatures all have fled," perhaps frightened away by the Maples' screams of "oppression."[10]

The shift to 4/4 after Verse 3, however, establishes an extended instrumental section that initially features a plaintive, woodwind-like synthesizer solo (1:45–2:17) beginning in A major (quite diatonically) and ending at A's dominant, E major. Lifeson and Peart respectively play quiet, angular, electric guitar figurations and rhythmic, wood block drum sounds. These evoke hammering woodpeckers, which prove insufficient for the task of equalizing the two groups of trees. A passage in 5/4 shifts the harmony back to B (2:17–2:53) and soon becomes louder and quite rhythmic (2:53–3:10). Lee plays bass rhythms highly reminiscent of the rhythms he sang in Verse 1 (the A section), and this section further merges the A and B sections by focusing on B minor, D major, and A major, and it also includes Lifeson's guitar solo (3:10–3:29) over the continuing 5/4 material. A section in 6/8 then further recalls the formerly sung rhythms (3:29–3:49), with the band also musically expanding the song's precarious balancing act by interrupting with brief, ascending (A-based) versus descending (D-based) scalar passages in the bass versus guitar, both in rhythmic unison with Peart's woodpecker wood block sounds.[11] These passages produce something like "stop-time" effects (by briefly highlighting certain instruments), and they also parallel the tonal areas of the B and A sections in very close proximity, thus inscribing a heated, contra-

---

[10] In addition, Lifeson voices the F# chords as barred, major power chords, thus extending the secondary dominant of B into the new, hard rock version of the A section (Verse 3).

[11] The band bases this distinctive and virtuosic section on G major and F# minor chords, with very prominent thirds. G major normally functions as "flat-7" in the pivot to A major in the B section.

puntal volley of arguments. The section then returns to the earlier 5/4 riff (3:49–3:58) but now with F# major chords in order to contrast the 3/4 pivot to the B section that this elaborate instrumental section already expanded and enriched.

After the instrumental section, Verse 4 outlines the Maples forming a union and "demanding equal rights" (3:58–4:28). At the end of this verse, Lee sings equal quarters on the words "trees are all kept equal" (4:20–4:23, on F#s). As this rhythm had not been sung at any point earlier in the song, it underscores the fact that an external, artificial agent had provided the "equality." The vocal melody, bass, and guitar then follow this with an ascent from F# through A, but instead of cycling back to 6/8, D major, and the A section the song ends abruptly—though ambiguously—on A major, with quiet bird calls recalling the song's opening sections. Peart strikes his wind chimes (4:28–4:42), but the fading pitches (G#, C#, and B, which are all very important elements in establishing A major) present an ominous effect, encouraging us to mock the song's sociopolitical "accomplishment."

The alternate time signatures, tonal juxtapositions, and contrary motions of the song's instrumental section suggest a kind of "Royal Commission." In Canada, such a publicly funded inquiry (or deliberation) normally concerns such thorny issues as language laws, the misappropriation of public funds, and the sale of publicly owned companies. In the middle section of "The Trees," Rush similarly presents material in ways not adequately argued elsewhere. One could thus interpret the eventual narrative solution of this song—legislated equality—as critical of Canadian Content regulations as a variant of affirmative action. In any case, the entire song achieves a kind of "critical mass" in its obsession with balance and equality. It provides aural and intellectual meaning because it "works through" its contradictory rhythms, tonalities, and textures instead of merely presenting them. Neil Peart later downplayed the song's meaning:

> It was just a flash. I was working on an entirely different thing when I saw a cartoon picture of these trees carrying on like fools. I thought, "What if trees acted like people?" So I saw it as a cartoon really, and wrote it that way. I think that's the image that it conjures up to a listener or a reader. A very simple statement.[12]

---

[12] Cheech Iero, "Neil Peart," *Modern Drummer*, April/May 1980; <http://yyz.com/NMS/HTML/artindex.html>.

Despite Peart's insistence on the simple statement of his lyrics, the resultant song is anything but simple, and I hope to have provided a reasonable interpretation of its meaning.

In a less extensive engagement with Canadianness also found on *Hemispheres* (1978), the hard-rock anthem "Circumstances" uses French (Canada's second official language) for the recurring phrase "Plus ça change, plus c'est la même chose" ("The more that things change, the more they stay the same"). The three members of Rush all studied French during the late-1970s, the band began recording at Quebec's Le Studio in 1979, and Peart bought a house in the area. In a comparable multicultural way, a section of the same album's "La Villa Strangiato" is named after Toronto's Greek neighbourhood: Pape and Danforth.

Moving Pictures, "YYZ," and *Grace under Pressure* (1981–84)

Moving Pictures (1981) stands as Rush's best-selling—and arguably best—album.[13] The album gained its favorable reputation largely based on the four songs on its first half: "Tom Sawyer," "Red Barchetta," the instrumental "YYZ," and "Limelight." These continue the succinct individualism embodied in the band's 1980 songs "The Spirit of Radio" and "Freewill," but they also pursue a more picturesque (or personal) idiom in keeping with the album title's filmic reference. Hugh Syme's album cover for *Moving Pictures* (see below) combines a title pun on the band's early 1980s' cinematic/picturesque approach to songwriting with a multiple visual play on words: people moved emotionally by pictures being moved physically. The picture at the front of the cover depicts Joan of Arc (portrayed by one of Syme's associates), the middle picture reproduces C.M. Coolidge's "A Friend in Need" (a.k.a. "Dogs Playing Poker"), and the picture at the rear comprises the "man against star," anti-collectivist logo from the cover of Rush's album *2112* (1976). These pictures are displayed in front of the distinctive three-arch entrance of the Ontario Provincial Legislature in Toronto's Queen's Park (see Figure 21.1).

---

[13] As with *Permanent Waves* (1980), the band recorded *Moving Pictures* at Le Studio in Morin Heights, Quebec, co-producing it with Terry Brown and recording it with engineer Paul Northfield. In 1995, the Recording Industry Association of America certified the album as quadruple platinum: four million copies sold in the United States.

Figure 21.1. *Moving Pictures* (1981), cover art by H. Syme

The three pictures, the three arches, and so on also visually play on the fact that Rush comprises three members, which is a recurring motif on a number of the band's album covers in the 1980s and 1990s. As for the album cover invoking Toronto, in addition to being home to the business offices of Rush's Anthem Records, all three members of Rush had houses either in upscale Toronto areas (Geddy Lee in Rosedale and Neil Peart in Forest Hill) or on an estate just north of the city (Alex Lifeson near Markham).[14]

The third track of *Moving Pictures*, "YYZ" (pronounced Y-Y-"Zed"), comprises Rush's best-known instrumental work. The band has often used unusual time signatures and complex rhythms in order to make a point or sometimes just to "mix things up," and it

---

[14] Peart also had a house in rural Quebec for several decades. Lifeson also had a smaller, second house in Florida, near where he was arrested on 31st December 2003 for participating in a disturbance at a New Year's Eve party. (The charges were later dropped for lack of sufficient evidence.) Peart's daughter and spouse died in 1997 and 1998, in a car crash and from cancer, respectively. Around 2000, he sold both of his houses and moved to Santa Monica, California with his second wife, who is an American photographer.

bases the opening of "YYZ" on Morse code for the radio call letters
of Toronto's Pearson International Airport:[15]

YYZ= -.- - -.- - - -..

= 7/8 + 7/8 + 3/4 (or 5/4 + 5/4 or 10/8 + 10/8)

= q(uarter-note) e(ighth-note) q q q e q q q q e e

At the quarter-note level, one could also interpret this as two measures of 5/4, which is how it is usually transcribed by third-party
engravers. Building a metrical structure around an airport code fits
with Richard Middleton's expansion of Gino Stefani's 1973 work on
musical semiotics: "There is a range of codes operating in any
musical event, some of them not even strictly musical but emanating from general schemes governing movement, gesture, rhetoric,
affect, and so on."[16] "YYZ" presents a coded meaning because the
band "transliterated" these non-musical elements musically. Rush
played "YYZ" about one thousand times between 1981 and 2011.
Thus, this particular piece of music inscribed one of the band's perpetual, affective "home connections," which is then emotionally
highlighted in the work's bridge section.

After a series of textually-contrasting sections (such as unison,
melody and accompaniment, contrapuntal, and "antiphonal"), its
guitar solo ends with an unaccompanied descending sequence,
similar to those found in Vivaldi's violin music. The solo leads into
a slower, cut-time section with bass pedal and brassy synthesizer
chords (2:51-3:20), providing what Neil Peart calls the "big sappy
. . . bridge in the middle that is really orchestrated, really emotional,
really rich [to] half symboli[se] the tremendous emotional impact of
coming home."[17] This section of the composition (and, arguably,
the entire work) demonstrates that David Brackett's idea of the
importance of "media image, biographical details, mood, and historical and social associations" can even hold for an entirely instrumental work.[18]

---

[15] Many Rush fans collect "YYZ" baggage tags. Canadian airports typically use
identifiers based on earlier weather transmitter codes, instead of on city names.

[16] Richard Middleton, *Studying Popular Music* (Open University Press, 1990), p. 173.

[17] Quoted in Bill Banasiewicz, *Rush: Visions—The Official Biography*
(Omnibus, 1988), p. 54.

[18] See David Brackett, *Interpreting Popular Music* (Cambridge University Press,
1995), p. 9.

After the bridge, the band reprises the pre-solo sections and ends with a Morse Code-like gesture that recalls the song's opening. On the whole, the work evokes mechanical signals followed by: complicated hesitancies, the excitement of traveling somewhere new, and a new set of signals at the end. This affirms Peart's comments that "The song is loosely based on airport-associated images. Exotic destinations, painful partings, happy landings, that sort of thing."[19] Peart elsewhere explains that this provided a "shorter, more concise instrumental that was actually a song with verses and a chorus...à la [jazz-rock band] Weather Report."[20]

In 1983, Rush moved on from its 1973–1982 co-producer, British-born Canadian Terry ("Broon") Brown, and engaged former Supertramp producer Peter Henderson (British) to co-produce the album *Grace under Pressure* (1984). However, as if to compensate for this change, the band arranged for the internationally renowned Canadian portrait photographer Yousuf Karsh to take the band's inner-sleeve album photo. Karsh was best-known for his World War II photograph of a grumpy Winston Churchill and had never before photographed a rock band.

Stylistically, from 1981 to 1987 Rush often engaged with such music technology as synthesizers, samplers, and electronic percussion, but the band then backed away from this starting around 1988, preferring to use technology within its computer-based songwriting process instead of with the sounds of its new music. After 1980, Geddy Lee also often sang in his natural, high-baritone voice, as opposed to the intense, very high, countertenor style in which he had frequently sung in the 1970s. Lee's modified and moderated vocal style (and his related vocal melodies) also suited Peart's more picturesque and less "preachy" lyrics. Rush's new music from 1996 to 2007 achieved a balance of a relatively traditional rock-trio aesthetic (guitar, bass, and drums) with complex structural and lyrical elements still inspired by 1970s' progressive rock. This resulted in songs and albums that were at least somewhat consistent with alternative rock and progressive metal, and throughout this period the band continued to perform for a large, international "cult" following, but with very little mainstream attention.

---

[19] Neil Peart, "The Drummer Sounds Off," *Rush Backstage Club newsletter*, March 1990; <http://yyz.com/NMS/HTML/artindex.html>.

[20] Quoted in Banasiewicz, *Rush Visions*, p. 54.

Later Rush (1996-2004)

Hugh Syme's cover for Rush's *Test for Echo* (1996, see Figure 21.2), shows three tiny figures, presumably representing the members of the band, climbing a massive, human-shaped rock structure (an inukshuk) in a barren, arctic tundra.

Figure 21.2: Test for Echo (1996), cover art by H. Syme

The North American arctic Inuit people traditionally used the inuk-shuk (meaning "in the image of man") in hunting practices and to mark trails and geographical directions. Such rock totems are usually no more than a meter or two high (the size of a child or adult), but in Rush's context an absurdly oversized version represents the band's long, complicated engagement with rock music. Although Syme's appropriation of the inukshuk as an image for this album does seem to stretch the boundaries of multicultural sensitivity, this issue is certainly not confined to Rush, for the 2010 Winter Olympics (based in Vancouver, British Columbia) appropriated the inukshuk as its primary symbol (see Figure 21.3)—and arguably with even less of a justification than the visual pun on the cover of *Test for Echo*.

Figure 21.3. Vancouver 2010 "Pac-Man" Inukshuk

Although some native groups have responded favorably to the circumstances of the Olympics, the organization's version of an inukshuk has also been compared by one Chief as resembling an image from the 1980s' video game Pac-Man. On the front cover of Rush's *Test for Echo*, Syme's version looks considerably more like the "real thing," and, moreover, the album includes additional northern or arctic images. The back cover technologically updates the front cover's symbol with three large satellite dishes within the same setting. The first page of the CD booklet features a digitally altered ancient map of the northern hemisphere (in Latin, but modified to refer to Rush). Each song lyric also receives a visual treatment, a few of which also reference inukshuks and/or other arctic imagery (a dog sled, the northern lights, and an image of Inuit stone carvers), and the credit page of the CD booklet also includes a snowman family of three. The album's acknowledgements of Inuit culture are thus presented in earnest (even self-effacingly), and at least some of the band's followers may have become at least slightly more informed about such aspects of Canada's multicultural identity. The same can probably not be said of the Olympics' "Pac-Man."

Regarding the album's song "Driven" (and a 1993 Rush song called "Stick It Out") and the band's partial interest in underlying funk- and groove-oriented playing, Geddy Lee self-effacingly described the band's success in this as being "about as funky as white Canadians get."[21] In the same album's "Time and Motion," the bridge uses the word "loon" to refer to the northern lake bird so common in Canada (such as near Peart's Quebec country house), but it also suggests "loony" (derived from "lunatic") or the nickname of Canada's one-dollar coin: the "loonie," which was introduced in 1987 and initially featured a loon (bird) on one of its faces.

Musically, by 1996 Geddy Lee was quite comfortable with over-dubbing his voice in contrasting ranges (in this case, baritone combined with countertenor), which is something that he had earlier avoided. On the other hand, this particular bridge retains Rush's established tendency to use an asymmetrical time signature (in this case a lurching 5/4) within a contrasting song section.

Outro

In 2004, Rush celebrated its thirtieth anniversary as a professional band with an eight-track CD of British and North American psychedelic and blues-rock songs that the band's members had played in cover versions during the half-dozen years leading up to 1974. The album, *Feedback*, includes a new version of Cream's version of Robert Johnson's "Crossroads" and a new version of Blue Cheer's version of Eddie Cochran's "Summertime Blues," each of which thus resulted in a "cover of a cover." Rush's rarely-heard first single, "Not Fade Away" (1973, backed with the original song "Don't Fight It"), is also a "cover of a cover," because Buddy Holly's 1957 song had already been covered by the Rolling Stones in 1964. Rush's version of "Summertime Blues" was used in 2004 as the theme for a pay-TV, pro-wrestling event held at Toronto's Air Canada Centre.

Feedback also includes songs by the Who ("The Seeker") and Love ("Seven and Seven Is"), two songs by the Yardbirds ("Heart Full of Soul" and "Shapes of Things"), and two songs by Buffalo Springfield: "For What It's Worth" and "Mr. Soul"—the last of these having been written by Rush's fellow Canadian, Neil Young. Many critics were pleasantly surprised that for its thirtieth anniversary as a professional entity, Rush chose to acknowledge its distant past (1968–74) of genres and styles not usually associated with the band instead of producing something along the lines of a ponderous,

---

[21] Philip Dawdy, article-interview with Geddy Lee, "You Can't Hurry Change," *Bassics* 6:2 (1996); <http://yyz.com/NMS/HTML/artindex.html>.

multi-CD boxed set of its own professional accomplishments of the sequent three decades. On the other hand, the band may also have wished to make the point that there was not much Canadian hard rock—and not really even much of a music industry—before Rush made its self-titled debut (1974) in Toronto in 1973.

The Canadian Music Awards Association was founded in 1974–75 and renamed the Canadian Academy of Recording Arts and Sciences (CARAS) in 1977. The Juno awards were first presented in 1971 (taking over from RPM music magazine's Gold Leaf awards, 1964–70), and they continued to be selected by RPM readers until 1974. The US National Academy of Recording Arts and Sciences (NARAS) began in 1957 and administered the first Grammy awards in 1958. Canadians have often created "new" institutions based on variations of existing U.S. institutions, such as the Canadian Recording Industry Association (CRIA, 1964– versus RIAA, 1952–) and CARAS. On the other hand, the Canadian music industry evolved fairly quickly from its humble origins in the early 1960s, when numerous musicians still had little choice but to leave. For its part, Rush effected a quite Canadian compromise in this matter by maintaining its own companies in Toronto (Moon, then Anthem) and by often recording in Canada (such as at Quebec's Le Studio), while also co-signing deals with major, international music labels (Mercury, then Atlantic).

Co-Produced By

RANDALL E. AUXIER lives with his album collection, spouse, and a lot of cats near Carbondale, Illinois. He teaches philosophy at Southern Illinois University, and especially likes to teach aesthetics and metaphysics at the same time. He is also a singing bass player, and privately fancies himself the "Gary Weinrib" of his hometown, except without all the money, and fame . . . and talent.

MELISSA BECK received a B.A. in Classics at Siena College in 1995 and an M.A. in Classics at the University at Buffalo in 1998. She also completed most of a Ph.D. at Buffalo for which her specialty was Seneca and Roman Tragedy. But she stopped writing her dissertation after the first chapter so that she could live a life of wealth and prestige by teaching Latin and Ancient Greek to students at Woodstock Academy in Northeastern Connecticut. Now she uses all of her money and copious free time to go to Rush concerts.

Besides teaching social studies to his eighth graders at Shaker Junior High, **JIM BERTI** teaches that non-conformity is okay, much to the chagrin of the "powers that be." He agrees with Chester Cheetah that "there is no f**king drummer better than Neil Peart." Jim credits Rush songs "Hersey" and "Manhattan Project" for helping him through his freshman history courses at Cortland State. His favorite songs are "Tom Sawyer," "Subdivisions," "Analog Kid," "Xanadu" and he is still on the "Passage to Bangkok". You can find Jim at any Rush show in the Upstate New York area, or on the jam scene (phish, moe).

NICOLE BIAMONTE has a BFA in piano from SUNY Purchase, which she earned despite using the time-honored technique of not practicing until the day of her lesson. This approach did not work well in graduate school, where she was compelled to employ more drastic techniques such as a hermitlike retreat from society, followed by moving back in with her parents. She eventually earned a PhD in music theory from Yale, where she was dissuaded from writing a dissertation on the music of Rush and is trying to make up for it now. Currently she teaches at McGill University in Montréal, and her hope is to make rock music an essential part of music-theory teaching everywhere. Her favorite Rush songs are "Free Will," "Jacob's Ladder," and all of the songs discussed in her chapter.

DURRELL BOWMAN completed his Ph.D. in Musicology at UCLA in 2003, with a dissertation entitled "Permanent Change: Rush, Musicians' Rock, and the Progressive Post-Counterculture." (You should read it, because he spent five years on it!) He has published a number of scholarly articles, presented various conference papers, and taught dozens of music history courses—mostly not involving Rush, actually. One of his ongoing projects is a book about music in *The Simpsons*, but he has also worked as a professional choral singer and as a music encyclopedia reference article writer. In 2009-10, Dr. Bowman got up at seven and went to school at eight, in order to study computer applications development and thus possibly become a working digital net boy and make some reasonably big money for once. See http://durrellbowman.com.

ANDREW COLE drums, DJs, and is a member of the noise outfit, Collective Media Project. He's a professor at Princeton, has been spotted carousing in Athens, Georgia, with him a hundred and thanks his pals Nick Bielli of Japancakes, Phil Dwyer of Inkwell, Joel Martin of Subrig Destroyer, and Aidan "Auden" Wasley for talking about music.

MITCH EARLEYWINE is Professor of Clinical Psychology at the University at Albany, State University of New York. He has over 100 publications on the addictions. He is the lone person to publish books with both Oxford University Press (*Understanding Marijuana*) and High Times Press (*The Parents' Guide to Marijuana*). He's a marijuana researcher and devoted Rush fan. Coincidence? You decide. He has been quoted in *The Economist, The San Francisco Chronicle, Chicago Tribune, New York Times, Los Angeles Times, USA Today, Time* magazine, *Sacramento Bee, Rolling Stone, Esquire, Salon,* and *The Nation*. He has also appeared on National Public Radio's "Talk of the Nation" and "Weekend Edition". Usually he discusses drugs but slips Rush references in whenever there's a chance for a good metaphor.

NEIL FLOREK lives on a small farm with his family in Northwest Indiana and teaches philosophy at Purdue University, Calumet. When he is not teaching Ethics or Philosophy of Religion, or coaching youth ice hockey, or blowin' harp in Chicagoland blues bands, he's still ruminating on whether to be the Analog Kid, the Digital Man, or the Ghost Rider.

NICOLAS P. GRECO wanted to become Alex Lifeson's guitar technician. Instead, he's an Assistant Professor of Communications and Media at Providence College in Otterburne, Manitoba. While he was hoping to carry Neil Peart's drum equipment, Dr. Greco ended up writing a dissertation exploring the enigmatic star image and the nature of fan desire in the case of British singer Morrissey. He really would like to help Geddy Lee with some of his keyboard lines, but he is instead a founding Fellow of the Canadian Institute for the Study of Pop Culture and Religion.

STEVEN HORWITZ grew up in the geometric order of the Detroit suburbs, where, as a teenager, Rush's music became the muse for the restless dreams of his youth. Since then, he has become Charles A. Dana Professor of Economics at St. Lawrence University in Canton, NY and the author of two books and dozens of scholarly articles. But everyone who knows him knows he'd still trade it all to spend a day hanging out with Rush. An active member of numerous online Rush communities since the mid-90s, where he has long been known as "The Professor," Horwitz has also written on Rush for the *Journal of Ayn Rand Studies* and on libertarianism in both the scholarly and popular press. He counts among the highlights of his life sitting in the front row at Alex's feet for a 2007 show in Columbus, Ohio. (Alex still owes him a guitar pick from that show.) He thanks Geddy, Neil and Alex for being the soundtrack to his life and for demonstrating that in any walk of life talent and integrity can transcend the false dichotomy of being "cool" or being cast out.

KAYLA KREUGER is currently working on a Ph.D. in English Literature at West Virginia University specializing in the Victorian era. When told about her piece in *Rush and Philosophy,* her advisors kindly pointed out the lack of a connection between Rush and Victorian literature and made various threatening noises. Though the bridge between prog rock and parasols continues to elude her, Miss Kreuger plans to continue as a Victorianist and a Rush fan—even if that raises eyebrows in both camps. After all, Neil Peart *did* cite "Dover Beach" on the latest album!

CHRIS MCDONALD is proud to be an ethnomusicologist because seven-syllable disciplines sound so impressive. He completed his doctorate at York University in 2002, having completed a dissertation titled "Grand Designs: A Musical, Social and Ethnographic Study of Rush." In 2009, his book, *Rush, Rock Music and the Middle Class: Dreaming in Middletown*, was published and was (predictably) panned by music critics and loved by fans. McDonald currently teaches at Cape Breton University and wonders if Rush will ever again play a concert less than five hours from where he lives!

GEORGE A. REISCH got to be a much better guitar player in 1976 after he started copying Alex Lifeson's riffs (instead of Peter Frampton's). Since then he has learned never to copy anyone's riffs (especially Plato's) and now teaches philosophy and history of science at Northwestern's School of Continuing Studies and edits the Popular Culture and Philosophy series for Open Court Publishing Company.

JOHN REULAND is a PhD candidate in English at Princeton University. When he's not trying to figure out Neil Peart licks, he studies late-nineteenth and early twentieth-century American literature, specifically the convergences between novels, poems, and American pragmatism. Despite his best efforts, he'll probably never nail the drum part to "YYZ."

JOHN J. SHEINBAUM is an associate professor of musicology at the University of Denver's Lamont School of Music, where he teaches courses on both classical and popular musics. He earned a PhD at Cornell University in 2002, where he completed a dissertation on the symphonies of Gustav Mahler, though his first extended project in analyzing music was his junior-high-era attempt to figure out all the guitar parts on *Permanent Waves* and *Moving Pictures*. In addition to his work on Mahler, he has published scholarly articles and presented papers on progressive rock, Bruce Springsteen, Aretha Franklin, and the Beatles. He gets a special thrill — and laughs embarrassedly—at his daughter Andie and son Jamie walking around the house screaming "SNOW Dog . . . is vic-TOR-i-ous!!!"

TIM SMOLKO earned a B.S. in Computer Science at Indiana Univ. of Pennsylvania when he discovered that they did not have a degree in air-drumming. At the University of Pittsburgh, he resigned himself to earning a Master of Library Science degree when he learned that they too did not have a degree in air-drumming. He now works as a music librarian, cataloging music scores, CDs, and DVDs at the University of Georgia. After learning that this third institution also does not have a degree in air-drumming, he is settling for a Master of Arts degree in Musicology. His fields of interest include progressive rock, J.S. Bach, Olivier Messiaen and Richard Wagner. He is writing his thesis on Jethro Tull's *Thick as a Brick*, seeing that his idea about tracing the history of air-drumming was met with some consternation from his advisors.

TODD SUOMELA is an independent scholar from Minnesota, which is close enough to Canada to make him consider Rush fellow-citizens. He studied philosophy and English at Yale University as an undergraduate. Since then he has worked in information technology, retail, consulting, and education. His interests include creativity, technology, libraries, classification, ontology, epistemology, ethics, interpretation, sociology, psychology, astronomy, meteorology, programming, business, music, postmodernism, juggling, metaphor, mutation, and more. He also has a master's degree in information science from the University of Michigan and is working on a

PhD in communications and information science at the University of Tennessee. His personal website is at http://toddsuomela.com.

LIZ STILLWAGGON SWAN, philosopher and writer, has been fascinated by Rush's music, and even more so by their superbly crafted lyrical stories, since her high school days. She's used insights from Rush's *Hemispheres* in her classroom teachings about human consciousness and human nature. She finds "sensitive, open and strong" (from "Natural Science") very good words to live by. Her son, Freeman J., enjoyed his first Rush show in utero (when Liz was eight weeks pregnant) at Red Rocks in Denver, summer 2010, and she's sure he loved it.

DEENA WEINSTEIN, Professor of Sociology at DePaul University, and **MICHAEL WEINSTEIN**, Professor of Political Science at Purdue University, join together as a collaborative team whenever their interests converge. Bonded at a common center in critical theory and philosophy, Deena specializes in studies of rock music and popular culture, and is a rock journalist; Michael concentrates on contemporary political philosophy and has been the front man for a punk rock band. They naturally come together when they encounter bands with philosophical import, like Rush, with its lyricist Neil Peart, and his problematic ties to Ayn Rand. Separately and as co-authors Deena and Michael have published books in the fields of philosophy, political theory, sociology of organizations and rock music studies, in addition to more than one-hundred [and fifty] scholarly articles, and a multitude of reviews, interviews and journalistic features.

Index

absurdity, 150–51
AC/DC, 290; "It's a Long Way to the Top (If You Wanna Rock'n'Roll)," 191
Adams, Bryan, 287, 288, 290
adaptive thoughts, 94
African American musical traditions, 63, 69
'Ahava Rabba' scale, 196
albums, online downloading of, 133
alētheuein, 226
Alexander the Great, 122
analytic philosophy, 206
Apocalyptica, 38
Apollo, 160–62, 166
Arden, Jann, 288
"The Aristocrats" vaudeville joke, 107
Aristotle, 81, 242; ethics, 140; *Nicomachean Ethics*, 225; on technology, 225–26; on virtue, 141
art, as virtual, 14
Art of Noise, 184
Atlantic1001, 83
Autonomous Technology, 230

Bad Company, 292
Bakhtin, Mikhail, 37, 293
The Band, 288
Baraka, Amiri, 63–64, 69; *Blues People*, 63
Barenaked Ladies, 27, 29, 35, 37, 288, 291; "Grade 9," 35, 41–42
Barthes, Roland: on "cruising," 214–18; on distraction, 217–18

Barton, Rachel, 30, 37–39; *Storming the Citadel*, 38
bass guitar, cancelation effect of, 8
Battersby, James, 243, 252
Baudelaire, Charles, 80
Baudrillard, Jean, 230
Beatles, 189; *Sgt. Pepper's Lonely Hearts Club Band*, 107–08
Beauvoir, Simone de, 183
Beck, 29–30
Beck, Aaron, 89, 94
belief, 201; behaviorists on, 205–06, 210; collecting evidence of, 203–04; as internal state, 205
Bellow, Saul, 292
Benjamin, Walter, 76; on distraction, 220; on film, 220; on translation, 80–81, 83, 86
Bennett, H. Stith, 177
Bieber, Justin, 107
The Birds (movie), 185
Bit Torrent, 133
Black, Jack, 105
Black Sabbath, 197
Blue Cheer, 82, 304
Booth, Wayne, 251
Bourdieu, Pierre, 67–70 on habitus, 188
Bowie, David, 38 "China Girl," 192
Bowman, Durrell, 61, 64–65, 67, 213
The Boys in Brazil (documentary), 133
Brackett, David, 37, 300
Breeders, 29

Brown, James, 53
Brown, Terry, 36, 173, 301
Bruce, Jack, 106
Bruner, Edward M., 251
Bryant, Kobe, 261
Bucholtz, Mary, 70–71
Burns, Gary, 216
Busch, Andrew, 99
Bush, Kate, 38
The Byrds, 189

Caesar, Julius, 127
Camus, Albert, 150
Camus, Renaud: *Tricks*, 217
Canada: as hybrid, 289; music
    industry, 305
Canada for Asia (TV show), 35
Canadian Content regulations,
    287–288, 293, 297
Capehart, Jerry, 82
Capote, Truman, 292
Capra, Frank, 258
Carmen, Eric, 19
Catherine Wheel, 37
Chalmers, David, 159
Chamberlin, Wilt, 261
Charlton, Katherine: *Rock Music Styles*,
    29
Chuck (TV show), 35
Churchill, Winston S., 301
class, and cultural markers, 67–69
Clinton, George, 53
Cochran, Eddie, 82, 304; "Summertime
    Blues," 304
cognitive-behavioral therapy, 89, 99
The Colbert Report (TV show), 35, 86,
    109, 136, 290
Coleridge, Samuel Taylor: "Kubla
    Khan," 193
Collins, Peter, 181
Coltrane, John, 65
Comte, Auguste, 242–43
consciousness: easy problems of,
    159–160; hard problem of, 159,
    164; and music, 16
conservatives, 256
Constantine, J.D., 212
Coolidge, C.M.: "A Friend in Need,"
    298
"coolness," in youth culture, 70
Corgan, Billy, 109
Cream, viii, 292, 304
Croot, John, 101
The Crying Game (movie), 184
Cygnus, 166

Deadsy, 27, 29, 41–43
Deal, Kim, 29
Death Organ, 29
Delaney, Samuel R., 292
depression, studies of, 90
Derrida, Jacques, 129–130, 134;
    Différance, 129–130; on signs, 137
Descartes, René, 163, 201–02, 209
Desmond, Paul, 63–64
Devo, 143
'diabolus in musica,' 196
dichotomous thinking, 94–95
Dio, Ronnie James, 106
Dion, Celine, 288
Dionysus, 160–62, 166
Disarray, 27, 30, 36, 41–42
DJ Z–Trip, 27, 30, 36, 41–42
Donne, John, 232
Dostoevsky, Fyodor, 5, 145
Dream Theater, 29, 36
Dr. Strangelove (movie), 176
Dubois, Page, 185
Dudley, Anne, 184
Dunst, Kirsten, 35
Durst, David C., 281
Dylan, Bob, 199
dystopia, as genre, 274–75

The Eagles, 132
Easlea, Brian, 183
Ellis, Albert, 89, 94
Ellul, Jacques, 230
emotions, technological metaphors
    for, 232–33
Enlightenment, 242–43
Epictetus, 89
Epicurean philosophy, 121–24; on
    atoms, 124
Epicurus, 121–22, 125, 126
ethics, 140, 152
eudaimonia, 140, 141
Eurythmics, 180
existential consciousness, 148
existential truths, 152
Exit . . . Stage Right (tribute album)
    36, 37, 39–40

faith, 155
Family Guy (TV show), 35
Fanboys (movie), 35
Fast, Larry, 180
Feenberg, Andrew, 229
finitude, 148
Fleetwood Mac, 132

Forster, E.M.: "The Machines Stops," 274
Fourier, Charles, 217
Frankenstein, 230
Frankie Goes to Hollywood, 181, 184
Freaks and Geeks (TV show), 35
Freud, Sigmund, 90
Frye, Northrop, 253
The Full Monty (movie), 184
Futurama (TV show), 35

Gabriel, Peter, 180
Gary Lewis and the Playboys: "This Diamond Ring," 37
Geddicorn, 121
Genesis, 105; "Watcher of the Skies," 64
Gillan, Ian, 106
Glaucon, 76
Goethe, Johann Wolfgang von: *The Sorrows of Young Werther*, 281; *Wilhelm Meister*, 281
Goldblum, Jeff, 230
Greenspan, Alan, 6
groove, characteristics of, 52–53
Guaraldi, Vince, 35
The Guess Who: "American Woman," 288
Guggenheim Museum, 9
Gump, Forrest, 112

Halloween (movie), 35
Halper, Donna, 134
Handel, George Frederick, 39
Hayek, Friedrich A., 264–66; *The Constitution of Liberty*, 260; *The Fatal Conceit*, 265; *Individualism and Economic Order*, 262; on scientism, 264; "The Use of Knowledge in Society," 262
Hegel, Georg, 280
Heidegger, Martin, 226; *The Question Concerning Technology*, 225
Hemingway, Ernest, 180, 292
Henderson, Peter, 174, 301
Hendrix, Jimi, viii; "Foxy Lady," 82
Herbert, George, 232
Herculaneum, 126
"Hey No, Nobody Home" (song), 193
Hine, Rupert, 211
Hitchcock, Alfred, 185
Holly, Buddy, 304
"hook," musical, 215–16, 218
humanism, 242, 251–52; in mythical language, 252; and need for enchantment, 251
A Humanist Manifesto II, 245
Humanities, 242
human nature, reason and passion in, 166
Hume, David, 242
Hush, 43
Huxley, Aldous: *Brave New World*, 275
hypermeter, 48
hyper-whiteness, 70–71

idealism, 77
ideology, 293
I Love You, Man (movie), 35, 67, 76, 136
imitation: philosophical views of, 76, 79; and variation, 79
inukshuk, 302–03

Jackson, Joe, 38
Janovich, Andre, 40
Jesus, 276
Jillette, Penn, 107
Joan of Arc, 298
Joel, Billy, 29, 37–38; "It's Still Rock'n'Roll to Me," 37
Johnson, Robert: *Crossroads*, 304
Jones, Howard, 180
Jurassic Park (movie), 231

Kamen, Michael, 38, 287
Kantor, Jonathan, 99
Karsh, Yousuf, 301
Kerman, Joseph, 293
Kerouac, Jack, 292
King Crimson, 180
Kinks, 189
Kiss, viii, 109, 131
klezmer, 39
Klosterman, Chuck, 3
Korn, 29
Kot, Greg, 105–07
Kramarae, Cheris, 169–170
Krupa, Jean, 180
Kubrick, Stanley, 176

lang, k.d., 290
Lange, Mutt, 287
Langer, Susanne, 9, 22, 23; on art, 13; assimilation principle, 9; on time, 16

"language forest," 80, 82
Led Zeppelin, viii, 18, 25, 102, 131, 199, 292; "Kashmir," 193; "Stairway to Heaven," 11, 35
Lee, Geddy, viii, 7, 10, 18–19, 30, 32–33, 36, 43, 45, 46, 48, 62, 66, 83, 106, 114, 139, 144, 145, 153, 177, 219, 221, 234–35, 248, 270, 277, 289; critics on, 211–13; in "Cygnus X-1," 196; influences on, 180; on *Signals*, 171–72; on syn thesizers, 170, 174–75, 177, 179, 182, 184; on technology, 234; on "Tom Sawyer," 34; on "The Trees," 294–96; voice of, 15, 211–13, 218, 221
Lennon, John, 107
Leonard, Smalls, 212
Lewis, Gary, 37–38
liberal education, 242
liberals, 256
libertarianism, 255–56; on competition, 266; on complexity, 262, 265–66; on market economy, 267–268; on science, 266–67
Lifeson, Alex, viii, 10, 18–19, 30, 32–33, 39, 40, 42, 43, 45, 46, 48, 54, 58, 62, 64, 66, 83, 84, 106, 136, 172, 177, 193–94, 219, 220, 234–35, 270, 277, 289, 291; on "Tom Sawyer," 34; on "The Trees," 294–95
Lindley, David: *Win This Record*, 180
listener competence, 190
literalness, and low cultural status, 67, 69
Living Colour, 29
Locrian mode, 197
Loder, Kurt, 64
London, Jack, 292
Love, 304
Lucas, George, 178, 281
Lucretius, 121–22; *De Rerum Natura*, 122, 123, 125; on religion, 125–26
lyrics, and instrumentation, 8

machines, and emotions, 234
The Making of Snakes and Arrows (documentary), 133
maladaptive thoughts, 93–95
Mallet, David, 176
Mann, Aimee, 186–87
Manson, Marilyn, 29
Marx, Karl H., 266; *Das Kapital*, 227

The Matrix (movie), 202
Max Webster (band), 6, 289
McCartney, Paul, 19, 38
McDonald, Chris, 50, 51
McKenzie, Bob, 290
McKenzie, Doug, 290
McKinney, Devin, 216, 218, 221
McLuhan, Marshall, 231, 289
memories, vagaries of, 91
Meshuggah, 29–30
Metallica, 29, 197; "One," 39; *S&M*, 38; "Wherever I May Roam," 190, 191
metaphysical conceit, 232
Michelangelo Buonarroti, 11; *David*, 9
Middleton, Richard, 300
Miles, Michael, 273
Mill, John Stuart, 268–69, 274
"Ming Hing, Laundry Man," (song), 193
Minimoog, 170
minor chords, 190
Mitchell, Kim, 289–290
Moog Taurus II, 175
Mornay, Rebecca De, 7
Mr. Deeds Goes to Town (movie), 198, 258
Mumford, Lewis, 227; *Technics and Civilization*, 227
Murray, Anne, 288
music and consciousness, 16; evoking evil in, 196–97; illusions of, 14–16, 22; and processed sound, 23; and stylistic conventions, 190; symbolizing otherness in, 189–190; and time, 16; ubiquity of, 8
musical time, philosophies of, 46–50

negative rights, 245–46
Negus, Keith, 292
nerdiness, 70–71
New Grove Dictionary of Jazz, 50
Newman, Randy, 29–30
The New Rolling Stone Album Guide, 211
Nickelback: "How You Remind Me," 288
Nietzsche, Friedrich, 278
non-contradiction of identity, 81
Norman, Richard: *On Humanism*, 251
Northern Lights: "Tears Are Not Enough," 290
Nozick, Robert, 256; *Anarchy, State, and Utopia.* 260
Nuttall, Carrie, 153

Oberheim OBX–a, 170
Objectivism, 257
Oppenheimer, J. Robert, 183
Oriental riff, 192
Orwell, George, 5; *Animal Farm*, 275; *Nineteen Eighty-Four*, 274–75

Paganini, Niccolò, 39
pain, as subjective, 205
Page, Richard, 19
Parales, Jon, 64
Parker, Charlie, 63–64
Parker, Dorothy, 180
Paul, St., 155
Pavement, 29
Peanuts (TV specials), 35
Peart, Neil, viii, 5–6, 10, 18, 32–33, 36, 40, 42, 43, 45, 48, 50, 54, 55, 57, 58, 62, 64, 66, 76, 78, 105, 122, 171, 198, 212–13, 218, 220–21, 235, 243, 291; critics on, 212–13; electronic drums, 177; ethics in, 141, 143, 145–47; on faith, 125; *Ghost Rider*, 109, 111, 119, 153, 236; humanism of, 241, 251; idealized capitalism in, 247; influences on, 180; journals of, 115, 117–18; as left libertarian, 271; motorcycle journeys of, 111, 114–15, 117–18, 124; *New Musical Express* interview, 273; and Rand, 5–6, 10, 273; *Roadshow*, 121; and technology, 178, 225, 226, 231–32; Technospeak in, 233; tragedies of, 111, 139, 152–55, 236; virtuosity of, 61; writing style of, 232; on "YYZ," 300–01
Peart, Selena, 236
performance, as dissembling, 73
Petty, Tom, 3
Philodemus, 126–27
physicalism, 162–63; and qualitative experience, 165
Pickett, Wilson, 37–38; "In the Midnight Hour," 37
Pine, Rachel Barton. *See* Barton, Rachel
Pink Floyd: "Comfortably Numb," 11; lyrics of, 11
Pixies, 29
Plant, Robert, 11, 107
Plato, 81, 179, 242; cave allegory, 77–78; on Forms, 103–04, 107–09; on imitation, 76–77; and music

criticism, 102–03, 105–09; *Phaedrus*, 103; *Republic*, 76, 140; theory of knowledge, 103; *Timaeus*, 103
Police (band), 18, 30
Pompeii, 127
popular music criticism, assumptions of, 63–64
Portnoy, Mike, 36
positive rights, 246–47
Postman, Neil, 227, 231
post-punk, 30
PPG Wave, 2–3, 175
Premonition, 37
Presley, Elvis, viii
Price, Carol Selby: *Mystic Rhythms*, 233
Primus, 29
principle of assimilation, in art, 9
Procol Harum, 38, 39
progressive rock, 17
prolepsis, 122
Protagoras, 242
Provenza, Paul, 107
Pseudo-Dionysius, 81
psychoanalysis, 90
Public Choice Theory, 262
pure language, 81

qualia, 205
qualitative experience, 164

Radiohead: *OK Computer*, 107
Rand, Ayn, 24, 51–52, 173, 292; *Anthem*, 259, 273, 282–85; —as dystopia, 282; —and "2112," contrast between, 282–85; *Atlas Shrugged*, 257; *Capitalism: The Unknown Ideal*, 257; *The Fountainhead*, 258; *The Virtue of Selfishness*, 257
Reagan, Ronald, 176
Red Hot Chili Peppers, 29
Red Star: Tribute to Rush (album), 36
Renaissance, 242
res cogitans, 163
res extensa, 163
Rheostatics, 29
Richards, Andy, 181, 184
Richards, Keith, 10
The Rick Mercer Report, 291
Risky Business (movie), 7
Robertson, Ed, 35, 291
Rock Band (video game), 84, 136

rock music: and classical music,
  combining, 38–39, 43; and post-
  counterculture, 65; and repetition,
  16–17
Rock'n'Roll Hall of Fame, 28
Rojcewicz, Richard, 226
Roland Jupiter-8, 171
Roland TR-808 rhythm composer, 176
Rolling Stone (magazine), 64, 211, 213
Rolling Stones, 290, 304
romance of social disillusionment, 281
Romantic Movement, 274
Roosevelt, Franklin D., 263
Rosetta Stone (band), 37
Royal Commission, in Canada, 297
Rubenstein, Todd Mark, 39–41
Rusch, Laura, 99
Rush: absurdity in, 150; acoustic/elec-
  tric contrasts in, 198–99; adaptive
  thinking in, 89; aesthetics of
  replicability, 60, 67, 71–73;
  "Afterimage," 99, 146, 149; as
  "album–oriented" rock, viii;
  "Alien Shore," 269; *All the
  World's a Stage* (album), 293; on
  American Revolution, 243;
  "Analog Kid," 84, 100, 270;
  "Animate," 98, 219; "Anthem," 24,
  246, 257, 273, 275; "Armageddon,"
  165; "Armor and Sword," 125–26,
  240, 259; on artisanship/mass
  production, 229; and artistic
  integrity, 22; assimilation of lyrics
  to music, 10–11; and audience
  participation, 45–46; "Available
  Light," 248; on awareness, 203;
  "Bastille Day," 24, 91, 106, 243,
  263; "Beneath, Between, and
  Behind," 226, 243, 258; "Between
  Sun and Moon," 94, 99; "Between
  the Wheels," 93, 146, 219, 228;
  "The Big Money," 264; —video,
  182, 184; "The Body Electric,"
  178, 233; —codes in, 72;
  "Bravado," 119; "Bravest Face,"
  93, 123; "By-Tor and the Snow
  Dog," 24, 46, 107; "The Camera
  Eye," 100, 173, 203, 228; as
  Canadian, 287, 289, 291, 293,
  298, 299, 305; Canadian awards,
  290–91; *Caress of Steel* (album),
  106, 129, 132, 197, 244, 263;
  "Carve away the Stone," 91, 98;
  "catches" in, 215; "Chain
  Lightning," 100; changes in, 75,
  301; "Chemistry," 233; "Cinderella

Man," 25, 198, 258;
  "Circumstances," 298; and class,
  66–68; and classical music, 38–40;
  "Closer to the Heart," 10, 25, 35,
  45, 79, 107, 173, 198, 226, 229,
  263; compassion in, 145–47; contingency in, 149–150;
  "Countdown," 173, 232;
  Counterparts (album), 219, 268,
  269, 270; *Counterparts* tour, 194;
  and critical acclaim, 29; critical
  disparagement of, 62–65, 67,
  102–03, 131; "Cut to the Chase,"
  248; "Cygnus: Bringer of
  Balance," 165–66; "Cygnus X–1,"
  24, 93, 134, 196; desire and
  ambition in, 248; "Different
  Strings," 190; "Discovery,"
  277–78, 294; "Distant Early
  Warning," 94, 98, 146; —video of,
  176; distrust of politicians in,
  263–64; "Don't Fight It," 304;
  "Double Agent," 95; "Dreamliner,"
  232; "Driven," 57, 248, 303;
  drumming as 'distraction' in, 219;
  The Earthquake Album, 35;
  "Earthshine," 97, 153; "Emotion
  Detector," 95; and Enlightenment,
  243–45; "Entre Nous," 97, 99,
  199; Epicurean ideas in, 123–26;
  and error analysis, 79; "Every
  Day Glory," 100, 146–47, 270;
  evocation of evil in, 197; *Exit . . .
  Stage Left* (album), 39, 64; —
  video, 46–47, 75; "Face Up," 112;
  "Faithless," 126, 154, 241, 259,
  269; fans of, 28, 51, 63, 67; "Far
  Cry," 54, 125, 240; *Farewell to
  Kings* (album), 10, 193, 196, 244,
  258, 263, 292; "Farewell to Kings"
  (song), 24, 198; *Farewell to Kings*
  tour, 3; —playlist, 24–25;
  Feedback (album), 82, 136, 304;
  "Feedback" (song), 82; finitude
  in, 148–49; "Fly by Night," 25, 93,
  101, 107, 232; "Force Ten," 83,
  185–86; "Freewill," 84, 100, 112,
  114, 125, 139, 141–42, 259, 298;
  on French Revolution, 244; genres of, viii, 28, 30, 213, 287, 289;
  "Ghost of a Chance," 125, 147,
  150, 153; "Ghost Rider," 232;
  Grace under Pressure (album),
  64, 146, 174, 176, 178, 180, 203,
  219, 301; —cover art, 174, 182;
  Grace under Pressure tour

(DVD), 75, 83; "Grand Designs," 226–27, 263; "Grand Finale," 280; groove in, 52, 55; "Hand over Fist," 269; *Hemispheres* (album), 54, 95, 293, 298; "Hemispheres" (song), 159–162, 165–66, 173, 194, 250, 255; "Heresy," 267; *Hold Your Fire* (album), 45, 83, 132, 185, 191, 203, 210, 269; "How It Is," 120; humanism in, 241, 245, 248, 252; "Hyperspace," 195–96; ideology of, 293; imitations of, 76; individualism in, 50, 51, 64, 245–46, 270–71; influences on, 180, 188, 193, 292; internal/external worlds in, 202–03, 210; "In the Mood," 25; on intolerance, 268–69; invisibility of, 101, 102; "Jacob's Ladder," 249; —rhythms in, 55–56; kick-drum and bass in, 18; "Lakeside Park," 24, 99, 292; "The Larger Bowl," 92, 121, 124, 125, 128, 146; libertarianism in, 257–58, 260–63, 270–71; "Limbo," 79; "Limelight," viii, 46, 54–55, 73, 78, 97, 134, 143, 203, 298; —rhythms in, 56; literalness of, 67, 72; "Losing It," 96, 145; love in, 153–54; Love and Reason in, 160–61; on machines, 231–32; magic in, 250; "Manhattan Project," 183–84, 230; "Marathon," 45, 58, 248; and meritocracy, 71–72; metaphor in, 232; meters in, 51–52, 54–55, 58; "Middletown Dreams," 203; "missions," 248, 259, 270; mixing of sound in, 8; *Moving Pictures*(album), viii, 10, 27, 33, 46, 57, 102, 142–44, 197, 203, 267, 298; —cover art, 298–99; and musical autodidacticism, 60, 65–67, 71; in musicians' magazines, 43; and "musicians' music," 30; mysticism in, 241–42, 250; "Mystic Rhythms," 184, 250; —video, 184; mythical ideas in, 250, 252–53; "Natural Science," 195, 230, 259, 266, 294; "The Necromancer," 134, 198; negative rights in, 247; and nerdiness, 70, 72; "New World Man," viii, 29, 134, 231, 290; "Nobody's Hero," 268; "Not Fade Away," 304; "One Little Victory," 97, 154; "Oracle: The Dream," 279; origins of, viii;

otherness in, 191–94; "Out of the Cradle," 153; "The Pass," 114, 146, 241; "A Passage to Bangkok," 132, 192–93; performance in, 73; *Permanent Waves* (album), 27, 30, 102, 135, 189, 190, 195–96, 254, 258–59; philosophical concepts in, 4; poking fun at, 106; popularity of, 109; and post-industrialism, 67; *Power Windows* (album), 181, 184, 192, 203, 236, 264, 269; —cover art, 181–82; "Presentation," 278; *Presto*, 203–204, 241, 250, 269; and progressive rock, 169, 180, 191, 220, 234, 250; pure language in, 82; and racial issues in music, 63; and Rand, 4, 10, 258–59; and readers' polls, 65; "Red Barchetta," 47, 57, 98, 267, 298; "Red Sector A," 45, 146; —video, 177; on religion, 239–240; "Resist," 98; rhythms in, 17, 50–52, 54–58; "Rivendell," 193–94; "Robot Plus," 160; rock critics on, 28–29; *Roll the Bones* (album), 81, 236, 250, 267; "Roll the Bones" (song), 91, 97, 100, 125, 147, 150; romantic tragedy in, 280–81; 7/8 meter in, 51–52, 54, 58, 173; "Show Don't Tell," 203; *A Show of Hands* (concert DVD), 45, 444, 75, 83; *Signals*, 50, 171, 173, 180, 203, 263, 270; *Signals* tour, 235; signs and signals in, 130; *Snakes & Arrows*, 83, 122, 124, 127, 152, 239–241, 245, 259, 269; *Snakes and Arrows* tour, 121; "Soliloquy," 195, 279; "Something for Nothing," 24, 99, 120, 190, 246, 250, 258, 267; space sounds in, 194–96; "The Spirit of Radio," 27, 30–31, 35, 36, 37, 79, 84, 99, 134, 135, 236, 258, 298; —adaptations of, 39, 40; —ending of, 32–33; —stylistic analysis of, 30–32; spiritual overtones in, 249–250; "The Stars Look Down," 142, 147, 151; "Stick It Out," 270, 303; "Subdivisions," 50, 52, 54, 96, 171–73, 203, 270; —metrical shifts in, 175; —rhythms in, 56, 61; —video, 172; success of, 288; "Summertime Blues" cover art, 82; "Sweet Miracle," 99, 139, 152;

synergy in, 145; synthesizers in, 169–171, 204; "Tai Shan," 191, 269; "Tears," 191; technocracy in, 228–29; and technology, 23, 169–173, 177, 182–85, 188, 225, 226, 230–31, 234–36, 301; Technospeak in, 233; "The Temples of Syrinx," 276; "Territories," 192, 264, 269; *Test for Echo* (album), 57; —cover art, 302–03; "Test for Echo" (song), 231; *Test for Echo* tour, 111, 194; as thought-provoking, 121, 123; as three-piece band, 18–19; "Tide Pools," 195–96; "Time and Motion," 304; time in, 227–28; *Time Machine* tour, 84; "Time Stand Still," 91, 100, 132, 147, 148, 153; —video, 186–87; "Tom Sawyer," viii, 27, 35, 93, 99, 102, 134, 143, 185, 214, 218, 236, 298; —adaptations of, 36, 37, 40–42; —distraction in, 221; —drumming in, 220–21; —guitar in, 220; —keyboard in, 221; —stylistic analysis of, 33–34; "Totem," 91; translation/variation in, 83–84; "The Trees," 10, 116, 198, 247, 261–63, 293–97; tributes to, 27–28, 35–36, 39–40, 44, 75, 83; tritone in, 197–198; "Turn the Page," 47, 83, 91, 210; *2112* (album), 3, 4, 132, 190–92, 194, 195, 234, 273, 276–285, 292; —dystopia in, 276–285; —as serious rock, 276; "2112" (song), 25, 91, 101, 134, 146, 198, 228–29, 231, 247, 257, 259, 260, 273, 275, 294; —romantic disillusionment in, 281; unhappy consciousness in, 279–280; in US, 289–290; value of, 131–32, 136; "Vapor Trail," 147, 149; *Vapor Trails*, 23, 120, 133, 134, 142, 152–53, 236, 250, 270; in video games, 84–86; videos of, 176; "La Villa Strangiato," 40, 45, 54, 193, 298; "Virtuality," 233; virtuosity of, 58, 61–66, 72, 106, 169; "Vital Signs," 91, 93, 98, 142, 143, 144, 145, 232; "War Paint," 204; "The Way the Wind Blows," 126, 240, 259, 269; "The Weapon," 263; "We Hold On," 98; "Witch Hunt," 83, 92, 93, 197, 247, 267, 268; "Working Man," 25, 99, 109, 134,

227–28; "Xanadu," 24, 101, 106, 193–94, 294; YouTube covers of, 59–62, 71, 72; "YYZ," 61, 75, 197–98, 298–301; —Morse code in, 62, 66, 236, 300–01; —tritone in, 197–98; —virtuosity of, 66
Rush, A.J., 94
Rush: Beyond the Lighted Stage (documentary), 102–103, 105, 106, 109
Rush in Rio (DVD), 29, 109
Rutsey, John, viii, 43, 212

Sachs, Jonathan: *The Dignity of Difference*, 269
Sandler, Adam, 35
Sargent, Martin, 234
Sartre, Jean-Paul, 118, 121, 152; *Existentialism and Human Emotion*, 112; on freedom, 113–14
Saul, Scott, 65
scientism, 264
Scott, Raymond: "Powerhouse," 197
The Screensavers (TV show), 234
Seeger, Bob, 7
Segel, Jason, 46
Sepultura, 29
Shakespeare, William, 50, 78
Shelley, Mary, 230
Shenker, Michael, 106
Simmons, Gene, 109
Simon, Paul, 32
Simon and Garfunkel, 136; "The Sounds of Silence," 32
Simple Minds, 180
skepticism, 201, 202, 206
Slayer, 29
Small Soldiers (movie), 35–36
Smashing Pumpkins, 29
Smith, Adam: *The Theory of Moral Sentiments*, 265
Socrates, 76–77, 140
solipsism, 202, 206, 210
songwriters, as readers, 10
Soundgarden, 29
space music, 194
Spinoza, Baruch, 249; *The Ethics*, 249
Springfield, Buffalo, viii, 304; *For What It's Worth*, 136
Stalling, Carl, 197
Star Wars (movie), 178
Stefani, Gino, 300
St. Etienne, 37
Sting, 19

mpin' Tom Connors, 288
.auss, Richard: *Thus Spoke Zarathustra*, 194
Straw, Will, 292
Subdivisions (tribute album), 36, 37
subjective experience, 159–160, 163
Superstandard English, 70–71
Supertramp, 173
Syme, Hugh, 130, 174, 181, 182, 298
syncopation, 48

"Take Off (to the Great White North)," 290
Tchaikovsky, Pyotr Ilyich: *1812 Overture*, 192
technē, 225–26
technocracy, 229–230
technological determinism, 230
technology: and masculinity, 169, 183; modern, 226; as pervasive, 225
Technology and Women's Voices, 169
text-painting, 189
Thatcher, Margaret, 176
Théberge, Paul, 177
30 Foot Tall, 37
thoughts: access to, 201–02; as altering perception, 91–93; examination of, 92–94
THX-1138 (movie), 178
'Til Tuesday, 186
time, subservience to, 227–28
Tobias, Patricia, 40
Tobias, Paul, 40
Tolkien, J.R.R., 292; *The Lord of the Rings*, 193
Tolstoy, Leo, 5
Toronto's Flying Bulgar Klezmer Band, 39
The Tragically Hip, 288, 291
tragic consciousness, and faith, 154–55
Trailer Park Boys (TV show), 291
Trailer Park Boys: The Movie, 291
trauma, and healing, 115
tritone, 196
Twain, Mark, 5, 33
Twain, Shania, 287
2001: A Space Odyssey (movie), 194

UFO (band), 6, 106
Ultravox, 180
value, deferral of, 132–33, 135
Van Halen, 18
video vertigo, 231
Villiers, Nicholas de, 217
Vivaldi, 300
Voltaire, François Arouet, 242
Vonnegut, Kurt: "Harrison Bergeron," 261

Wajcman, Judy, 169–170, 183; *Feminism Confronts Technology*, 169
Walser, Robert, 27, 43
The Waterboy (movie), 35
Waters, Roger, 6, 11, 19
Wayne's World, 86
Weather Report, 180, 301
"Weird Al" Yankovic, 35
Wells, H.G.: *The Time Machine*, 275
Western aesthetics, 65
Whatever (movie), 35
Whitman, Walt: "I Sing the Body Electric," 178
The Who, 18, 19, 84, 304
Wild, David, 28–29
Wittgenstein, Ludwig: on language, 210; on meaning as reference, 207–08; *Philosophical Investigations*, 206; private language argument, 207–08; *Tractatus*, 206
Working Man (tribute album), 36, 37
Wright, Frank Lloyd, 9

The Yardbirds, 304
Yes, 25, 105; "Roundabout," 64; *Tales from Topographic Oceans*, 17
Young, Neil, 288, 290, 304

Zagorski-Thomas, Simon, 52
Zamyatin, Yevgeny: *We*, 275
Zandt, Ronnie van, 3
Zappa, Frank, 35
Zola, Émile, 5
Zombie, Rob, 35
ZZ Top, viii, 18